Primal Roots
of Horror Cinema

PRIMAL ROOTS OF HORROR CINEMA
Evolutionary Psychology and Narratives of Fear

Carrol L. Fry

McFarland & Company, Inc., Publishers
Jefferson, North Carolina

LIBRARY OF CONGRESS CATALOGUING-IN-PUBLICATION DATA

Names: Fry, Carrol L. (Carrol Lee), author.
Title: Primal roots of horror cinema : evolutionary psychology and narratives of fear / Carrol L. Fry.
Description: Jefferson, North Carolina : McFarland & Company, Inc., 2019 | Includes bibliographical references and index.
Identifiers: LCCN 2019008864 | ISBN 9781476674278 (paperback : acid free paper) ∞
Subjects: LCSH: Horror films—Psychological aspects. | Horror films—History and criticism. | Fear in motion pictures.
Classification: LCC PN1995.9.H6 F79 2019 | DDC 791.43/6164—dc23
LC record available at https://lccn.loc.gov/2019008864

BRITISH LIBRARY CATALOGUING DATA ARE AVAILABLE

ISBN (print) 978-1-4766-7427-8
ISBN (ebook) 978-1-4766-3531-6

© 2019 Carrol L. Fry. All rights reserved

No part of this book may be reproduced or transmitted in any form or by any means, electronic or mechanical, including photocopying or recording, or by any information storage and retrieval system, without permission in writing from the publisher.

Front cover image of screaming woman © 2019 Joe Therasakdhi /Shutterstock

Printed in the United States of America

McFarland & Company, Inc., Publishers
  Box 611, Jefferson, North Carolina 28640
    www.mcfarlandpub.com

Table of Contents

Preface	1
Introduction	3
ONE: *2001: A Space Odyssey*	17
TWO: The Territorial Narrative	27
THREE: The Assimilation Narrative	52
FOUR: The Tribal Narrative	74
FIVE: The Mating Narrative in the Gothic Romance	100
SIX: The Predator Narrative	125
SEVEN: The Other Narrative: Ghosts, Slashers, Witches and Robots as Other	151
Conclusion	187
Chapter Notes	191
Bibliography	201
Index	207

Preface

When I was a child, my father, who was a dedicated film fan until television seduced him away from the movie theater, took us to see *The Wolf Man*. As was customary in those palmy pre-mall days, I sat down in front with the other kids, our parents in the back. I was fine with Larry Talbot killing the four-legged werewolf with his silver wolf's-head cane because we didn't see much of the monster. When the exotic looking old gypsy lady told Talbot, "Even a man who is pure at heart and says his prayers by night, may become a wolf when the wolfbane blooms and the autumn moon is bright," I was a little less sanguine, since I was, at least by self-perception, pure at heart and had no desire to be transformed into a slavering beast. Then when Talbot started sprouting fur and fangs as the full moon rose, I ran back to sit by my parents. I was afraid of the dark for a long time afterward.

But my fears didn't keep me from the Saturday double features with the other Universal monsters of the day. I remained a fan of horror movies and the irrationally pleasurable fear that they inspire right to the present day. In the 1950s when the horror genre morphed into the alien invasion science fiction film, I was equally taken with *It Came from Outer Space*, *The Thing*, etc.

As the intensity of horror has increased, *The Wolf Man* seems like pretty tame stuff compared to, say, *An American Werewolf in London* and many others of the horror genre. But *The Wolf Man*, *Frankenstein*, *Dracula*, *The Mummy* and the plethora of horror movies of my youth planted the seeds for my enjoyment of the genre, even in its contemporary sensationalism, and led me to write about film in my professional life.

But my book is not a history of film horrors. Another influence led to my writing *Primal Roots of Horror Cinema*.

Many years ago, I was a member of a book discussion group which chose Desmond Morris' *The Naked Ape* as a topic. It inspired a lively debate in the group, pretty much along the lines of that in the greater national audience with some members offended at its premise that humanity is just another species of the animal kingdom. The book's argument, built on Charles Darwin's theory of evolution, asserted that humans evolved through the same forces of survival-of-the-fittest and natural selection as did all species. As it turns out, Morris' book was a popularization of an ongoing discourse in the fields of biology, anthropology and psychology that had been around for some time. But *The Naked Ape* stuck in my mind and percolated for 20 years. Later, as I began reading similar works, I came to see that they were presenting a new view of human nature and behavior. Also I have found that evolutionary criticism, as it is sometimes called, is a lively field of analysis in the arts, and my book offers another approach in that dialogue.

I wrote three articles over the years adapting sociobiology and evolutionary psychology. I thank the editors of the following journals for permission to adapt parts of them: "'We Are Legion': Primal Dreams and Primal Screams in the Satanic Film," published in *The Journal of Literature and Film* (19:2, 2015); "The New Naturalism: Primal Screams in Abraham Stoker's *Dracula*," appearing in *Midwest Quarterly* (47:1, 2004); and "From Technology to Transcendence: Humanity's Evolutionary Journey in *2001: A Space Odyssey*," published in *Extrapolation* (44: 2001). In addition, I thank Sandra Fry for valuable help in editing, technical assistance and advice and my friend and frequent collaborator Dr. Robert Craig of Central Michigan University for suggestions. Both were good sounding boards for my ideas.

Primal Roots of Horror Cinema is both an adaptation of the findings from evolutionary psychology and sociobiology to explain our long love affair with the horror film and also to point out how the narratives imbedded there remain in our behavior and culture. Evolutionary criticism offers much more than a new approach to film and literary criticism. Scholars in the field agree that for all our civilized veneer, there are primal minds in our skulls that whisper to us. Edward O. Wilson sums up the power of the evolutionary whispers from our ancient ancestors: "The evolutionary epic is probably the best myth we will ever have. It can be adjusted until it comes as close to truth as the human mind is constructed to judge the truth."[1] We can perceive echoes of that epic in the primal narratives embedded in the horror film, narratives that impact our lives and behavior as well as our taste in the arts.

Introduction

> *Where there is human nature, Hastings, there is drama.*
> —Agatha Christie, "The King of Clubs Mystery"
>
> *The arts are not solely shaped by errant genius out of historical circumstances and idiosyncratic personal experience. The roots of their inspiration date back in deep history to the genetic origins of the human brain, and are permanent.*—Edward O. Wilson, *Consilience*

The TV promo for a recent horror movie proclaimed that it is "so disturbing that you won't sleep for weeks." The ad suggests an enduring question. Why do we pay to be frightened by films that make us lose sleep at night? It is a conundrum that has engaged generations of literary critics, and it is central to the topic of *Primal Roots of Horror Cinema*. Findings from the fields of sociobiology and evolutionary psychology suggest that our attraction to and enjoyment of narratives in the arts in general and the horror genre in particular are influenced by our evolutionary heritage and are built into humanity's genetic package. They offer a new approach to understanding our response to literature and film often referred to as evolutionary criticism. I will call my approach "primal traits criticism" because I focus on specific elements of evolutionary adaptation. The horror film and the works of fiction that filmmakers adapt offer a useful example for an adaptation of a primal traits critique, and *Primal Roots of Horror Cinema* is an analysis of why we respond to primal narratives that are imbedded in the genre.

"Its moldering walls of dark grey stone, rendered it a gloomy and sublime object."

So Ann Radcliffe described Castle Udolpho in her 1794 gothic novel *The Mysteries of Udolpho*. Radcliffe and other eighteenth-century purveyors of the gothic romance were inspired by Edmund Burke's 1757 book *A Philosophical Enquiry into Our Ideas of the Sublime and the Beautiful*. Burke called the pleasures of vicarious fear "sublime": "Whatever is fitted in any sort to excite the ideas of pain and danger, that is to say, whatever is in any sort terrible, or is conversant about terrible objects, or operates in a manner analogous to terror, is a source of the *sublime;* that is, it is productive of the strongest emotion which the mind is capable of feeling."[1] He gave a variety of examples of the sublime: mountains, storms at sea, ruins, and even various colors and smells, all conducive to create unease. His theory on the pleasures of vicarious fear influenced generations of gothic novelists. Echoes of the Burkean sublime recur in the horror film.

Modern behavioral studies offer theories that are both similar to and different from Burke's. Freud's writings on the tripartite psyche inspired critical analysis of literature and film. Carl Jung described what he called archetypes, primordial images imbedded in the human mind that influence our lives and create a response to art, literature and of course film. Earnest Jones adapted central Freudian concepts in his seminal 1910 essay "Hamlet and Oedipus," arguing that if we imagine literary characters are real people, we should be able to psychoanalyze them. Literary critics continue to find new adaptations of Freud's writings, even though they have long been relegated to the lumber room in the field of psychology. Writers and filmmakers, on the other hand, have found his works useful as a frame for *their* work. Maud Bodkin's *Archetypal Patterns in Poetry* (1934) is an early adaptation of Jung's writings for literary criticism. Northrop Frye and his followers have further adapted Jung's work. The premise of both is that the unconscious, be it the individual as in Freud's writings or the collective in Jung's, drives some human behavior and can create a response to literature or film. Burke's description of the sublime bears similarities in the assertion that powerful emotions override reason to create pleasure.

Literary criticism has splintered into a kaleidoscope of approaches in the past 50 years, with Jacques Lacan's resurgent Freudianism, Michel Foucault's discourse on power, Jacques Derrida's work in deconstruction and other postmodern critical theories. Writings in these fields are often more about "theory" than actually literary analysis. More recently, literary criticism has focused on the influence of culture in creating response to literature and film. Douglas Cowan, for instance, describes horror films as "sociophobic artifacts, the artistic traces of a wide variety of fears that continue to haunt us." Put differently, he writes, "our culture teaches us in a variety of ways what to fear [in the horror film], and through a variety of cultural products reflects and reinforces the fears we have been taught."[2]

Stephen Prince also attributes the power of the horror genre to culture: "The horror film may be viewed as a visualization of the dialectic between linguistic and socially imposed systems of order and the breakdown of those systems through their own internal contradictions.... Rather than signifying the projection of repressed sexuality or some other psychological process, the monster represents those unmapped areas bordering the familiar configurations of the social order."[3]

New fields in the study of human nature offer a fresh insight. Terry Burnham and Jay Phelan sum up the central point: "Our brains have been designed for genetic evolution.... To understand ourselves and our world, we need to look not to Sigmund Freud but rather to Charles Darwin."[4] But Joseph Carroll points out the value of both cultural and evolutionary criticism: "Evolutionists insist that genes constrain and direct human behavior. Cultural constructivists counter that culture, embodied in the arts, shapes human experience. Both these claims are true, but some evolutionists and some cultural constructivists have mistakenly regarded them as mutually exclusive."[5]

A series of books and essays that extrapolate on Darwin's theory began to appear in the 1960s. Their writers meld the disciplines of biology, sociology, anthropology and psychology to establish fields that came to be called sociobiology and evolutionary psychology. In describing sociobiology, John Alcock asks, "What role did natural selection have in shaping this society or that social behavior? ... Sociobiologists want to know the evolved function or purpose of whatever society they are studying."[6] The University of California–Santa Barbara Center for Evolutionary Psychology website defines the field: "Evolutionary psychology is based on the recognition that the human brain consists of a large collection of functionally specialized computational devices that evolved to solve the adaptive problems regularly encountered by our hunter-gatherer ancestors."[7] Sociobiology is rooted in animal and insect studies that parallel human behavior, while evolutionary psychology focuses more on evolved brain development and chemistry.

The two fields differ in methodology, but their core findings about human behavior are similar. They postulate that evolution has created a response in the *Homo sapien* mind to the adaptive behavior of our primal ancestors that enhanced their chances for survival. Since for the most part, evolutionary psychologists have led the way in adapting critical analyses of film and literary criticism, I'll refer to that field for the common findings of the two when discussing film and literary works. Their conclusions offer a fresh approach to understanding why we take pleasure in the vicarious fear inspired by the horror genre. Mathias Clasen writes that fright scenes in film or literature "successfully target ancient evolved defense mechanisms and short-circuit prefrontal mechanisms. Horror fiction works, in other words, throw a live wire into ancient structures in the audience's central nervous system."[8]

But beyond criticism of the horror film, the findings of evolutionary theory offer a fertile approach to film and literary criticism in general. In recent years, Joseph Carrol, Jonathan Gottschall, David Sloan Wilson, Brian Boyd and others have amassed an impressive body of work in evolving, so to speak, and adapting Darwinian evolutionary findings to form a coherent school of evolutionary criticism. Their work and my primal traits critical approach in some ways run counter to cultural criticism but also adapt it, suggesting that whispers from our early ancestors may contribute to the very formation of culture and tastes in the arts.

"Know thyself... The proper study of mankind is man."

Alexander Pope's 1734 poem *An Essay on Man* is one of many attempts to define ourselves. Countless treatises have been written on the subject. Perhaps somewhere a simian relative of ours ponders this question and has found his or her own version of "I think, therefore I am." But so far as we know, humanity differs from other species in our ability to even ask questions about our nature, despite our failure to answer them. Most attempts were written by philosophers and theologians or poets and novelists, and the mythologies of all cultures tell their own versions of our origins and nature.

Many creation myths portray human nature and humanity's condition as fallen from an earlier time of innocence and bliss. The Greek myth of the three ages of the world—from gold to silver to iron—traces the successive deterioration of our nature. The Fall, as described in Genesis with the original sin passed to succeeding generations, might be seen as an explanation for humanity's capacity for extraordinary violence and cruelty. True, the Romantic Movement's dictum that human nature is good until spoiled by civilization still survives, but it is a relative latecomer in the dialogue. Central to most mythologies and religions is the conviction that however much or little we have fallen from original innocence, humanity was nonetheless the special creation of the divine. In Christianity, this comfortable belief was anchored in "the argument by design."

In *Natural Theology* (1802), William Paley proposed a metaphor that explains the concept. He describes a watch designed by a craftsman to perform its task: "It requires indeed an examination of the instrument, and perhaps some previous knowledge of the subject, to perceive and understand it, but being, as we have said, observed and understood, the evidence, we think is inevitable; the watch must have a maker."[9] The symmetry of the universe—with the cosmic dance of the planets, the balance of nature and species seemingly formed to fit their niche in the environment—demonstrates, he postulates, the existence of a creator and a design.

"Natural selection is the blind watchmaker."

With his 1859 book *On the Origin of Species,* Charles Darwin brought a new dimension to perceptions of human nature, one based on science rather than philosophy or religion. Humanity developed, he wrote, from our species' adaptation to the environment. The iron laws of survival of the fittest and natural selection molded the clay of our physical forms as it did for all other species. The core of his theory is simple enough. Species and individuals within them adapt to the environment due to favorable survival traits and evolve through natural selection, breeding with others like them. Individuals and whole species without the needed traits simply die out. Denise Cummins puts the process succinctly: "Natural selection is a straightforward process: The genes of those who live long enough to reproduce remain in the gene pool. The genes of those who don't, don't."[10]

In *Origin of Species*, Darwin depicts a savage nature with his description of a "tangled bank," in which each individual plant tries to choke out others so that it and its progeny can survive. Some do, but most don't. In nature's toy box, only those species survive that have physical characteristics enabling them to adapt and pass their fortuitous traits on to their progeny through natural selection. Richard Dawkins sums up this view as a reaction to Paley: "Natural selection is the blind watchmaker, blind because it does not see ahead, does not plan consequences, has no purpose in view. Yet the living results of natural selection overwhelmingly impress us with the appearance of design as if by a master watchmaker, impress us with the illusion of design and planning."[11]

Darwin's theory and harsh interpretations of it such as that of Dawkins caused a case of spiritual indigestion in his time that remains with us today. It supplants the concept of a loving God who made us with a description of random creation of species by the forces of nature. The Victorian English poet Alfred Tennyson foresaw the spiritual emptiness of this view in his 1849 poem "In Memoriam," and agonized over "nature, red in tooth and claw and ravine." Stephen Crane articulates the sense of loss felt by many in his 1897 short story "The Open Boat" when the narrator, stranded in a tiny craft with three others after their ship sinks and is tossed about by wind and wave, laments: "When it occurs to a man that nature does not regard him as important and that she feels she would not maim the universe by disposing of him, he at first wishes to throw bricks at the temple, and he hates deeply that there are no bricks and no temples."[12]

Darwin proposed that our forebears were not given, as Genesis proclaims, "dominion over the fish of the sea and over the fowl of the air, and over every living thing that moveth upon the earth" in the Garden of Eden. Rather they were one more species in the Garden of Nature. One might contemplate the giraffe for an imaginary scenario of Darwin's concept. Conservative Christians, Jews and Muslims following the argument by design believe that God created this species with the gift of a long neck and long legs to fit its place in the environment, allowing it to browse on foliage that others could not reach. The Pew Research Religion and Public Life Survey found that one-third of the American population today accepts this view of creation and believes that the Earth is about 6000 years old. Fifty-seven percent believe that humanity has always "existed in its present form."[13] Evolutionary theory takes a different view. Over the millennia, Darwin proposed, millions of species have failed to adapt. Others, however, have succeeded in surviving and evolving because of some adaptive trait that the environment favored.

For instance, the giraffe might have been just another species of antelope on the veldt of Africa eons ago. In the Darwinian scenario, when a great drought struck and there was no forage, the antelopes were forced to browse on the leaves of trees. Only those antelopes with somewhat longer necks and legs could reach this tasty greenery. The longer reach was their adaptive trait, enabling individuals of the species to survive. The antelopes with shorter reach perished. The long-necked members passed on their advantage to their progeny through natural selection, breeding with other surviving antelopes with longer reach. And as the lower foliage receded, only those with the longest necks and legs remained. In a few hundred thousand years, we have a giraffe, created and shaped by the environment through adaptation, survival of the fittest and natural selection.

Matthew Ridley steals a line from Victorian sage Thomas Henry Huxley when he asserts that life "is a chess tournament in which if you win a game, you start the next game with the handicap of a missing pawn."[14] The process is not quite that simple, of course. Ridley continues: "Sex brings together mutations, constantly rearranging genes into new combinations until new fortuitous synergy results. One ancestor of a giraffe, for example, might have invented a longer neck while another invented longer legs. The two together were better than either alone."[15]

The theory of evolution, as originally proposed, explains only its role in the development of species' physical characteristics. Darwin had speculated that there might be more to evolution than the process that built physical forms of life. In *The Expression of Emotion in Man and Animals*, he wrote: "I have often felt much difficulty about the proper application of the terms, will, consciousness and intention. Actions which were at first voluntary soon become habitual, and at last hereditary and may then be performed even in opposition to the will."[16] But he didn't take this idea much further.

> "Before the curtain is drawn and the play unfolds, the stage has already been partly set and much of the script written."

The new Darwinists begin with the hypothesis that if evolution created our physical forms, behaviors from our primal ancestors that favored survival and adaptation through natural selection would have been incorporated into our genetic heritage from hundreds of thousands of years of evolution and would at least influence, but not totally control, our actions, decisions and thoughts today. Such were the conclusions of Robert Ardrey's *African Genesis* (1961) and Konrad Lorenz's *On Aggression* (1963) as well as W.D. Hamilton's widely circulated essay "The Genetical Evolution of Social Behavior" and John Maynard Smith's similar essay "Group Selection and Kin Selection," both published in the journal *Nature* in 1964. Robert Ardrey's *The Territorial Imperative* (1966) raised the hackles of both conservatives and liberals. Desmond Morris brought the new Darwinism to the larger audience with his bestseller *The Naked Ape* in 1967. The controversy culminated with Edward O. Wilson's *Sociobiology* in 1975, followed three years later by the more reader-friendly *On Human Nature* and has continued to the present.

The field of sociobiology and evolutionary psychology began with the recognition that humans are members of the animal kingdom and evolved under the same conditions as all other species that have instinct. If they, why not humanity? Sociobiologists and evolutionary psychologists differ in methodology, but they agree on a central assumption: that promptings for human behavior bubble up in our brains from the adaptive experiences of our distant forebears that have become imbedded in our genetic inheritance. They share a common goal: to understand more fully our nature and our behavior as we have inherited it from our primal ancestors. Edward O. Wilson sums up their theory: "Before the curtain is drawn and the play unfolds, the stage has already been partly set and much of the script written."[17]

Evolutionary psychology and sociobiology, then, are an extension of Darwin's findings. Might not survival of the fittest and natural selection through adaptive traits, they propose, do more than create giraffes with long necks, the physical effect of evolution? Might not adaptation to the environment involve behavior patterns of species, including our own, in addition to physical form? Might not humanity to some degree be subject to the same laws of evolution that created adaptive instinctual behavior in all species, from migration patterns, to territorial defense, to mating rituals? The central argument of this book is that the adaptive behaviors that enabled survival of our primal ancestors—such as territoriality, tribalism, mating, fear of the predator, assimilation and distrust or hated of the Other—remain in *Homo sapiens'* genetic inheritance and whisper to us today, influencing our response to timeless narratives imbedded in film and fiction. Edward O. Wilson writes: "Artistic inspiration common to everyone in varying degree rises from the artesian wells of human nature.... It follows that even the greatest works of art might be understood fundamentally with knowledge of the biologically evolved epigenetic rules that guided them."[18]

"One of the greatest pains to human nature is the pain of a new idea."[19]

Evolutionary biologists might be rather arbitrarily divided into two camps, adaptationists and pluralists. They disagree on the extent of adaptation's effect, not only on the evolution of physical forms but in creating human nature. The extreme views of adaptationists are rather determinist. Richard Dawson speaks for them in this oft-quoted passage: "Like successful Chicago gangsters, our genes have survived, in some cases for millions of years, in a highly competitive world. This entitles us to expect certain qualities in our genes. I shall argue that a predominant quality to be expected in a successful gene is ruthless selfishness" in creating behavior that ensures their survival and propagation.[20] Jay Gould's writings articulate the extreme of pluralists. Evolution, he asserts, involves a number of factors, and he doubts that adaptation has molded human behavior. Daniel Dennett takes a convincing middle ground between the two. He notes that environmental constraints on humanity as builders of culture would seem greater than for most species, but nonetheless adaptation must have some influence on us.[21]

Both adaptationists and most pluralists, however, agree on the fundamental hypothesis explored in this book: that to one extent or another, the adaptive strategies of our ancestors exist in the unconscious mind as narratives that influence our behavior. And it follows that our response to film and literature is a part of that behavior. Janet Richards writes, "The disagreement between [evolutionary psychologists and sociobiologists] and the standard social science theorists is not about *whether* environment influences what we are, but only about the extent to which an understanding of our evolutionary origins can help to show *how and to what* extent this happens."[22]

Evolutionary scientists are, after all, academics and subject to the sort of "acrimony of the scholiast" that Samuel Johnson described in the eighteenth century: quarrels about matters in which they are wholly invested but that are not of much interest to the mass of people. So the findings of scholars in these fields have been savagely attacked by other academics. Jay Gould writes that those conclusions are a reactionary justification for racism. Daniel Dennett, on the other hand, suggests an imbedded reason for this hostility in the academy: "Today we can see that not only Aristotle's divisions but also other cherished compartmentalization's of science are threatened by its territorial expansion."[23] At Harvard, where Edward O. Wilson is a professor, students with bullhorns picketed his office demanding his dismissal, and he was shouted down at professional conferences (even doused with ice water) for challenging the view that only society molds human nature and behavior. A 1975 article in *The New York Review of Books* weighed in: "We think that this information [in Wilson's *On Human Nature*] has little relevance to human behavior, and the supposedly objective, scientific approach in reality conceals political assumptions. Thus, we are presented with yet another defense of the status quo as an inevitable consequence of human nature."[24]

The hostility to the new Darwinism results from the field's calling to question the assumption that humanity has few if any instincts and differs from other species in the animal kingdom. John Tooby and Leda Cosmides give this perspective a name: the Standard Social Science Model. "The SSSM proposes a fundamental division between biology and culture. Biology endows humans with the five senses, a few drives like hunger and fear, and a general capacity to learn. But biological evolution, according to the SSSM, has been superseded by cultural evolution."[25] John Locke (1632–1704) articulated an early version of this view in *An Essay on Human Understanding*. He postulated that the mind is "a white paper, void of all character without any ideas. How comes it to be furnished? To this I answer in one word, from Experience."[26] This *tabula rasa*, or blank tablet of the brain, according to Locke, may come into the world programmed with elemental desires such as need for food and sex, but the mind is created by experience, especially through association. In various forms, Locke's version of the mind has exerted a powerful influence on those who study human behavior down to the present.

In the 1950s, B.F. Skinner, the father of behaviorism in psychology, took Locke's *tabula rasa* concept a step further. He insists that the behavior of individuals can be engineered through programmed learning. In his utopian novel *Walden Two*, his hero Frazier says, "In the long run, *man is determined by the state* [italics are his]. A *laissez faire* philosophy which trusts to the inherent goodness and wisdom of the common man is incompatible with the observed fact that men are made good or bad and wise or foolish by the environment in which they grow."[27] Skinner assumes the blank tablet concept he had inherited from Locke, but his political spin on behavioral engineering was labeled as brainwashing by many, both liberal and conservative.

Lockian and Skinnerian assumptions on the malleability of the human mind long ruled in the social sciences. Richard Wrangham and Dale Peterson point out Margaret Mead's errors in convincing generations of anthropologists in this view: that "culture alone—nature without nurture—serves as impervious markings on the blank state of human character."[28] Daniel Dennett writes, "People ache to believe that we human beings are vastly different from all other species—and they are right! We are the only species that has an *extra* medium of design preservation and design rudiments of culture as well, and their capacity to transmit information 'behaviorally' in addition to genetically is itself an important biological phenomenon."[29]

Despite opposition, over the years the general concepts of evolutionary psychology and sociobiology have gained wide popular acceptance. For example, the January 16, 2016, *Time* article "The Science of Why People Snap in Anger" explains the phenomenon as evolved brain chemistry in language from evolutionary psychology that would have been anathema not many years ago: "We evolved these neural circuits for survival in the wild. We still need them." And the October 10–17, 2011, issue of *Newsweek* attributes the volatility in financial markets and politics to instant online communication: "The brain of *Homo sapiens* remains pretty much the same organ that evolved in the heads of African hunter gatherers 200,000 years ago." This sort of casual reference to behavior being rooted in evolution is routine today. It seems generally accepted that the *tabula* is not so *rasa* after all.

Evolutionary scientists believe that these ancestral voices, located in our genetic inheritance, whisper to us of behavior that was certainly adaptive in aiding the survival of our species but may not be now. But this evolution does not leave us in the thrall of the whispers, as is the case for most species. The process of evolution gifted *Homo sapiens* with a very large brain. With the spread of education and culture, modern humans can choose to reject narratives that are no longer adaptive. Thus, from an evolutionary perspective, our actions are influenced by both nature and nurture: both from our nature as it lies in the experience of our Paleolithic and Neolithic forebears and nurture as it comes from education, peer relationships and culture in general. John Milton's words from *Paradise Lost* in describing the sin of Adam and Eve make an excellent metaphor for our condition from an evolutionary perspective: We are "sufficient to have stood but free to fall" in our freedom to follow or reject evolutionary behavioral urges (though evolutionists might disagree on the extent of that freedom).

Primal Roots of Horror Cinema is not Evolutionary Psychology 101. If I may recast Mark Antony's line in Shakespeare's *Julius Caesar*, I come to adapt evolutionary research for criticism of film from the horror genre, not to add to it. For the most part, I exclude description of the multitude of animal studies by sociobiologists and experiments in brain chemistry that evolutionary psychologists cite as the basis for their findings. Rather, I focus on a central assumption: Although humans have free will, we are deeply influenced by whispers from the adaptive behavior of our distant ancestors.

Following this hypothesis, I propose that if the findings of evolutionary scientists are true, or maybe even true-ish, we are to some degree wired not only to feel the promptings of evolutionary adaptive behaviors but to respond to stories that re-enact the survival experiences of our forebears. And we can understand the appeal of those stories and something about ourselves through perceiving how primal narratives underpin them. Wilson's findings support the underlying premise of a primal traits critical methodology in the study of the arts in general and film in particular:

Gene-culture co-evolution is, I believe, the underlying process by which the brain evolved and the arts originated.... This much can be said with confidence, however: The growing evidence of an overall structured and powerful human nature, channeling development of the mind, favours a more traditionalist view of the arts. The arts are not solely shaped by errant genius out of historical circumstances and idiosyncratic personal experience. The roots of their inspiration date back in deep history to the genetic origins of the human brain, and are permanent.[30]

But how would early instances of artistic endeavor that paved the way for film, literature, art and music contribute to survival? There is general agreement on "the art instinct" and the species' need for play. But evolutionary psychologists disagree on whether art was adaptive and contributed to the survival of the species or invented later as a sort of evolutionary byproduct to become part of our generic heritage. Dennis Dutton adapts a quotation from German aesthetician Eckart Voland to explain the latter position in the origin of the arts: "We might think of a moth circling a lantern at night. With the arts, perhaps we should regard ourselves like moths who have succeeded in inventing a lantern in order to have fun circling it. If the arts are like the lantern, the Darwinian question is why we work so hard to invent them and why we have such fun circling them in the first place."[31] John MacKinnon takes the position that the arts were adaptive, not a later development: "If a behavior is adaptive, i.e., helps the individual to achieve evolutionary success, then selection will find an appropriate motivational pathway to ensure that the behavior occurs. Of what evolutionary benefit can artistic expression be to us? ... The brain must be able to swing instantly into fourth gear. It must be kept well tuned for such important moments, and art and intellectual stimulation are ways by which we keep it in mind."[32]

Whether the arts were adaptive in the sense of tribalism and territoriality or a later add-on, they seem to have been with us early in the origin of *Homo sapiens*. Cave paintings in Europe from 35,000 years ago (and longer in other locations) reflect primitive religion, with horned gods prominently featured along with carvings of squat, pregnant goddess figures as early vestiges of religion and hunting scenes that united tribal groups. The arts became increasingly powerful as language developed, creating the images of heroism that reverberate in our psyches today. Oral tales were circulated in humanity's beginnings. They were probably far less polished than those finally set into writing by the author of *Gilgamesh* in the eighteenth century BC or by Homer (if there was such a man) in his tale of the Greek conquest of Troy and the hero Odysseus' journey home afterward, dating to the eighth century BC. The folk epics' celebrations of the deeds of great heroes were of course entertaining, but they also reflect the early development and transmission of tribalism and warrior culture as adaptive behavior. Evolutionary psychology and sociobiology would suggest that echoes of primal voices whisper to us today in the art instinct and contribute to both the creation of culture and to our response to film and literature. But they may also have destructive effects in real life among tribal societies in Africa and the Middle East and even in the racial, ideological and ethnic divides in the United States.

The horror and science fiction–horror film and the literary sources that inspire them seem particularly appropriate for a primal traits critical approach, since their appeal lies in the realm of unreason, the unconscious. Joseph Carroll refers to the evolved human brain having "'cognitive modules' designed to solve adaptive problems specific to the statistical regularities of the ancient environment."[33] Brian Boyd expresses the same concept: "Evolution builds many specific learning tracks into minds, preparing them to expect certain kinds of situations and to understand them by making rich inferences from particular information patterns."[34] I adapt this concept to organize this book on six of the modules or learning tracks that I will call primal narratives in film and literature that have evolved from the experiences of our forebears and continue to whisper to us in the horror genre—and in life: (1) territoriality; (2) fear of assimilation and protection of the group and gene pool; (3) tribalism; (4) mating; (5) fear of the predator; and (6), woven through all of these narratives, distrust or hatred of the Other who might invade our territory, corrupt our genetic heritage and take our possessions. These are by no means the only such narratives, but they are a fruitful approach to analysis of the horror genre. Evolutionary psychologists and sociobiologists hold that these whispers from our ancient ancestors are stored in our genetic material and remain as factors in our lives and choices. It follows that such narratives can bring vicarious and pleasurable fear in film for viewers and literature for readers.

In *Hard Times* (1854), Charles Dickens criticizes the treatment of workers in Victorian England and also Jeremy Bentham's soul-crushing utilitarianism. In the novel, Dickens gives his view of utilitarian philosophy through satirizing his character Mr. Gradgrind as the pattern Benthamite. In lecturing the teachers of a school he has established, he says: "Now what I want is facts. Teach these boys and girls nothing but facts. Facts alone are wanted in life. Plan nothing else, and root out everything else. You can only form the minds of reasoning animals upon facts."[35] In contrasting Gradgrind's philosophy to the novel's circus players and the entertainment they bring others, Dickens' dialogue in the novel is a predecessor to evolutionary psychologists' comments on the human need for play. John Tooby and Leda Cosmides echo Dickens: "We think the human mind is permeated with an additional layer of adaptations that were selected to involve humanist aesthetic experiences and imagined worlds, even though these activities appear to be non-functional, and even extravagantly non-utilitarian."[36]

"A tale which holdeth children from play and old men from the chimney corner"

In George Eliot's *Middlemarch,* the pretentious scholar Edward Casaubon seeks to explain almost everything with his ambitious projected work *A Key to All Mythologies.* I have no such ambition, and if I may quote a line that was a cliché even when the poet Longfellow wrote it in "A Psalm of Life," "Art is long, and time is fleeting." So my approach to the horror film is not intended to be encyclopedic. I limit my topic to analysis of a small selection of horror and horror-science fiction films and in some cases to the literary sources that inspired them: works that offer a rich seed ground as models for adapting my critical approach and bring whispers of the primal narratives.

This book will focus on film and fiction in the horror and science fiction horror genres that have powerful visceral appeal inspired by the six primal narratives on which the book focuses. Genre films are more fruitful sources of the ancient whispers of adaptive behavior than more artistically conceived works with cerebral appeal, as we might see in comparing *Twilight* with *Last Year at Marienbad.* My modest proposal is that we can recognize these primal dreams imbedded in our human nature to explore our response to film and literature, using the horror genre as an example. Also, by tracing the whisper of these dreams, we can hope to understand more about ourselves.

Although it not a true horror or science fiction horror film, Stanley Kubrick and Arthur Clarke's *2001: A Space Odyssey,* both novel and film, serve well as an introduction to primal traits criticism in Chapter One. This splendid film is unique in its adaptation of primal narratives in a fictional primal environment, and it will be referred to throughout this book. Chapter Two focuses on territoriality with discussion of the satanic film—a narrative that has inspired vicarious fear for centuries—and science fiction films that fall into the horror category beginning with H.G. Wells novel *War of the Worlds* and its film adaptations. The invasion story offers an example of how culture reshapes the narrative, while the central elements remain unchanged.

Chapter Three centers on the assimilation narrative as it developed in the 1950s science fiction–horror film and on the zombie apocalypse meme with its origins in Voodoo folklore. Richard Matheson transformed the zombie into something quite different in his novel *I Am Legend* and its film adaptations. George Romero's *Night of the Living Dead* owes a debt to Matheson's novel but created the zombie meme in film as it has developed. Chapter Four analyzes the vampire meme as an example of the tribal narrative, beginning with Bram Stoker's novel *Dracula* and a sampling of the multitude of adaptations it has inspired in film as well as other versions of the vampire narrative. Chapter Five centers on the mating narrative, using the gothic romance subgenre of the horror film for an analysis of how its appeal springs from our adaptive evolution.

Fear of the predator, be it animal, human or alien, has inspired many horror films, a narrative passed to the human consciousness as a subject for vicarious horror from the experiences of our primal ancestors. Chapter Six explores this narrative with discussions of the *Predator* and *Alien* franchises and a sampling of the multitude of other predators portrayed in film. Interwoven throughout the discussion of all these films is the human evolutionary narrative of fear of the Other. Some films are more firmly rooted in this narrative, and Chapter Seven explores it as developed in the ghost, robot-computer, witch and slasher films. The Conclusion offers a perspective on primal narratives not only as an influence in the appeal of the horror film but their impact on the future of our species.

These primal narratives and the films and the fiction that inspired them tell us much about ourselves in our response to them. They are imbedded in our human nature and can create our response to conflict, the basis of drama and fiction. As Agatha Christie's canny sleuth Hercule Poirot opines in "The King of Clubs Mystery," "Where there is human nature, Hastings, there is drama."

ONE

2001: A Space Odyssey

"Dave ... I have the greatest enthusiasm for the mission."

2001: A Space Odyssey (1968) provides an introductory example of evolutionary concepts adapted for film and a fine opening subject for a primal traits critique. It is, in fact, a portal to discussion of all the primal narratives to be addressed in this book, and it will also be a reference point throughout this book as a kind of touchstone. Director Stanley Kubrick worked closely with science fiction novelist Arthur Clarke in developing his film. Indeed, two separate texts, film and novel, evolved from the collaboration. So in addition to serving as a model for a primal traits critique, it is a fascinating example of film adaptation and the interaction of fiction and film.

Just who adapted whom remains an open question because at Kubrick's insistence, the novel appeared shortly after the release of the film, although it was ready for publication earlier. *2001* offers two approaches on the subject of adaptation: both to adaptation of novel to film and to Darwin's theory of evolution through adaptation to the environment with the expansion of that theory by sociobiologists and evolutionary psychologists. *2001* is unique among the films discussed in this book in that it seems an intentional appropriation by Clarke and Kubrick of Darwin's ideas and of those who applied them to human nature rather than filmmakers' and authors' response to primal narratives bubbling from the unconscious and their genetic heritage as combined with their cultural experience.

Most of those who saw *2001* when it opened in 1968 were inspired with a sense of awe at its visual splendor but were left scratching their heads as to just what it was about. Perhaps if the word "evolution" had appeared at some point in the dialogue, all would have become clear for viewers. Clarke's novel answers many of the questions. Both Clarke and Kubrick acknowledged the philosophical core of the film. Clarke referred to the "metaphysical, philosophical and even religious questions" that it poses. And Kubrick found the introduction of religious thought into the film inevitable because of the enormous diversity of the universe and the potential for the evolution of highly advanced aliens. "All the essential attributes of such extraterrestrial intelligences," he commented in an interview, "are the attributes we give to God. What we are really dealing with here is, in fact, a scientific definition of God."[1] While the core of the film and novel focuses on evolution, both in the strict Darwinian sense and from the early perspectives of sociobiology and evolutionary psychology, Kubrick's film, more than Clarke's novel, adds spiritual dimensions. This theme begins with the segment "The Dawn of Man" and its Biblical symbolism, culminating in allusions to the New Age paths of the 1960s.

The evolution theme develops through three patterns of images: one pattern persistent in the beginning, another in the middle, and a third in the final portions. All are especially revealing as visual tropes that connect the theme of human evolution to the "metaphysical" qualities that Kubrick and Clarke as well as critics mention. The "Dawn of Man" segment tells the story of humanity's genesis, quite appropriately through the ironically presented visual suggestion of a Darwinian Garden. The segment portrays the origin of adaptive elements of the human form as well as behaviors that have been both essential for our survival in the past and potentially destructive to our survival today.

"The Dawn of Man" establishes both filmmaker's and novelist's appropriation of evolutionary adaptation. Clarke's novel relies on authorial explanation. Kubrick's approach is visual. He gives the viewer repeated visual suggestions of the Garden from Genesis, a natural enough choice of metaphor for humankind's beginnings. But Kubrick's Garden allusion remains wholly ironic, for it is a post–Darwinian version: an anti–Eden, a place of eating and being eaten. The camera repeatedly pans across bones. We see the man-apes competing for food with the tapirs as they forage together, a demonstration that they are at about the same place on the food chain; and we see a great cat attack one of our ancestors, who has no survival traits for self-defense. The film shows us that both apes and tapirs are prey, an ironic reversal of the Genesis dictum of humanity having dominion. We see our evolutionary forebears huddled at night in a cave, frightened at the "terror by night" to which the psalmist refers, though in their evolutionary history they will soon be endangered by "the arrow that flies by day" from their own species.

The film's opening connects to basic Darwinian theory, as developed by evolutionary psychologists and sociobiologists. The scenes are powerfully reminiscent of the opening pages of Robert Ardrey's *African Genesis*, in which he traces our evolutionary history to the plains of Africa: "Here we came about—slowly, ever so slowly—on a sky-swept savannah glowing with menace.... Even in the first long days of our beginnings we held in our hand the weapon, an instrument somewhat older than ourselves."[2] In addition to competing with other species, the group of proto humans must also fight for territory with their own kind, a competition enacted through growling and posturing sessions at the water hole in a scene suggesting a Biblical allusion to Genesis 2:10: "And a river ran out of Eden to water the garden." The two alpha males confront each other with violent gestures, but no blows are landed. The proto humans have not yet mastered aggression as we know it in this anti–Eden. The territorial battle at this stage of their evolution resembles that of the great majority of male animals today: confrontation without a fight to the death. The scene demonstrates a perspective on what would become human narratives: aggression, territoriality, tribalism and distrust of the Other, human adaptive traits described in the literature of evolutionary science. The incursions of the cat as predator add another narrative.

The monolith suggests the Tree of Knowledge from Genesis. In a shot as night falls before it arrives, Kubrick centers a tree in the middle of the frame to cue the viewer's eye. When the proto humans discover the monolith and excitedly dance about it the next morning, the alpha male ("Moon Watcher" in Clarke's novel, so named because he is fascinated with the moon in the night sky) touches and actually tastes this symbolic Tree. Then, appropriately, he is the first to experience the epiphany of knowledge in the scene that follows as he forages for food. He finds the bone that will become the first tool and, importantly so far as our evolution is concerned, the first weapon. Two separate close-ups of his fist raising the bone emphasize his hand and center on the gift that may have led the aliens to find our species a fit subject for evolution: the opposable thumb, which enables us to be tool users and tool makers. Jonathan Gottschall sums up this central development of our evolution: "Other animals, with their thumbless extremities, can merely paw at the world, or butt and scrape it with their hooves. But because we humans have thumbs, we can seize hold of it and manipulate it to our ends."[3]

It may not be entirely coincidental that a line in *The Naked Ape*, which achieved notoriety at about the time the film was in production, so clearly reflects the epiphany scene when Moon Watcher "gets it." In noting the inferiority of the human body as opposed to that of other species, Desmond Morris observes that our ape ancestors could not compete with big cats and other carnivores with their body: "Instead, an entirely new approach was made, using artificial weapons instead of natural ones, and it worked."[4] In the novel, following their transformation and successfully killing tapirs, Moon Watcher and his fellow tribal warriors do just that, attacking and killing the big cat that has long invaded their cave for prey.

Moon Watcher's epiphany is surely one of the great scenes in cinema history. We see him contemplate the bone. Clarke spells out what is happening to the proto human in quite explicit fashion, describing him held spellbound while the monolith "trains" him. Later, after his victory at the water hole, Clarke tells us in his novel, "He rightly sensed that his whole world had

***2001: A Space Odyssey*:** **Moonwalker's epiphany after the monolith has changed him.**

changed and that he was no longer a powerless victim of the forces around him."[5] Later, other members of this early version of a tribe get the same treatment. Kubrick adapts this scene to let us comprehend it the same way Moonwalker does. Like him, we use our intelligence to *see*, rather than being told as in the novel, the connection between (a) the proto human holding the bone, looking at it and the tapir's skull speculatively, and (b) the close-ups of the opposable thumb on his right hand that will make him a tool maker. Now that the proto humans have intelligence and the ability to make tools, they use them for aggressive purposes of promoting their own species against an Other. Clarke gives us a rather detailed description of the proto humans' perilous condition. But Kubrick demonstrates his theme visually, forcing us, in a nice bit of irony, to use the same mental critical thinking processes as Moon Watcher's: the perception of analogy and discovery of patterns.

We see a reenactment of the territorial narrative in the battle at the water hole. Moon Watcher has become the alpha male, the leader of the tribal hunting pack and territorial defenders. The ground rules at the water hole change in the second meeting of tribes. The camera underscores Moon Walker's transformation and that of his pack by showing him in an upright stance as he and his fellows confront the rivals, who are noticeably still in the shambling posture of their fellow man-apes at the start of the film. From an evolutionary perspective, of course, tool makers and users would have to be erect to see properly and use implements. Jay Gould, no friend of evolutionary psychology or sociobiology but a famed scholar in the field of evolution, writes,

"Upright posture frees the hands from locomotion and for manipulation.... Complete freeing of our hands for using tools preceded most of the evolutionary enlargement of our brain."[6] But now the hunting tool that the alpha male discovered in his epiphany has become a weapon used against his own species. And we return to "Genesis," with an ironic allusion to a memorable line after the eviction from Eden: "Cain rose up against Abel his brother, and slew him" (4:8). The shots that follow, however, show the Cain figure triumphant, not outcast like the Biblical Cain.

The water hole scene makes a commentary on evolved human behavior. David Barash notes that most animal species have instinctual inhibitions against killing their own kind. The wolf who submits to a dominant member of his species, for instance, exposes his throat, which saves his life. Humans seem to lack this inhibition. He suggests that cultural development of weapons may have far outstripped evolutionary behavior.[7] But this opening sequence rests on the primal narratives of tribalism, territoriality, fear of the predator and willingness to kill those perceived as Other who are not part of our tribe: narratives that continue in the remainder of the film. They are narratives that are endemic in the horror genre and unfortunately in human relations today.

The million-year segue to *2001* links the two sections by transforming the bone that Moon Walker jubilantly throws into the air into a spaceship and also a pen floating in free fall: the lineal descendants of the first tool and perhaps a sly reference to the pen being mightier than the sword. The entire segment underscores the development of technology since the use of the first tool-weapon by Moon Walker. In the millennia separating the two parts, humanity has established bases on the moon. Heywood Floyd, an American official, has been summoned there to inspect a strange monolith. The journey involves a stop at a space station before proceeding to the moon, where we see a counterpoint with the opening episode: a re-enactment of the territorial battle that ends the "Dawn of Man" sequence, with males from two tribes confronting each other. The Russians, who also have a moon base, are concerned about rumors regarding expansion of American lunar territory and some kind of find there. A Russian official pumps Floyd; the encounter ends in a standoff, with a steely-eyed Floyd responding, "I'm not at liberty to divulge that information." Viewers in 1968, when children were taught to "duck and cover" in school, would have understood the significance of this modern version of confrontation between international tribes and alpha males. The "Dawn of Man" watering hole encounter links to yet another watering hole, a futuristic lounge. But the evolution of technology and suggestion of aggression in this territorial confrontation offer a comparison to the battle with bone clubs.

Parallels to the first segment continue. We repeatedly see humans eating through the first three segments and Dave's last meal before he loses his mortal form. Most animals in the wild spend their entire lives foraging for food and battening when it is available, an instinct we encourage in food animals. It is an instinct that may be a cause for high levels of obesity among humans today. We see this behavior by Moon Walker and his tribe in the opening scenes as they forage for insects and plant food. Later we get close-ups of the tribe munching tapir flesh. The film emphasizes human functions, as seen when Floyd anxiously looks at instruction on how to use a toilet in zero gravity on the space shuttle. Later we see Floyd and his companions eat sandwiches with artificial material that "tastes sort of like chicken" while on the way to view the monolith, and Dave and Frank eat chemical-looking goop on *Discovery*. Kubrick emphasizes these human functions from our evolutionary past that will be lost for Dave when he is transformed.

The "Jupiter Mission" segment enacts the final stage of humanity's technological evolution, and in this largely non-verbal film, one passage of dialogue is a focal point for the theme that the director will show us visually. After a long establishing shot of the *Discovery*, another underscoring of the technology theme, the film introduces us to the crew: Dave Bowman, mission commander; Frank Pool, his deputy; three scientists in prophetically coffin-like hibernation boxes; and the film's only really interesting character, the artificial intelligence computer who runs the *Discovery*'s systems, HAL 9000. Its name is an acronym for Heuristically Programmed Algorithmic Computer and he comes to us with a wink and a nudge since the following letters of HAL would spell IBM. Dave and Frank watch an interview they had given the BBC some time before, which is now broadcast to them. The interviewer introduces HAL as a computer that "can reproduce, though some experts still prefer the word 'mimic,' most of the activities of the human brain and with incalculably greater speed and reliability." The line signals the end result of technological evolution: a machine that equals or exceeds human intelligence and far excels humanity in ability to absorb and process information.

But the following lines suggest the potential problem with such technology. The interviewer asks whether HAL has genuine emotions. Dave responds, "Well, he acts like he has genuine emotions.... As to whether or not he has real feelings is something I don't think anyone can answer." The remainder of "Jupiter Mission" will provide that answer visually. The adaptive traits that permitted humanity to survive—defense of territory and tribal conflict between alpha males—have been passed on to their creation, our evolutionary child, so to speak. He does, as the BBC interviewer suggests, "reproduce ... most of the activities of the human brain" as it has evolved.

When devices on the ship mysteriously fail, Dave and Frank plan a shutdown of HAL, a machine given human instincts from our primal narratives, and he responds as a human would. His omnipresent eye reads the conversation between Dave and Frank as they plot to at least temporarily end his consciousness. The film has twice demonstrated the territorial imperative; thus, like Moon Watcher, HAL defends his territory and his life. He kills the crew members in hibernation and schemes to get Frank and Dave out of the ship, managing to kill Frank when he leaves to replace a part.[8]

A careful viewer, then, will see the irony of the final battle between Dave and HAL. The film demonstrates what evolutionary scientists would call a fundamental trait of human nature with another territorial conflict between alpha males, one human and the other a human creation, linking us to the battle at the water hole and the confrontation of Russians and Americans on the space station. In this case, unlike Victor Frankenstein, the human succeeds in destroying his monster when Dave is able to return to the ship after failing to rescue Frank. The cybernetic male's death throes provide ironic punctuation with his pathetic rendition of "Daisy" and the final lines referring to "a bicycle built for two," a regression to a primitive technological device. Humanity and its technology have been partners to this stage of *Homo sapiens*' evolution and have had a "stylish marriage." HAL's demise symbolizes the end of the union of humanity and technology begun with Moon Watcher's epiphany. Also, the episode has brought us to the final limits of technology, and the visual imagery demonstrates that the limitation of the machine is the limitation of human nature. On this subject, Kubrick said,

> Most advanced computer theorists believe that once you have a computer which is more intelligent than man and capable of learning by experience, it's inevitable that it will develop an equivalent range of emotional reactions—fear, love, hate, envy, etc. Such a machine could eventually become as incomprehensible as a human being, and could, of course, have a nervous breakdown, as HAL did in the film.[9] In other words, the machine would parallel human evolution.

The ironic tone that dominates the visual imagery of the Moon journey and "To Jupiter" ends with "To the Infinite—and Beyond." Irony will not do for death and transfiguration, an evolution away from the human primal narratives. Clarke's novel verbalizes the transition, reporting Dave's experiences as he realizes that he is traveling at faster-than-light speed and then describing his arrival at a switching station. Here he sees graveyards of spaceships (apparently brought there through the Star Door) and perhaps the alien entities as energy forms moving about a star. It is the conventional stuff of science fiction. Kubrick abjures such explicit description to achieve the mystical tone of his conclusion.

But finding visual images for Dave's transformation offers a greater challenge than visualizing man's genesis and final development as a tool maker and user. As Kubrick and Clarke both suggested in interviews, a truly poetic visualization of this process of death and rebirth would almost certainly have religious connotations. In addition to the film's adaptation of the early findings of sociobiology, *2001* is also a product of the spiritual soup of the late

1960s. It was a time of religious searching. The New Age was aborning. The conclusion of *2001* seems a melding of science fiction and transcendentalism, strange bedfellows influenced by the New Age spirituality that was just appearing the 1960s.

Kubrick establishes religious symbolism in the "Dawn of Man" segment with the ironic portrayal of an evolutionary Genesis. Then in the last of his triad of image patterns, he uses a metaphor of death and reincarnation as inherited from Eastern and Christian mysticism by the New Age as metaphor for Dave's transformation brought about by the unseen aliens. When *2001* appeared, it was, in the words of the Fifth Dimension's song "the dawning of the Age of Aquarius" (included in the Broadway musical *Hair*), a time when new religious movements gained hundreds of thousands of followers and millions of interested observers. Maharishi Mahesh Yogi's Transcendental Meditation practice (adopted by the Beatles and the Beach Boys), A.C. Bhaktivedanta Swami Prabhupada's Krishna Consciousness, Zen Buddhism and other Eastern paths found uncounted and uncountable followers. If the New Age was not born during the mid– to late 1960s, it enjoyed a rapidly increasing popularity; and a focus on Eastern religions was fundamental to the movement, if so amorphous a group of belief systems can be called a "movement."[10] Moreover, Arthur Clarke lived much of his life in Sri Lanka, where the population is over 70 percent Buddhist.[11] While he did not use the same religious imagery that we see in the film for his novel, Clarke might well have suggested it for the screenplay as a means of visualizing Dave's transformation. In evolution, for every new species that develops, old ones may die. Clarke, in fact, had proposed such an evolutionary change in *Childhood's End*, when the Earth Children move to the next step in their evolutionary transcendence.

Kubrick visualization of Dave Bowman's metamorphosis as brought about by the alien masters continues the religious symbolism from the opening segment of the film. If the monolith suggests the Tree of Knowledge in the Genesis portion of the film, it has now become the Tree of Life. Dave reaches out with his mechanical hands from the pod, a shot offering another visual counterpoint from the first and second parts and a reminder of the increasing level of technology humanity has achieved, from Moon Watcher touching and tasting the monolith and his transformation to Floyd making contact with it in his spacesuit on the moon. After what seems a faster-than-light trip, we see him age in his corporeal form. The film shows him as an old man eating a meal in a sumptuous apartment, a final reference to food as part of our evolutionary need. We see him dying in a bed with the monolith poised to end his mortality. He then begins his journey back to Earth as the Star Child.

The visual imagery of the film's conclusion offers interesting ambiguities, strongly suggesting a metaphor of death and reincarnation from New Age

2001: A Space Odyssey: **The monolith at the end of Dave Bowman's (Keir Dullea) mortal life.**

beliefs and adapted for a science fiction vision of evolution to another stage of being. Buddhist and Hindu traditions offer an appropriate frame of visual reference in creating the film's religious or mystic tone to which both critics and Kubrick refer. These traditions focus on detachment from the material world and reincarnation. Clearly, Dave has been transformed and reborn to another evolutionary stage, and Eastern mysticism offers a stunning visual metaphor for his death and rebirth.

The writings of Christian mystic, Jesuit priest and paleontologist Teilhard de Chardin (1881–1955), whose work was adopted by the New Age, seem another possible source in *2001*. His thinking melds evolution and transcendental mysticism (which nearly caused him to be defrocked). His writings were long suppressed by the Church, and his books and essays began appearing posthumously in the late 1950s, with *Living in the Divine Milieu* published in 1957 and *The Phenomenon of Man* in 1959. They were adopted by the New Age at the time of Kubrick's development of *2001*.

Evolution, de Chardin proclaims, is much more than the change of the material form as created by adaptation to the environment through natural selection and survival of the fittest, as envisioned by Darwin. In *The Phenomenon of Man*, he describes the origins of thought in terms reminiscent of Moon Watcher's epiphany: "The access to thought represents a threshold which had to be crossed at a single stride, a 'transcendental experimental interval' about which scientifically we can say nothing."[12] His words might describe the experience of Dave at the conclusion of *2001*. At the same time we see him captured by the alien entities, we also see his evolution to another transcendental level, an evolution quite different from the evolution that formed the primal narratives.

2001: A Space Odyssey can be summed up as a story in which aliens come to Earth to find a species that might be evolved to intelligence and change it. Then, after the species progresses enough to achieve primitive space travel, the aliens lure one of them through a Star Door for a faster-than-light journey to their home world where they change the individual thus trapped to a level beyond the physical realm and return him. Kubrick assures us that such is the bare-bones plot of his film.

But to simplify *2001: A Space Odyssey* to a mere plot summary is tantamount to saying that John Keats' "Eve of St. Agnes" is a poem about a boy who tricks his way into a girl's bedroom, and after having his wicked way with her persuades her to elope with him. In each case, the work, both film and poem, is far greater than its plot. Perhaps the title of Kubrick's final film *Eyes Wide Shut* (1999) offers an appropriate metaphor. That film's hero has failed to realize the complexity of life because he has walked through it, in the words of the title, with "eyes wide shut." When he opens his eyes, he discovers a new and troubling level of experience. So it goes for the viewer of *2001*. Those who encounters it with eyes, and mind, wide open will find many rewards in its insights into human nature and humanity's relationship with its technology.

Two
The Territorial Narrative

"This Land Is Your Land"

Woody Guthrie's 1940 song remains stirring today. Evolutionary psychologists might trace the continuing power of the lyrics to the territorial imperative. We respond to the seduction of the words for about the same reason that the fictional Moon Walker's tribe in *2001: A Space Odyssey* claim their water hole and do battle for it. Evolutionary theory maintains that the desire to establish and defend territory is deeply ingrained in the adaptive behavior of our primal ancestors. Edward O. Wilson observes,

> Territoriality is one of the variants of aggressive behavior that can be directly evaluated by the new insights of biology. Students of animal behavior define a territory as an area occupied more or less exclusively either directly or by overt defense or indirectly through advertisement. This area invariably contains a scarce resource, usually a steady food supply, shelter, space for sexual display.[1]

Richard Wrangham and Dale Peterson define territory similarly as "a range that is forcibly occupied, i.e., defended from trespassers of the same (or sometimes other) species. *Range* on the other hand, is a piece of land that is occupied whether or not force is employed." They note that chimpanzees are our closest relatives in the animal kingdom and that we share their territorial instincts. They describe male chimpanzees "as defenders of a group territory, a gang committed to the ethnic purity of their own set" that invades the territory of other chimps to kill their competitors.[2] Our simian cousins can be ruthless in defending and acquiring territory. Edward O. Wilson wryly observes that if hamadryas baboons had nuclear weapons, "they would destroy the world in a week."[3]

The parallel to territorial behavior among humans is unmistakable. We see it in the building of empires in the ancient world. We see it in the desire to conquer new territory for their expanding populations and natural resources by Japan and Germany leading up to World War II. We see it in the almost religious adherence to the manifest destiny philosophy of nineteenth-century America, which maintained our right to claim territory from the East to the West Coasts, no matter that it was already occupied by Native Americans. And we see it in the visceral ties of many Jews to Israel as their ancient territory. In twenty-first–century America, we have seen it in the demand to build a wall on our southern borders to defend our territory.

If the instinct for establishment and defense of territory is common throughout the animal kingdom, the early proponents of sociobiology and then evolutionary psychology asked, why should humanity, having evolved through the iron laws of survival of the fittest and natural selection in the same manner as other species, be different? Territorial boundaries and defense through tribal allegiances against Others would have been a significant evolutionary advantage for primal humans. Desmond Morris notes that our ancestors in hunter-gatherer groups endured long and dangerous hunting forays. Thus, the change for *Homo sapiens* from a nomadic life to establishment of a settled territory where they could practice agriculture to supplement and soon replace hunting would have been an adaptive development. "A home base was necessary, a place to come back to with the spoils, where the females and young would be waiting and could share the food.... So the hunting ape became a territorial ape."[4]

Evolutionary psychologists and sociobiologists posit that the territorial imperative remains with us today in both subtle and obvious forms, expressed in a variety of ways, some harmless and others potentially destructive. College students sometimes put a line of tape down the middle of their dorm rooms to separate territories, and we often see fences or hedges separating properties in the suburbs. Robert Ardrey writes: "We act as we do for reasons of our evolutionary past, not our cultural present.... If we defend the title to our land or the sovereignty of our country, we do it for reasons no different, no less innate, and no less ineradicable, than do lower animals. The dog barking at you from behind his master's fence acts for a motive indistinguishable from that of his master when the fence was built."[5] The territorial battle at the water hole in *2001* is a metaphor to demonstrate the transmission of territorial defense from the time of our primal ancestors throughout human history. Robert Frost wrote in his poem "Mending Wall," "Something there is that does not love a wall." Yet it seems to be our nature to build them.

"Thy lot is given charge and strict watch": Defenders of the Portal in the Satanic Horror Film

Humanity's adaptive drive to defend land or to take that of the Other has long inspired stories dramatizing both the successful defense of territory and the conquering of that of Others, from the Greeks' attack on Troy in the

Homeric epic to western films with the cavalry-and-Indian plot. In the horror film, this Other who would invade our territory and corrupt the gene pool is often of supernatural origin, from vampires or werewolves to zombies, and the narrative inspires vicarious and pleasurable fear whispered from the adaptive behavior of our earliest ancestors.

Satan is a model for a territorial invader, one of the most ancient of Others in religion; and in horror literature and films that the myth has inspired, he remains a pervasive presence. Genesis identifies the serpent as only a tempter, but John Milton builds on a tradition in his epic poem *Paradise Lost* that gradually evolved to create the Father of Evil. We meet Satan later in the Old Testament in the Book of Job. Carol Newsom estimates it was written somewhere between 500 and 700 BC.[6] Here Satan is introduced as one of the "sons of God," presumably angels. There is no sense that he is evil in the theocratic sense. Rather, he is a sly instigator who, when God praises Job for his righteousness, asks, "Doth Job fear God for naught?" (1:9), bringing about Job's trials. According to Howard Schwartz, Jewish myth made a distinction between Satan as "tempter and heavenly prosecutor," who often cooperates with God, and Lucifer, the outcast who rebelled.[7] Jeffrey Russell links the evolution of Satan's role as the personification of evil to the Jews' captivity in Babylonia where they were exposed to the intensely dualistic Zoroastrian religion, which portrays nearly equal forces of light and darkness locked in eternal struggle.[8] Zoroastrianism exemplifies the ultimate tribalism: the battle of light against powerful darkness, Them against Us. By the time of Jesus, Satan and Lucifer had been melded into the enemy of man and God. In this version, Satan gets credit for overthrowing Eden, as described in *Paradise Lost*. He left the Hell to which he and his minions had been consigned and invaded the Garden, a territorial incursion.

Some historians speculate that many pagans of pre–Christian Europe worshipped a Goddess and a horned, tailed hunting god, Cernunnos, both of whom are portrayed on cave wall paintings. The church, they believe, created the image of Satan from those paintings of Cernunnos to eliminate competition and burned the priestesses of the Goddess as witches and the Devil's servants. A reaction to the tyranny of the church, they suggest, created a cult of Satan rooted in worship of Cernunnos in the countryside during the Dark Ages. Arthur Lyons summarizes the theory of the Horned God as the origin for the Satan figure.[9] James Frazer's discoveries of horned gods through many mythologies spurred interest in this concept. Satanic worship died among the peasantry by the eighteenth century, but the black mass continued to be celebrated among the elite in circles like the Hellfire Club, the Medmenham Abbey group in England and similar Satanic enthusiasts on the continent. Then during the Romantic Movement, Satan became the embodiment of freedom and rebellion against authority in the works of romantic poets, who took Milton's Satan's stirring lines "Better to reign in Hell than serve in Heaven"[10] out of context. In "Cain," the poet Byron ennobles Satan when he has him exclaim, "Through All Eternity and the Unfathomable Gulfs of Hades.... All, All Will I Dispute." We hear echoes of the words Byron gives Satan from Ahab in *Moby Dick* when he exclaims at the last battle with the whale, "From Hell's heart I stab at thee; for hate's sake I spit my last breath at thee."[11] Then Khan in *Star Trek II: The Wrath of Khan* quotes Melville in his concluding lines before blowing up his ship. William Blake and Percy Bysshe Shelley in England and later Charles Pierre Baudelaire in France similarly sided with Satan as a symbol of energy and personal freedom. The evolution of Satan's image from emblem of the ultimate Other to a more sympathetic portrayal offers an example of the changes culture can exert in the primal narratives.

The groundwork for the Satanic invasion plot had been firmly established by the time film became an art form, rooted in the folklore of Satanism from the Middle Ages and the modern urban legends that spring from it. Contemporary media give us lurid stories of Satanic cults that kidnap and sacrifice blond, blue-eyed children. Conservative Christian author William Viser writes of "a highly organized, very secret network.... The odds are this is happening in your town."[12] Stories of Satanic rituals and symbols often involve reversals of Christian practice: desecration of the Christian mass with a Eucharist of blood and urine; the upside-down cross; the pentagram with the two horns up; the goat's head symbol; the number 666, which is briefly mentioned in The Revelation to John (13: 18); the ritual orgy; and other imagery and allusion as they can be traced in folklore. Dennis Wheatley adapted this folklore in his novels, as have Viser, Constance Cumbey and their ilk in sensational exposés for the conservative Christian market.

Satan is a central performer in the horror genre. Four plotlines dominate the Satanic film: territorial invasion; the Antichrist as invader; possession; and the Faust story. These narratives and the films' imagery whisper the primal fear of the Other as territorial invader and his hidden presence with his followers: an opposing tribe, a cult, imbedded in our territory dedicated to aid in Satan's invasion.

In Christian tradition, as told in *Paradise Lost,* Satan led one-third of the angels of heaven in a rebellion. All were cast down into Hell, prepared for them in advance. In Milton's cosmos, God may not necessarily predestine but he surely foreknows. Milton follows tradition in establishing Hell as another place with the potential of its inhabitants to invade and conquer our territory, as in the Judeo-Christian tradition that Satan escaped and invaded Eden. In films that have sprung from the tradition, this invasion often involves some kind of portal separating the two territories with defenders of the portal.

The confrontation implicit to invasion brings conflict, the central element of drama. Dennis Dutton observes, "[T]hrough all of known cultural history, stories have been about problems and conflict," and finds that conflict involves "(1) a human will and (2) some kind of resistance to it."[13] A story about Benjamin Braddock meeting Elaine Robinson, forced to take her on a date but falling in love and marrying her, is not the story we are adapted to want. But when we find that after Benjamin and Elaine fall in love and appear to be on their way to a happy ending, Elaine learns that Benjamin has been in an affair with her mother, we have conflict and a rattling good story for *The Graduate*. The central conflict of the Satanic film, however, is conflict over territory.

"Let no evil thing enter in": *The Sentinel, Prince of Darkness, Cabin in the Woods, Poltergeist* and *Insidious*

In *The Sentinel*, Satan's minions, a cult, plan their master's invasion through such an entryway. In the Satanic film, Satan and his servants are often opposed by a secret society dedicated to preventing the invasion, an example of the tribal defense of territory against Others. Thus, we have the primal equivalent of two tribes in many Satanic films, one seeking to bring about an invasion of territory and the other defending it. *The Sentinel*'s opening shots show priests praying, "Let no evil thing enter in." The scene shifts to Alison Parker, a successful model who rents a lovely apartment in a luxurious building for a suspiciously low rent. Strange things happen. Alison goes into trances, in one of them writing a passage in Latin although she has no knowledge of the language. Boyfriend Michael takes the Latin sentence to a church for translation. He finds that it is from *Paradise Lost* (a little misquoted) in which the angel Gabriel gets his charge from Uriel as guardian of the gate of Hell to keep Satan from Eden: "Thy lot is given charge and strict watch that to this happy place no evil thing approach or enter."[14]

Alison discovers Father Halliran, an elderly blind priest who lives in the top floor of the building. We learn that he is the Sentinel, the most important member of a secret society charged with protecting the gate between Heaven and Hell. Halliran is the latest in a line to take on the work of Gabriel. The portal is located in Alison's apartment building. The Satanic cult living in the apartment house is dedicated to bringing about their master's return. Alison learns that she is intended as the new Sentinel to defend the portal and humanity's territory against the invader.

Kendall Phillips observes that John Carpenter's films are often invasion stories, citing *Assault on Precinct 13*, his remake of *The Thing from Another World, The Fog* and others as examples.[15] *Prince of Darkness* adapts this plotline in another portal defense of territory approach, with a twist from H.P.

Lovecraft's Cthulhu mythos, tales of the Old Ones striving to re-enter from a different dimension. But here, Carpenter combines Lovecraft with a vaguely Christian spin on Satan and a bit of science fiction. A priest, Father Loomis (Donald Pleasence), discovers that the Brotherhood of Sleep order (another tribe of defenders) has for 2000 years guarded a vessel that contains the essence of Satan, now located in a Los Angeles church.

Loomis recruits Prof. Birack (Victor Wong), a physicist, and his students to analyze the vat, which if opened would free Satan to enter, open the portal and bring an Anti God into the world. The film uses the hoary "discovered manuscript" plot, the diary of the last priest, a member of an order of territorial defenders who guarded the container that the students find. It ends with the exclamation "The Sleeper Awakens!" a warning of an invasion from Hell. The vicarious horror of the film stems from the culturally inspired fear of Satan, whom we have been taught to regard as the great enemy of mankind, and the Anti God as territorial invaders, aided by hordes of street people taken over by the cylinder. At the conclusion, team members Danforth and Kelly serve as sacrifices to save the world, a familiar theme described by evolutionary psychologists of characters who give up their lives to save their kin group.

Cabin in the Woods (2012), directed by Drew Goddard with a script by Goddard and Joss Whedon, gives a unique meta spin to the portal and invasion of territory film, a horror movie based on horror movies and yet another adaptation of H.P. Lovecraft's Cthulhu mythos. It begins with clichés from the genre, introducing the familiar plot of a group of five college students getting away for a weekend at a secluded cabin. Each represents a type from the genre: Jules (Anna Hutchison) the good girl, a virgin; Dana (Kristen Connolly) the wild child; Holden (Jessie Williams) the straight arrow; Curt (Chris Hemsworth) the hunky jock; and Fran (Marty Mikalski) a stoner. These conventional roles would be important at the conclusion, transformed from convention to archetype.

When they stop for gas, they meet a strange old man, Mordecai, who sneers at them and tells them they are doomed if they proceed but gives them directions to the cabin. Whedon might have named the character for the Biblical Mordecai from the Book of Esther who brought warnings, once to save the king and once the Israelites. But from a narrative perspective, the scene echoes similar warnings through the history of literature that serve as foreshadowing, from the prophet in *Oedipus the King* to the villagers who warn Jonathan Harker in *Dracula*. Getting to the cabin involves passing through a tunnel, in effect leading the students to another territory where they will find an environment where the laws of nature as they understand them are changed. The scene frequently shifts to a headquarters under the cabin where the controllers manipulate the environment above in a variety of ways. We are told repeatedly in control room scenes that the students must make choices. One of the directors says, "They have to make choices or the system doesn't work."

The film gradually reveals the purpose of the cabin and the reasons for having the students there. We learn that the students are intended as a ritual sacrifice to the Lovecraftian ancient gods who sleep beneath the earth of the cabin, one of many such events worldwide to take place on a chosen day. So the students' ritualized deaths are a sacrificial offering in humanity's defense of the portal. They represent specific archetypes (a nod to Joseph Campbell) for the ritual: the virgin, the whore, the athlete, the scholar and the fool. They must die with their blood funneled below, the whore first and the virgin last, or the Old Ones will awake and invade. So when the portal is breached and our territory invaded, Fran, the wise fool, opines, "Maybe that's the way it should be. If you've got to kill your friends to survive, maybe it's time for a change."

Poltergeist (1982) develops a unique twist on the portal invasion plot. The evil entity comes to our territory through a television. After Steve and Diane Freeling find their young daughter Carol Anne conversing with the TV, the home is plagued with a variety of frightening supernatural incidents. Carol Anne is sucked into another territory, the spirit world, by one of childhood's most pervasive fears, the monster in the closet. Her frantic parents enlist the help of Dr. Lesh, a parapsychologist, and her two assistants. After an assortment of terrifying supernatural events, Dr. Lesh realizes she needs help and calls on Tangina, a medium.

Poltergeist: **Carol Anne (Heather O'Rourke) meets the spirits in the television.**

Tangina's story to the Freelings is the common wisdom of spiritualists: "There is no death. It is only a transition to a different sphere of consciousness." Carol Anne has been lured into a "bi-location," another territory, that of the dead who have not passed into the light. The house is plagued by angry ghosts. But Tangina also finds a demonic entity: "A terrible presence is in there with her. So much rage; so much betrayal.... I don't know what hovers over this house, but it is strong enough to punch a hole into this world and take your daughter away from you." This territorial invader has taken a child, a symbol of our genetic future.

The film ends with a reversal, a heroic invasion by "Us," Diane Freeling, into the territory of "Them" through the portal in the closet to rescue her child. We respond with pleasure to a mother's love and courage, one of the most important adaptations in the survival of humanity and a narrative we see over and over in the horror film. Catherine Salmon and Todd Shackelford observe, "The most intimate of mammalian relationships is that between mother and child, and it is the one with the greatest number of special-purposes anatomical, physiological, psychological mechanisms."[16] But the invasion of our territory by the Other provides the central conflict. The same invasion-of-territory plot underpins the three other films in the *Poltergeist* franchise.

The territorial invasion theme in *Insidious* (2010) resembles that of *Poltergeist*. Josh and Renai Lambert (Patrick Wilson and Rose Byrne) move into a new home with their three children. The move to a new territory where horror awaits is a common plot in the genre, especially to a strange house. When their son Dalton, who looks to be about ten years old, explores the attic, he falls when a ladder breaks and goes into a coma that the doctors cannot explain. After many poltergeist events and the appearance of a threatening figure, Renai insists that they move to another house. But the events and the figure follow them, leading them to enlist the help of Elise Rainier (Lin Shaye), a demonologist and an echo from Tangina in *Poltergeist*. She and her helpers find a supernatural presence.

Occult films commonly include a lecture to explain the frame, provided here by Rainier when she describes Dalton as a Traveler: one who explores the astral plane in his dreams, where he has become lost. This lecture emphasizes territory: "You son isn't in a coma.... His physical body is here. But his spiritual body is not. And the reason these disturbances followed you to a new home is because it's not the house that's haunted. It's your son." According to Rainier, Dalton is an empty vessel which ghosts are trying to get into as well as "other entities with insidious agendas to cause pain to others," here represented by a red-faced evil spirit seen at various points. Josh is the conventional disbeliever in films on the supernatural, a narrative device to provide conflict and lead viewers to gradually suspend disbelief along with the character. In another similarity to *Poltergeist*, it is the father instead of the mother who goes into the spiritual realm to rescue his child, though at the conclusion we find that he has brought the evil presence with him.

Insidious' horror element is remarkably similar to that of *Poltergeist*. In each case there is an invasion of the human realm by an Other, a supernatural being, as well as a child threatened by that Other and a parent who goes into the invader's territory to rescue the child. The invaders have the look of otherness: the Man with Fire on His Face and the Old Woman who appears in mirrors and photographs. Rainier describes her as "a parasite" that draws Dalton further into the spirit world.

The Sentinel, Prince of Darkness, Cabin in the Woods, Poltergeist and *Insidious* are but five films that adapt the primal narrative of invasion by Satan or evil spirits through a portal. Other portals for invasions by demons in film include Ouija boards, as in *The Exorcist* and a host of other low-budget Ouija board movies such as *Witch Board* (1986) and *Ouija* (2013), as well as mirrors (*Prince of Darkness, Mirror* [2008]). Evolutionary psychologists point out the centrality of tribal defense of territory in our nature. René Dubos traces territoriality to the Old Stone Age when hunter-gatherers camped near bodies of water as a place to leave women and children while the men hunted: "Long associations with a given region, a camp, or a shelter are probably at the origin of the very human tendency to develop emotional attachments which can get so strong as to constitute an organic bond to a particular place."[17] This sort of finding suggests that we respond with horror to the territorial invasion as we inherit it from primal ancestors. The Satanic portal plot triggers the pleasurable fear of this narrative.

"He came up from Hell and begat a son": *Rosemary's Baby, The Omen* Franchise, *Left Behind* and *Constantine*

The Antichrist story is a variation on the portal plot: a defense of territory on a cosmic level. For a body of myth so extensive as that of the Antichrist, the figure gets relatively little attention in the Bible, where the word is mentioned only five times. He appears first rather obliquely in the Book of Daniel; in 1 John ("You have heard that the Antichrist cometh") and 2 John; in 2 Thessalonians where he is described as the "man of sin" who will bring about the three stages of the apocalypse; and finally in the Revelation to John as "the beast rising out of the sea" given power by "The Dragon."

From an evolutionary psychology perspective, the Antichrist is another model for the territorial invader and the Other, a threat to our genetic heritage and a figure who stimulates our most primal and paranoid fears of hidden servants facilitating his coming. Conservative Christians see evidence of

Satan's work and the coming of the Antichrist everywhere, from the New World Order to the Protocols of the Elders of Zion. Evangelical author Constance Cumby writes exposés of what she calls the insidious New Age, "a movement that includes many thousands of organizations networking through every corner of our globe with the intent of bringing about the New World Order—an order that writes God out of the picture and deifies Lucifer."[18] Such paranoia reeks of the primal narrative of tribalism and fear of the Other as territorial invader. Stories of Satan and the Antichrist offer rich soil for the horror film and feed fears of the threat posed by the hidden enemy and his minions in our midst. *The Omen* and *Rosemary's Baby* are classics of the horror genre that trigger a primal response to the invader—an invader not just within the material world but from beyond—and the contamination of the gene pool. The *Left Behind* films present another level of paranoia aimed at a target audience of conservative Christians.

James B. Twitchell believes that the core attraction of the horror film lies in sex: "While the characters who populate horror myths may be from Fairyland, their interests are not startlingly new: they are concerned with sex and reproduction. I don't believe there is a horror myth in the West that is not entangled with the theme of procreation."[19] Evolutionary psychologists would agree that concerns about procreation and protection of the gene pool are central to primal instincts that are buried in our DNA, stoking the fear of males that their genetic heritage might be corrupted. Helen Fisher writes of this fear of a mate's fidelity: "It probably evolved for two essential reasons: to protect ancestral men from being cuckolded and raising another's child and to protect ancestral women from losing to a rival a potential husband and father to her children. This craving for sexual exclusivity enabled our forebears to protect their precious DNA."[20]

Our response of empathy for our group defending against the Other who invades our territory comes from genetic programming but comes mixed with cultural input. So the power of the Antichrist story lies in our inward fear of both territorial invasion and a threat to our tribal and genetic heritage mixed with centuries of legend and Christian tradition. In this version of the territorial narrative, the Antichrist is an invader and Other, coming from Hell to rule the earth, almost always supported by a cult, an opposing tribe. The portrayal of the Antichrist as threat is often intensified in these films with the invader coming to our world through the womb of a woman as a portal.

So it goes in *Rosemary's Baby* (1968), a film based closely on Ira Levin's novel and directed by Roman Polanski. When Rosemary and Guy Woodhouse (Mia Farrow and John Cassavetes) move into the Branford, an upscale New York apartment building, they come under the control of Satan worshipers who play on Guy's weakness and disappointment with his actor career, persuading him to allow Rosemary to be raped by Satan. The narrative line of the film has Rosemary gradually discovering the true nature of people in her building, a Satanic cult that murders those who seek to help her and lead her to understand her danger. After she gives birth, they withhold the child from her until she finally escapes her bedroom and confronts the group. Roman, the leader, brings her to the child's black-shrouded crib with upside-down cross hanging from the top. Then when she finally sees the child, she cries, "What have you done to his eyes?" Roman, the cult leader, responds, "He has his father's eyes.... Satan is his father, not Guy. He came up from Hell and begat a son!" Yet in the closing shots, she accepts her demonic child with a look of love. Evolutionary psychology holds that adaptation has led to a special bond between mother and child that is central to the survival of our species, and scenes of mothers sacrificing themselves for their children reflect a primitive drive. Mathias Clasen writes, "We still carry along ancient mammalian adaptations for mother-infant bondings,"[21] and the horror of *Rosemary's Baby* is to see a mother bonded with a demon child. The film gradually reveals the invasion plot, with imagery of darkness and satanic symbols. But a central horror is the successful corruption of the gene pool through the portal of Rosemary's womb. This and other Satanic films exemplify Carol Clover's assertion that "the portals of occult horror are almost invariably women."[22]

Rosemary's Baby has inspired conflicting critical interpretations, some suggesting that Rosemary's experience was just a dream. Lucy Fisher sees the film as heralding "both the birth of horror and the horror of birth in modern cinema.... It is also a skewed documentary of the societal and personal turmoil regularly attending female reproduction."[23] Her interpretation favors both a psychological and cultural approach. But *Rosemary's Baby* is a true horror film, and whether we see the plot as metaphor for cultural or psychological issues or take it literally as Ira Levin and Polanski give it to us, the film enacts the narrative of invasion of territory.

The Omen offers another example of the Antichrist portal film. Here the portal for Damien, the Antichrist, is not the womb

Rosemary's Baby: **Rosemary (Mia Farrow) sees her demon baby.**

of a woman but that of a jackal. When his own son supposedly dies at birth (actually murdered by a Satanic cult), Robert Thorn, U.S. ambassador to Italy, is persuaded by a doctor to secretly accept a foundling as a replacement, ironically assuring him, "God has given you something." The baby, Damien, is Satan's child, to be the Antichrist. The cult then supports and protects Damien and arranges for the death of anyone who threatens him. The film reeks of paranoia at the presence of Others imbedded in society to abet invasion of our territory. As in so many Satanic invasion films, they are opposed by defenders, eventually including Thorn himself when he finally understands. He is another conventional disbeliever in the horror film who must learn the truth. The film's central action is his gradual realization of his child's true nature.

Director Richard Donner's screen ambience supports the sense of otherness with sign and symbol from the Satanic tradition. Black birds spy on the Thorns. Black Rottweiler dogs guard Damien, animals associated with Hell in Dante's *The Inferno,* where Cerberus rends sinners on level three and in *Paradise Lost* where Sin, Satan's lover and daughter gives birth to Hounds of Hell at Hell's gate. The "Ave Satani" ("Praise Satan") music reflects the Satanic reversal of Christian worship, and it triggers the presence of evil and imminent violence. Thorn's discovery of "666," the *de rigueur* Satanic symbol (see the Revelation to John 13:18), on his son's scalp triggers the final confrontation with evil and the recognition that Damien is the Antichrist and Other.

Robin Wood condemns *The Omen* on ideological grounds: "In obvious ways, *The Omen* is old-fashioned, traditional, reactionary: the goodness of the family unit isn't questioned: horror is disowned by having the devil-child, a product of the Old World, unwittingly adopted into the American family: the devil-child and his independent female guardian (loosely interpretable in mythic terms as representing child liberation and women's liberation) as purely evil."[24] Yet the qualities Wood condemns in the film are those that trigger tribal loyalty and vicarious fear of invasion and the Other. The plot may be a bit trite, but director Donner brings the primal narratives to life with the power of the medium to inspire entertaining horror and achieve box office success.

Financially successful films generate sequels. *The Omen II* (1978) and *III: The Final Conflict* (1981) continue Damien's career as he gradually realizes his nature as Antichrist and becomes the leader of a New World Order until he is killed with the second coming of Christ. In all of the films, a Satanic cult supports the Antichrist's invasion while a few devoted opponents try to kill him, a typical Us against Them tribal and territorial conflict. A nearly shot-for-shot remake of the first film was released in 2004. *The Omen IV* (1992), an odd sort of sequel made for TV, has a cult attempting to bring Damien's daughter to power. The additions to the franchise lack the cinematic resonance of the original and target the Christian conservative audience more intensely.

Antichrist films abound, but the *Left Behind* franchise is one of the most interesting from a cultural perspective, aimed specifically to conservative Christians. *Left Behind: The Movie* and its sequel *Left Behind: Tribulation Force* were released in 2000 and 2002, and *Left Behind: The World at War* came out on DVD in 2005. A reboot appeared in 2014 as well as another sequel, *Vanished: Left Behind, the Next Generation*, in 2016. All are based on the Tim LaHaye-Jerry Jenkins' bestselling series of novels, and they amplify conservative Christian paranoia with a twist that illuminates the cultural divide in the U.S. A May 24, 2004, *Newsweek* article reports that 71 percent of the novels' sales were from the South and Midwest. Nicolae Carpathia is the Antichrist, but novels and film adaptations establish him as the emblem of the New World Order so ardently feared by conservative Christians and indeed by many secular conservatives.

The *Left Behind* novels and films begin with the Rapture predicted in the Bible, when the elect will be taken to Heaven and others are left behind (see 1 Thessalonians 4:16–18, for instance), and a "tribulation" will follow. After the event, a small Tribulation Force acts as a sort of underground (another group of defenders in the Satanic film) seeking to depose Carpathia, the Antichrist and leader of the New World Order, who comes to power after the Rapture. The Tribulation Force, like other tribal defenders in the Satanic film, exemplifies the human behavior that is central in the primal narratives. David Barash writes, "Efficient hunting often requires group coordination, obedience to authority and a high degree of conformity, especially if the prey is large and dangerous. During this stage of our evolution, those who fitted in and were good 'team players' almost certainly left more descendants than those who stubbornly insisted on individual action."[25] The Tribulation Force is such a band of warriors who oppose Carpathia—through the films and the 12 novels to date. It is worth noting that LaHaye and Jenkins have no trouble serving both God and Mammon. On a website, they specify that no one, including church groups, is allowed to use the films without permission and paying a royalty.

Antichrist films are, to borrow a term, legion. But two updates of this narrative deserve mention in combining narratives from the Satanic film. *Constantine* (2005), an adaptation of the graphic novel series *Hellblazer*, offers a unique spin on the Antichrist plotline. The film establishes a territorial plot frame: a world where demons are not permitted to cross through the portal from Hell but "half breeds," who are partly demonic, are among us. John Constantine (Keanu Reeves), who was condemned to Hell because of an attempted suicide but returned, is the warrior to battle them, hoping to good-deed his way into Heaven. Constantine is the territorial defender against the return of the Antichrist. *Devil's Advocate* (1997), based on Andrew Neiderman's novel, portrays Satan as John Milton (a not very subtle bit of literary allusion), a New York lawyer who plots to bring about a sexual liaison between Kevin, who we later learn is his son, and Christabella, his daughter, which would result in another point of entry for the Antichrist from the womb of a woman. Both films rest on the portal narrative as well as the birth of the Antichrist.

Mick Broderick sums up the power of the Antichrist plot as seen in films like those mentioned and *The Omega Code* (1999), *Lost Souls* (2000) and *End of Day* (1999) from a cultural perspective:

> In periods of uncertainty and anxiety, film narratives of apocalypse that represent a literal and identifiable Antichrist provide a historical mythic template for action and drama that simplify complex relations of alliances of either good or bad, or right and wrong, which unfold according to a predestined cosmic plan dramatizing us/them.[26]

The power of culture in influencing our taste in film is undeniable. The unease the turn of the century brought probably made the coming of the Antichrist as apocalypse in films more disturbing. But Broderick's reference to Us/Them applies in a greater sense. Evolutionary psychology would point out the added influence of the whisper within that tells us to fear the invader and corrupter of the gene pool.

"In my name they will drive out demons": *The Exorcist*

Jesus' words (Mark: 16:17) have inspired belief in possession of humans by demons through the centuries. Exorcism of them is a variation on the demonic invasion plot. Exorcism of evil spirits appears early in Christian tradition. The first four gospels and the book of Acts are replete with such examples. Today, the Roman Catholic Church retains the Roman Ritual for exorcism, though it has fallen into disfavor and is seldom used. Exorcism is much more common in fundamentalist Christian groups, especially Pentecostals. The success of the Other in possessing one of ours and the eventual triumph in driving the invader back to Hell is an engaging primal traits invasion narrative in the Satanic film.

William Friedkin's *The Exorcist* (1973), based on William Peter Blatty's novel, is surely the most powerful of the possession subgenre. It generated sequels (*Exorcist II*, 1977, and *Exorcist III*, 1990); an imitation *(Possessed,* 2000); a remake (2006); and a prequel (*Dominion*, 2005). The film establishes a powerful ambience with the opening sequence in Iraq. Father Merrin (Max Von Sydow) is on an archaeological dig there. A tracking sequence leads Merrin to the site through streets that reverberate alien otherness. He finds an amulet showing Joseph holding the Christ Child and also a small carving of a demonic-looking head from the excavation. The two discoveries symbolize Merrin's role as defender of innocence against the invasion of evil. He arrives at the site of the dig, where we see the giant statue of a winged, reptilian demon against a setting sun, the same image as that of the carved head he has found. The amulet and carved image of the demon Pazuzu in this opening sequence establish the primal narratives of invasion and defense of territory: not a house or other structure but the body of a young girl by an Other enacted in the film.

The demon's prey is Regan MacNeil (Linda Blair), another example of the horror in film inspired by the threat to a child. A Ouija board provides a portal for the invasion and possession, leading to bizarre and violent behavior from Regan. In desperation, Regan's mother Chris (Ellen Burstyn) asks the Church for an exorcism. The extended scenes in Regan's Georgetown bedroom, with Father Merrin, aided by Father Karras, doing battle with Pazuzu, show their defense against the invading Other in what looks like a netherworld between Earth and Hell. The visual ambience of darkness, the intense prayers of the priests and the gyrations of the possessed Regan could hardly make the struggle between Us and Them clearer. The primal narrative of invasion of the Other and staunch defenders against it has the twist that the portal is a girl on the threshold of womanhood. That it takes place in her bedroom underscores the sexual and rape implications of the invasion. The visceral horror of the story is rooted both in the defense of territory, a female child

The Exorcist. Father Merrin (Max Von Sydow) confronts the demon Pazuzu.

on the verge of womanhood, and the threat of pollution of the gene pool by an Other. The film's Biblical allusions enhance the battle of good and evil, Other and defender, and provide a rich backdrop of dramatic conflict. Father Karris takes up the battle after Father Merrin's death, and demands the demon's name. It responds, "My name is Legion," a reference to the line in Mark 5:9 when Christ exorcises demons who respond, "We are Legion, for we are many": a story repeated in Matthew and Luke. The passage might be a source for the concept from folklore that knowing true names can give command, as Ursula LeGuin adapted it in the *Earthsea* novels. In the Bible narrative, Jesus casts the demons into swine (unclean animals for Jews) after getting their names, and they then rush off a cliff. The film parallels the Biblical passage when Karras, who has experienced an unresolved spiritual crisis of faith, demands that the demons take him and leave Regan. They possess him, and like the Biblical swine, he rushes out to meet his end when he leaps off the back stairs of the apartment to his death. And so the invasion is ended with the demons vanquished and returned to their own territory.

The exorcism theme has inspired many other films, for instance *The House of Exorcism* (1975), *The Possession of Gail Powers* (2006) and *The Last Exorcism* (2010). The theme has also been adapted in a flood of made-for-TV and DVD movies with amusing titles such as *High School Exorcist* (1991) and *Shark Exorcism* (2015). While all exorcism films follow the same pattern—the battle between an exorcist figure (our territorial and tribal warrior) and the invading demon possessing one of Us—none of them approach the power, complexity, and visual impact of *The Exorcist*.

"I'll burn my books!": *Dr. Faustus, The Devil and Daniel Webster* and *Angel Heart*

The Faust legend began in the sixteenth century, the story of a historical figure who made a deal with the Devil. Gordon Melton calls him "a wandering magician or necromancer whose picturesque character won him notoriety."[27] He was supposedly carried away to Hell in a noisy confrontation with Satan. The legend inspired a 1587 chapbook in Germany, followed by its entry into the canon of great literature in Christopher Marlowe's 1604 play *The Tragical History of Dr. Faustus* and Johann Von Goethe's drama *Faust, ein Tragödie* (1804). Both classics have been adapted for film, and the Faust story has inspired many more.

Robert Singer observes that the Faust legend "is consistently renewed by the presence of four elemental motifs: the Faust-Mephistopheles relationship; the pact; ritual magic; and the relationship between Faust and Helen of Troy–Marguerite."[28] These plots fit well into a primal traits critique. From an evolutionary psychology perspective, the power of the legend lies in one of Us becoming an outcast, voluntarily becoming one of Them and ultimately being torn from our territory and social kin group for the sake of gain: money, power and sex, all of which are included in Singer's appraisal. In Matthew 4: 1–11, Jesus goes into the wilderness to be tempted by Satan, whose final offer is power: "All these I will give to you, if you will fall down and worship me." The passage is repeated in Luke. It has inspired a central element of the Faust legend: the offer of wealth, sex and power if the character will forsake loyalty to his own kind, with the proviso that he will ultimately pay the price.

Richard Burton's 1967 *Dr. Faustus* is a direct filming of Marlowe's drama. In play and film, Faust considers the various arts but rejects them in his desire to make himself a demigod through magic. But to achieve his goal, he must strike a deal. Both the Good Angel and Mephistopheles warn Faust of his error. In some adaptations of the Faust story, the Tempter expresses regret that he has been expelled from his own angelic kin group and territory in Heaven because he failed to resist temptation, as does Mephistopheles in the Marlowe-Burton telling of the ancient story. But Faust's pride and desire for power and wealth and his lust for the demonic version of Helen of Troy lead him to reject his own people and be placed in the territory of the Other. Marlowe's Faust's piteous plea for forgiveness when that moment comes epitomizes the horror of becoming Other voluntarily: "I'll burn my books," he cries when devils come to claim him. "Let Faustus liue in hel a thousand yeers, a hundred thousand ... and at last be sau'd. No end is limited to damned souls!"[29] Humanity's territorial and tribal imperatives lead us to feel for one who has made a decision that banishes him from his own kind.

The Faust narrative appears very early in film with a 1917 version, adapted from Marie Corelli's 1895 novel *The Sorrows of Satan*, now a lost film. D.W. Griffith made a second version in 1926. In it, failed writer Geoffrey Tempest meets and seduces Mavis Claire, another struggling writer. Tempest fits the mold of the Faust figure, selling his soul and then changed by wealth. He forgets Mavis, the woman he had seduced and wanted to marry, and becomes involved with a slinky Russian princess, perhaps a literary descendent of Helen of Troy in the Faust legend. The film gives us another mournful Tempter in Prince Lucio de Rimanez, an interesting character with a touch of the Romantic Movement's melancholy and romantic Satan. He admires Mavis for rejecting him and longs through souls like hers to achieve redemption. He is an Other who lost his way while Geoffrey is one of Us who agrees to become Other. Our inborn need to belong to a tribe brings pity and horror from the situation of both outcasts in *Sorrows of Satan*: the Faust figure who has voluntarily left his kind and the tempter who has lost his heavenly community. The film dilutes the horror of the Faust character's inevitable situation when the bill comes due with a love-conquers-all conclusion.

Most Faust films adapt the character similarly. *The Devil and Daniel Webster* (1941), based on Stephen Vincent Benét's story, retains the familiar elements of pride, avarice and lust in the Faust tradition and combines them with a populist theme that speaks to Depression era issues. Poverty and desperation lead simple farmer Jabez Stone (James Craig) to exclaim that he'd sell his soul for money to support his family, bringing Scratch (Walter Huston) with his offer. Like Faust and Geoffrey Tempest, Jabez is seduced by a beautiful woman and does not use his wealth to help others, forgetting his ties to his community, to Us, in order to become a miserly money lender like the one who had persecuted him. The great orator Daniel Webster (Edward Arnold) agrees to give up his own soul should he lose in a trial to save Jabez, with damned souls as a jury and Scratch as prosecutor. The defender of his own kin group against a powerful Other, he saves his client with a patriotic and populist speech.

Edward O. Wilson writes, "We are ruled by a compelling urge—better, a compelling necessity—that began in our early primate ancestry. Every person is a compulsive group-seeker, hence an intensely tribal animal."[30] And tribes since primitive times have inhabited and defended territory. In some cultures such as that of the Amish, "shunning," or expulsion, is the ultimate punishment, and those shunned are unwelcome in the tribal territory. Be it rooted solely in genetic programming and tribal and territorial behavior or the power of culture, the expulsion from the tribe is a whisper that triggers horror. The Faust character exemplifies this vicarious fear.

Director Alan Parker's *Angel Heart* (1987), adapted from William Hjortsberg's novel *Fallen Angel*, is one of the most effective and richly complex adaptations of the Faust theme. The story begins with shady private detective Harry Angel (Mickey Rourke) taking an assignment from Louis Cyphere (Robert De Niro), a name sounding like "Lucifer," to find Johnny Favorite. Parker creates a dark, forbidding screen ambience in a horror film laden with Satanic symbolism that enhances the sense of otherness. Five-bladed ceiling fans throughout make images of a pentagram, often inverted to symbolize Satanic evil. Toots Sweet, the black musician Harry fights, has the inverted pentagram embedded in a front tooth. The opening segment showing steam rising from vents in the dark city streets conjures an image of Hell beneath, an other and alien territory. Scenes with Harry descending winding staircases are scattered throughout, suggesting his descent to Hell, as does his elevator ride down in the final shot: a journey to the new territory. The film dramatizes Angel's Oedipal path to self-discovery. We eventually learn that there are two souls in his body, his own and that of Johnny Favorite, the person Cyphere has hired Harry to find, knowing, no doubt, the outcome. Favorite was an accomplished occultist who had sold his soul in Faustian fashion. To escape Cyphere when payment is due, he placed it in the body of Harry Angel. From the primal traits critical perspective, we see the horror of one who not only becomes Other but brings another to his fate with him.

The film has racist overtones in its adaptation of Voodoo, which it incorrectly equates with Satanism. Harry's brutal rape and murder of Epiphany Proudfoot seem an example of a racist theme. Robert Singer disagrees, arguing that Harry is not consciously racist. But the film shows how "his fear of Black Power in the form of voodoo compels him to commit heinous acts.... The evil does not reside in the black man or the mambo priestess. The heart of darkness is within Harry Angel himself."[31] At a deeper level, however, Harry's implicit racism as projected in the film is rooted in willingness to do harm to the Other, a central element of racism.

Procreation is an important primal narrative, and the lust that brings about this Faust character's fall is as important as the desire for wealth and power in the narrative's various incarnations. David Buss writes, "Men seek attractive women as mates not simply for their reproductive value, but also as signals of status to same sex competitors and to other potential mates."[32] The whisper that demands procreation is complicated for humans by our cultures. Faust, Jabez Stone, Geoffrey Tempest, Harry Angel and others of their ilk are inspired not only by the promise of wealth and power but also of sex with the kind of woman Buss describes. They are accouterments of the power the characters desire. In a bit of irony, Faust's cry to the demonic version of Helen of Troy, "Make me immortal with a kiss," seems an early version of Dawkins' insistence that our genes lead us to find immortality through sex; Faust loses his soul for it. Yet culture teaches us that desire for beauty and the status a beautiful woman brings to a man or a powerful man to a woman is not just for procreation. The Faust myth also tells us to beware of submitting to unwise alliances with the likes of the Faust stories' devastating beauties.

"Watch the skies.... Keep watching the skies": The Science Fiction–Horror Film—*The War of the Worlds, They Live* and Other Invasion Narratives

The words of Scotty, the reporter in 1951's *The Thing from Another World*, sum up the invasion of territory theme in the science fiction–horror film. While scholars trace science fiction back for centuries, most agree that there could be no science fiction as we know it today before there was science. But many works of film and literature that we refer to as science fiction could also be called horror films. Brian Aldiss defines a basic element of the science fiction genre as "cast in the gothic or post gothic mode."[33] H.G. Wells' novel *The War of the Worlds* reflects both Darwin's ideas, so controversial at the time, and the potential of science for fiction in an example of horror–science fiction. It also reflects one of the most enduring themes in science fiction: the invasion of our territory by a new kind of Other, one from outer space.

Scholars disagree as to which were the first works of science fiction, from the Roman writer Lucian to Mary Shelley's *Frankenstein*. But H.G. Wells' novels are often cited as a starting place for what we think of as modern science fiction. John Clute calls him the most important science fiction writer.[34] *The War of the Worlds* (first published in 1897 as a serial in both *Pearson's Magazine* and *Cosmopolitan* and in book form a year later) is not only an early example of the invasion theme in science fiction but the first to link the genre to Darwinism. Wells' opening for the novel establishes the theme of invasion of territory and the battle for survival of our species:

> No one would have believed in the last years of the nineteenth century that this world was being watched keenly and closely by intelligences greater than man's and yet as mortal as his own; that as men busied themselves about their various concerns they were scrutinised and studied, perhaps almost as narrowly as a man with a microscope might scrutinise the transient creatures that swarm and multiply in a drop of water.... Yet, across the gulf of space, minds that are to our minds as ours are to those of the beasts that perish, intellects vast and cool and unsympathetic, regarded this earth with envious eyes and slowly and surely drew their plans against us.[35]

Wells, an ardent advocate of evolutionary theory, establishes a Darwinian and species struggle narrative that whispers to us fear of territorial invaders in a new way that could only appear when science had developed far enough for us to imagine alien invasion. Clearly, the Martians are intellectually fitter for survival from a Darwinian perspective than is humanity. Wells' narrator observes, "We men, the creatures who inhabit this earth, must be to them at least as alien and lowly as are the monkeys and lemurs to us. The intellectual side of man already admits that life is an incessant struggle for existence, and it would seem that this too is the belief of the minds on Mars" (125).

The narrator, separated from his wife by the invasion, flees and gives us the details as the alien tripod devices kill with death rays and "black smoke," easily destroying the army units that try to oppose them. During his journey, he meets the Artillery Man, whose ideas reflect concepts of Social Darwinists: those who applied Darwin's theory of survival of the fittest to politics, holding that the strong should increase in wealth and power and the weak should be left behind. The Artillery Man argues for such a new society: "The weak and cumbersome have to die. They ought to die" (267).

While he was interested in eugenics—the belief that the future of humanity would be better served if those who are more highly evolved were to populate the Earth—Wells does not seem to endorse the harsh world perspective of Herbert Spencer and others of the Social Darwinist camp. But his acceptance of Darwin's theory and the bleak view it presents is nonetheless apparent in the novel. Humanity, his narrator argues, has been as ruthless in invading territory and murdering those seen as Other and worthless as are the Martians: "Before we judge them too harshly, we must remember what ruthless and utter destruction our own species has wrought, not only upon animals, such as the vanished bison and dodo, but upon its own inferior races. The Tasmanians, in spite of their human likeness, were entirely swept out of existence in a war of extermination waged by European immigrants in the space of 50 years. Are we such apostles of mercy as to complain if the Martians warred in the same spirit?" (125–26). The evolutionary element of the plot culminates with the Martians being slain by bacteria against which they have no immunity while we have developed defenses through evolution. Humanity survived "by virtue of this natural selection of our kind" (288), he writes.

Orson Welles' *Mercury Theatre on the Air* radio production of *The War of the Worlds* on October 30, 1938 (the proximity to Halloween was no accident), demonstrates the power of the invasion narrative. Many of those who missed the opening monologue believed we had truly been invaded. The program's approach with what seemed to be continuous flashes from radio news announcers set off a widespread panic. The effect was enhanced by the absence of commercial interruptions until near the end of the program. The threat of invasion and the resulting alarms and confusion Welles' program created demonstrate the power of the invasion narrative.

The two film versions of *War of the Worlds* are revisions of Wells' novel. Both downplay the Darwinian theme Wells established, and each reflects the culture of its time. George Pal's 1953 production—heralded for groundbreaking special effects—omits the overt Darwinism of Wells' novel. But the narrative of invasion of territory remains, enhanced by the cultural context of the Cold War when the western world was locked in conflict with the Soviet Union, the Other of choice at the time.

Pal's visualization of the film's source brings the invasion plot to life, this version set in the United States. Dr. Clayton Forrester (Gene Barry), a scientist who had worked on the development of the atomic bomb, is vacationing in Southern California when the Martian ships arrive. Pal imagines them differently from Wells' tripods, screening them as some kind of hover craft with a gooseneck extremity that projects destructive rays. As in Wells' version, the army is unable to stop them, and the Martians ravage cities. Pal's film adds a romance theme, with Forrester falling in love with Sylvia Van Buren (Ann Robinson). She reflects the 1950s version of the good woman, serving coffee during an attack and making breakfast, screaming and hysterical when in danger and primarily there to be rescued.

The film reflects events and culture of the time it was made. Ideological and territorial confrontation with Russia inspired fear of invasion and subversion from within; and as is often the case, these cultural themes are inextricably tied to the primal narrative of territoriality. Before the Martian rampage begins, three people approach this spaceship, one with a white flag, saying "everybody understands the white flag." But they are incinerated by the craft. From the perspective of Cold War days, viewers might understand the subtext of the film: that we can't be friendly with the Russians and that they are potentially ruthless enemies. But from a primal traits perspective, both the Martians and the Russians might trigger vicarious horror as invaders of our territory by an Other, a primal response deeper than the cultural issue of the time.

The 2005 version retains few remnants of Wells' novel. But it has a different spin on the invasion of territory narrative. Here the aliens' ships have been buried far beneath the Earth, perhaps for centuries. The characters are clichés from the period. Ray Ferrier (Tom Cruise) is a cultural stereotype of the antihero, a feckless dockworker whose irresponsible behavior cost him his marriage and his two children. His ex-wife leaves him in charge of them for a weekend, and the film focuses on his desperate attempt to save them.

The alien ships are close in appearance to those Wells describes. Otherwise there is little similarity to the novel beyond the invasion of territory by an Other. These alien invaders harvest human blood and remains to grow a plant, red weed, which apparently nourishes them. The harvesting of humans for food plot occurs frequently in the history of science fiction, but as Brian Aldiss points out, aliens won't invade Earth to eat humans: "Beef animals make better sense, though [eating humans] amps up the horror motif."[36] Also, evolutionary psychology would suggest that the horror inspired by a predator who would hunt us for food must be deeply engrained in our primal memory. There is little discussion of science or evolution beyond the mad Harlan Ogilvy (the equivalent of the Artillery Man in the novel, played by Tim Robbins) crying, "We can't survive, Ray. We weren't built for it." Implicit in the story is the threat to the child, Rachel (Dakota Fanning), a motif that rings bells for viewers or readers in the threat to the gene pool.

The final voiceover from narrator Morgan Freeman is, considering the fact that several million people have died, a rather sanctimonious paraphrase of Wells' words and at least suggestive of Darwin's writing on survival of the fittest. The aliens were killed "by the tiniest creature that God, in his wisdom, made upon this Earth. By the toll of a billion deaths, man had earned his immunity, his right to survive among this planet's infinite organisms. And the right is ours against all challenges, for neither do men live, nor die, in vain."

The inspiration for the invasion theme in the 1950s may have been paranoia generated by the Cold War. But the invasion of our territory by an Other persists in great variety in the science fiction–horror film. There are far too many to mention. But a few stand out as examples of this primal narrative.

Roland Emmerich's *Independence Day* (1996) is a model for the invasion plot. Here aliens who travel from planet to planet to rape them of all natural resources attack Earth. Their ships have shields that render the Air Force impotent, but in what may be an homage to *War of the Worlds,* our intrepid heroes implant a cybernetic version of the disease that killed Wells' Martians, slain by Earth's bacteria. Emmerich's aliens are brought down, but it is a virus implanted into their mother ship's computer to make them vulnerable. These alien invaders return for a second invasion 20 years later in *Independence Day: Resurgence* (2016).

In *Cowboys vs. Aliens* (2011), a morphing of the conventional Western into a science fiction film, a coalition of cowboys, bandits and Indians battle aliens who seek to rob Earth of its gold. They are aided by another alien of a different species who understands that the invaders would bring sister ships to destroy Earth's population if they are not stopped. The film offers a unique adaptation of the tribal narrative with three groups—cowboys, Native Americans and outlaws—united to confront a territorial invader. The threat to natural resources might be seen as a horror plot for a more environmentally conscious film audience.

Many science fiction films reverse the invasion of territory narrative. Not all aliens in the science fiction film are evil invaders. Starman in the eponymously named 1984 film is Other but seems far more moral that those who want to capture and study him after his ship crashes, forcing him to take human form. Klaatu in the 1951 film *The Day the Earth Stood Still* and the 2008 remake reverses the 1950s portrayal of the alien as villain. While he has the power to destroy the Earth, Klaatu lectures against war and the hatred of Others. And of course there are the lovable, cuddly alien visitors like E.T. in Stephen Spielberg's film *E.T.: The Extra Terrestrial* (1982) and the multitude of adaptations of this plotline. The influence of culture has produced a contrary view to the portrayal of aliens as evil invaders, showing that the world they visit is in some ways in need of change.

More recent films portray humans as invaders of territory, as in James Cameron's *Avatar* (2009) in which a human army invades the planet Pandora for its natural resources, a reversal of the invasion-of-Earth narrative. Pandora is the home of an indigenous people, the Na'vi. Cameron's motion-capture CGI brings the blue, ten-foot tall Na'vi and their forest habitat to life in stunning visuals. The film reverses the usual portrayal of the alien as evil, and the post-colonial theme of taking territory from indigenous peoples to acquire their natural resources would be hard to miss. Cameron's film demonstrates that shifts in culture can change our perspectives on Them and Us and create empathy for those who would otherwise be seen as Other. The Na'vi are noble savages in the Rousseauian tradition. That we can cheer their victory over technology and corporate greed in defending their territory is a testimony to cultural changes that bring a different view of this narrative. But despite our empathy for the alien Other whose territory is invaded, the primal narrative remains, though changed in focus. In *Avatar*, it is the Other who is defender of territory.

John Carpenter's *They Live* (1982) gives a political spin to the hidden alien Other narrative with a quite different perspective on otherness. Set in a future that looks a little like the Great Depression, the film follows the Drifter (George "Buck" Flower), who stumbles into knowledge that hidden aliens have taken over American society when he gets a pair of sunglasses from a resistance group that reveal the truth. An electronic media device has masked the aliens and their subliminal advertising on television and street signs with advertisements reading "do not resist" or "be content" visible only with the glasses. The Drifter (he gets no name) begins a crusade against the aliens, whose monstrous faces are invisible to all but are unmasked by the sunglasses.

The invasion of territory by an Other narrative and the paranoia implicit to it seem quite obvious in the film. But a powerful ideological critique of modern society lies buried in its routine action-adventure plot. The Drifter hears a street preacher at the outset: "Why do we worship greed? Because outside of our sight, they are feeding off us." The film's ideological center equates the aliens with the ruling class, the top of the economic pyramid. Gilbert, a leader of a resistance group, says, "They have created a repressive society, and we are their unwilling accomplices.... We have been lulled into a trance." In the symbolic context of the film the aliens, or the ruling classes, "keep us asleep, keep us selfish, keep us sedated."

At the end, when the Drifter and Frank crash a banquet for aliens and wealthy humans in their thrall, they meet "the Bearded Man," as the credits describe him. Like so many humans, he sold out to the aliens. He points out that most humans who achieve any position of power "sell out right away" for money. The aliens encourage pollution because "they are turning our atmosphere into their atmosphere." And the Bearded Man preaches the doctrine of corporate greed: "It's business, that's all. There aren't no countries any more, no good guys. They're running the whole show. They own everything, the whole damned planet."

They Live turns the narratives of invasion of the Other from the horror genre into Carpenter's critique of economic injustice. The Other narrative still holds. It is not limited to aliens, as in most science fiction films, but to otherness between social and economic classes.

Edward O. Wilson notes that primitives separate their world into their known territory and that of others. "This elemental topography makes easier the distinction between enemies who can be attacked and killed and friends who cannot. The contrast is heightened by reducing enemies to frightful and even sub-human status."[37] This topography has expanded in the twentieth century science fiction film to make Earth our territory to be defended against fictional invaders of various types. But as you will see in Chapter Four of this book, there is more than one way to have our territory invaded. A simpler form of invasion would be assimilation and conquering of our gene pool, as we see in zombie and science fiction–horror films adapted from John W. Campbell, Jr.'s, novella "Who Goes There?" and its film versions or *Invasion of the Body Snatchers* with its four movie adaptations.

Three

The Assimilation Narrative

"Resistance is futile."

In the first season of the TV series *Star Trek: The Next Generation*, Captain Picard's persistent antagonist Q sends the *Enterprise* to a distant part of the galaxy where they meet the Borg, a mixture of cybernetic and species-specific beings who constitute a hive. Their mission is to bring all other sentient species into their collective, and the phrases "You will be assimilated" and "Resistance is futile" sum up their goal. The Borg episodes exemplify a persistent narrative in the horror and science fiction–horror genre: the fear of assimilation of our gene pool by an Other. Bram Stoker alludes to Leviticus 17:14 ("For the life of every creature is the blood of it") in *Dracula* when he has Prof. Van Helsing say, "The blood is the life"; for the vampire can assimilate his victim by exchanging blood. So too the zombie's bite assimilates its victim, and the werewolf turns those it attacks into a beast when the full moon rises. The assimilation story in film and fiction offers an example of cultural adaptation of a primal narrative. Perhaps humanity's tribal impulses account for the culturally inspired fears of miscegenation, another kind of fear of assimilation that has plagued cultures everywhere.

Evolutionary psychology proposes that the somehow pleasant and vicarious horror of the assimilation narrative rises from the whisper within warning us of pollution or loss of our genetic heritage. The assimilation theme provides the foundation of the zombie meme and also of an important branch of the science fiction–horror film. Richard Dawkins introduced the concept of the selfish gene in his book of that title. He argues that our behavior is closely connected to the preservation of our genetic kin's continuance. He uses the example of the bird that sounds the alarm to its group that a hawk is near. Why, he asks, would the self-sacrifice of the one who sounds the alarm, putting itself most in danger, be an evolutionary adaptation? His answer to this puzzle is that the bird is not altruistic. Rather, it protects the genetic heritage of its species.

Dawkins' findings have inspired both adherents and critics. Barry Schwartz agrees with his position, observing that the gene bringing about unselfish behavior is an apparent paradox, since it would seem that only the selfish should survive. But the individual organism is not the unit of selection; it's the gene. He writes: "Organisms are simply nature's way of making other genes." Following Dawkins' example of the apparently unselfish bird, he believes that the gene controlling alarm calls "is interested only in itself, not in the body it inhabits. If it's bad for the bird, that's too bad, as long as it's good for itself. Hence we have selfish genes, not selfish organisms."[1]

Edward O. Wilson disagrees with the extreme view of gene selection. In defining his concept of eusociality, he asks: "Do kin recognize one another and form altruistic groups, because relatives share the same genes and can still place those genes in the next generation, even if they fail to do so by having offspring of their own? Or finally, is it that hereditary altruists form groups so cooperative and well organized as to out-compete non-altruist groups?" In response to Dawkins, he postulates that it is not genes only that create social behavior and survival of the group but "the condition of multiple generations organized into groups by means of an altruistic division of labor."[2] Altruistic behavior, he argues, is in itself adaptive in preserving the genetic group as well as the species; but his findings still suggest that the narrative of a threat to the gene pool, be it species or group specific, might whisper pleasurable vicarious fear for reader or viewer as a primal narrative.

"We have met the enemy and he is us": "Who Goes There?," *The Body Snatchers* and Film Adaptations

Thus spoke that wise and witty philosopher Pogo in Walt Kelly's long-running comic strip. From the perspective of the assimilation narrative in the horror genre, we might recast the line to read, "We have met the enemy, and he wants to become us." Assimilation narratives abound in the horror and science fiction–horror fields. Most of these works of film and fiction include important elements of cultural significance. But evolutionary psychology suggests that such narratives are significant factors in creating culture. John Campbell's novella "Who Goes There?," its two film adaptations and a prequel and Jack Finney's novel *The Body Snatchers* with its multiple film versions furnish models for the assimilation theme in the science fiction–horror genre. All are rooted both in cultural and primal narratives.

John W. Campbell, Jr., is probably most often remembered for influencing a generation of science fiction writers as editor of the magazine *Astounding*. But his novella "Who Goes There?" (written under the pseudonym Don A. Stuart) has become a classic of science fiction literature. Campbell spins a tale with the action played out at the South Pole, a fine example of nature at its most hostile and primitive, where two competing species—a group of humans and an alien invader the characters call "The Thing"—engage in a battle for survival that is a metaphor on two levels. On the one hand, "Who Goes There?" reflects the culture of the time with a theme that became increasingly prominent from the story's 1937 publication date through the 1950s: the fear of corruption and assimilation within the body politic by Communist subversion. But beyond this cultural theme, Carpenter's novella portrays a Darwinian battle for survival of the fittest. If humanity loses, the alien would corrupt humanity's genetic heritage: it would become Us.

In "Who Goes There?," a scientific expedition studying the magnetic power of the South Pole discovers a spacecraft beneath the ice and a frozen alien buried nearby. Thirty-seven humans in the expedition confront this alien intelligence that is seemingly vastly superior to them and could literally assimilate the entire human race, not just its governments as in the fear of Communism but its gene pool. Campbell establishes the harsh environment for this struggle early and often in the story: "At the surface—it was white death. Death of a needle-fingered cold driven wind, sucking any warm thing."[3] The story's setting reflects a Darwinian harsh nature where the two species struggle to survive. This cold had frozen the alien whose ship had crash-landed there 20 million years ago. After finding the ship under the ice, the scientists accidentally destroy it and what might be three occupants in a failed recovery operation. But one of the aliens had left the ship, and remained frozen in the ice for those millions of years.

The alien has its own adaptive qualities. As the scientists learn, it seems to have some kind of telepathic abilities. It terrifies some with horrible dreams and may have influenced Blair, the biologist, more directly to persuade others to thaw it out, over the objection of some of his colleagues. His argument is pure Darwin. When crew members Connant expresses horror at its face, Blair responds, "That is just a different development of Nature, another example of Nature's wonderful adaptability" (47). Blair's error is forgetting that the Thing is part of a competing species that needs to eliminate his own through absorption.

Its most powerful adaptive quality is its ability to assimilate. After the crew members believe they have electrocuted the monster, they find that it has become the dog that had earlier attacked it. Blair says, "It digested Charnauk, as it digested, studied every cell of his tissue, and shaped its own cells to imitate them exactly" (57). Asked what the goal of the Thing might be, Blair replies, "Take over our world, I imagine" (54). But the humans have their own survival trait, their brain and ability to solve a puzzle. When they discover that some of them have been assimilated, paranoia sets in over the hidden enemy within the group with each crew member suspicious of the next. But they gradually arrive at a solution in what amounts to a detective story plot and save the world from invasion and assimilation.

The first film adaptation, *The Thing from Another World* (1951), adapts only the first half of Campbell's story and turns it into science fiction–horror and thrills rather than science fiction–horror mixed with speculation in the Campbell story. It ends with the electrocution of the alien. *The Thing from Another World* is interesting both from a cultural and a primal traits perspective. This alien is still a territorial invader who must be defeated by our tribal warriors. At the end, Scotty, the reporter, tells his listeners that it was "one of the world's greatest battles was fought and won today by the human race. Here at the top of the world, a handful of American soldiers and civilians met the first invasion from another planet." The assimilation plot is only briefly referenced in this first film adaptation.

But it was the height of the Cold War. The pilot of the Air Force plane, Captain Hendry (Kenneth Tobey), has no doubts as to what to do with the invader: kill it. But the scientist, Dr. Carrington, stands for the intellectual who demands that the Thing be saved. "If we could only communicate with it, we could learn secrets hidden from mankind.... Remember that it is a stranger in a strange land." *The Thing from Another World*, like Campbell's

The Thing from Another World: Dr. Carrington (Robert Cornthwaite) tries to reason with the Thing (James Arness).

story and the first film version of *War of the Worlds,* is a model for fear of Communist infiltration in the 1950s and reflects the culture of its time, when the Red Scare and McCarthyism were at their apex. Anyone who was even suspected of Communism or socialist sympathy might be swept up in the McCarthy witch hunt. Many in the Hollywood community suffered for their membership in radical clubs from their youth. Carrington stands for a squishy intellectualism that might be seduced by left-wing thought. But this cultural condition itself is at its root a primal narrative: evocative of fear of invasion, assimilation and suspicion of the Other, narratives that gave Senator McCarthy his power.

John Carpenter's adaptation of Campbell's story, titled *The Thing* (1982), continues the assimilation narrative with a different cultural spin. Carpenter completes Campbell's plot rather than only half of it and changes the opening. Also set at an American scientific base in the Antarctic, the story has the alien discovered by a Norwegian research team with all but one member killed and the alien brought to the American base in the form of a dog, leading to the battle of humans and Other.

The film's hero is MacReady (Kurt Russell), the intrepid helicopter pilot, one of several name shifts from the Campbell novella. While the 1951 adaptation makes a military officer a hero, as might have been expected during the Cold War, MacReady is a version of the 1970s antihero born from the Vietnam protest days, a hard-drinking outsider. But it is he who figures out the alien's intent. Carpenter cues the audience to its presence within the dog it inhabits as it looks about in close-ups in shadows creeping around the enclosure before it finally begins the change after a fight with other dogs in the kennel. The dogs' sense of smell and instinct, their evolutionary gift, enable them to recognize that the Thing is Other to them and no longer their genetic kin.

Carpenter used improvements in special effects technology developed since the 1951 film to create a thoroughly alien monster, writhing with tentacles, spewing fluid and changing into a variety of shapes in trying to convert its victims to its own form. The film settles into the fight against the invading Other's attempt to assimilate the entire planet, adapting Campbell's puzzle plot of how to distinguish invader from human. While Campbell and the 1951 film give the story a happy ending for humanity, only two Americans remain in Carpenter's version, hoping they have destroyed all the cells of the alien but facing certain death themselves after blowing up and burning everything at the base. Yet they are still not entirely sure if either of them is assimilated and Other.

The assimilation narrative is strong enough to have inspired yet another version. The 2011 film with the same title is a prequel set in the days before the action of Carpenter's version and in the Norwegian camp, where the

Thing was first discovered and the battle joined, leading to the pursuit of the infected dog that begins the 1982 film.

"They are here already!": *Invasion of the Body Snatchers* and Film Adaptations

At the closing minutes of the 1956 film *Invasion of the Body Snatchers*, Miles Bennell hysterically screams to all who will listen that we have been invaded by aliens who take over our bodies. The film and three remakes are based on Jack Finney's novel first published as *The Body Snatchers* in a 1954 *Collier's* magazine serial and as a book in 1955. Like "Who Goes There?" and its film adaptations, Finney's novel and the films it inspired are models for the invasion-through-assimilation narrative.

In the novel, the hero, Miles Bennell, a Mill City, California, physician, begins to notice changes in the behavior of his fellow townspeople. He and his love interest Becky discover copies of people they know, transformed by seed pods as soon as they go to sleep. The copies retain memories and are no longer Us but rather are assimilated into an alien entity's mental collective. As Miles and Becky realize what is happening, the novel becomes a fight, flight and pursuit plot. When they are finally captured and face being assimilated, they get a lecture from Budlong, a professor at the local college, who is one of those taken over, that establishes the aliens' otherness and evolutionary survival approach. He explains that the seeds have traveled through space for millennia from a dying planet and arrived by chance on Earth, where they have taken root to create the pods. Those assimilated lack emotions, cannot reproduce and die in a few years. When all life is assimilated and all die without offspring, the aliens leave a dead planet to seek more life elsewhere. Finney includes a nod to Darwinian theory: Budlong tells Miles that the aliens have "universal adaptability *to any and all other life forms, under any and all other conditions they might possibly encounter.*" They are "the perfect parasite, capable of far more than clinging to the host. They are completely evolved life."[4]

Finney provides a sort of tacked-on happy ending with our warriors defeating the invading aliens' pods through their communal intelligence, making them realize that "this little race would never receive them, would never yield." He quotes Winston Churchill's stirring wartime speech defying the invasion of an Other that would assimilate British culture: "We shall fight them in the fields, and in the streets, we shall fight in the hills; we shall never surrender." Finney indicates that the same fight had been fought elsewhere and won, discouraging the aliens.

The cultural implications for a book written at the height of the Cold

War and the Red Scare are obvious, similar to those of "Who Goes There?" and other science fiction films of the era. The aliens and those converted are a metaphor for the cells of Communists many believed to be imbedded in our society, working to corrupt it: another version of the paranoia inspired by fear of hidden cults in the Satanic film. But Finney's novel and the films that followed present a larger issue in their horror theme: the assimilation of our very genetic heritage. The invasion and assimilation narratives in the novel inspire a visceral horror that led to the film *Invasion of the Body Snatchers* a year after the novel was published.

Directed by Don Siegel, *Invasion of the Body Snatchers* retains the metaphor of Communist infiltration as well as the timeless invasion and assimilation narratives. Siegel's film follows the novel in most respects, with the Miles and Becky characters (played by Kevin McCarthy in his signature role and the luminous Dana Wynter) gradually coming to realize their danger, and a plot similar that of the flight-and-fight story of the novel results. The town has been changed to Santa Mira. And the film changes the novel's plot narrative, with the crazed Miles in the opening scene being examined in a hospital because of his raving about alien invaders and a flashback as he explains. The plot differs too because all of Miles' friends, including Becky, are assimilated at the end, and it substitutes a different conclusion, with Miles, after he escapes his assimilated pursuers, making it to the freeway where Kevin McCarthy enacts the memorable film scene when he screams at passing drivers, "They're here already!" On one level, the lines inspire vicarious fear of Communist subversion. But on a deeper level, the film whispers to us of the primal fear of invasion, assimilation and the destruction of our genetic heritage common to 1950s science fiction films.

The 1956 adaptation of Finney's novel has become a cult classic, but it has the production values of a "B" movie. By 1978 when the second version appeared, also titled *Invasion of the Body Snatchers,* innovation in special effects give the film much more interesting visual qualities. And it also reflects a change in American culture. The film's opening visualizes the spores leaving a dead planet, traveling through space and landing in a field near San Francisco, where they take root to grow pods. The structure of the source novel remains. The names and location shift from small town California to urban San Francisco, and the hero and heroine become Matthew Bennell (Donald Sutherland) and Elizabeth Driscoll (Brooke Adams). They work together at the public health office and are best friends. Elizabeth has a troubled marriage with a husband who is a bit too much of a free spirit. Then he changes to a pod-victim's lack of emotion. The plot follows the previous film and the novel with discovery of copy bodies, gradual realization of the situation, then flight and pursuit and an unhappy ending.

There's a repeat of the explanation for the pods' presence. Matthew's

THREE • *The Assimilation Narrative* 59

Invasion of the Body Snatchers: Miles Bennell (Kevin McCarthy) knows that the body snatchers have arrived.

psychiatrist friend Dr. Kibner (Leonard Nimoy), an early pod transformation, speaks for them: "We came here from a dying world.... We adapt and survive." We even get an homage to the first film with a brief shot of Kevin McCarthy as Miles running through the streets shouting "They're here already!" But this time, he is mobbed and trampled, presumably killed by pod people, signaling that things will not go well in this version.

The film changes the transformation metaphor from fear of Communist infiltration to the danger of conformity. By 1978, American culture, or at least the media presentation of it, was dramatically different. The counterculture movement of the late 1960s contributed to a transformation of the zeitgeist. Conformity was a primary value of the 1950s, but in the late 1960s and '70s, films like *The Graduate* and *Butch Cassidy and the Sundance Kid* valorized the Thoreauvian ethos of praise for the outsider who flaunts authority and marches to the beat of a different drummer. So we might see Matthew and Elizabeth in their flight from assimilation and failure as exemplifying the futility of attempting to retain individual freedom in a conformist society. But the assimilation narrative remains.

Body Snatchers (1993) is the third adaptation of the Finney novel, with another combination of the territorial primal narrative and cultural adaptation, including a bow to the youth market. Here we have teenager Marti Malone (Gabrielle Anbar) as heroine. Her parents move to a military base where her father will research the environmental impact of Army operations. As in the other adaptations, she discovers that everyone around her has been assimilated, even her father and stepmother Carol. Marti flees assimilation with other young people. They seem to escape to another Army base, but at the end, a voiceover repeats Marti's assimilated stepmother's words: "Where you going to go? Where you gonna run? Where you gonna hide? Nowhere, because there's no one like you left." Like the 1978 pod people film, this one takes a position on conformity, valorizing the rebellion of the young people against it. They are now Other and outsiders to the assimilated masses.

The cultural package of *Invasion* (2007), the fourth adaptation of *Invasion of the Body Snatchers*, develops yet another spin on the assimilation narrative, with a bit of speculation on the possibilities for life without destructive primal narratives. By 2007, the ideas of evolutionary psychology had spread, and the film alludes to them. As in earlier versions of pod people films, the infection comes from the sky, this time fungus from a fallen space vehicle. Carol Bennell (Nicole Kidman) is a psychiatrist with a son, Oliver, another threatened child in a narrative common to literature, especially beginning in the nineteenth century. Dickens held his readers breathless over the fate of children when the life of Little Dorrit hangs in the balance, Little Paul in *Dombey and Son* dies an episode at a time and the young David Copperfield, Oliver Twist and Tiny Tim face their own perils. Our evolution has programmed us to respond to this plot. Ellen Dissanayake describes the "undeniable satisfaction while caring for a small helpless thing—especially when it's our own.... Although most people take human mother love for granted, it was an important evolutionary adaptation."[5] So when Carol finds that her son is immune to the pod people infection (because of a childhood disease) and the pod people want to kill him because he is Other and a threat to their existence, we get the timeless narrative of a mother protecting a child.

The attack on the Twin Towers and the continuing violence in the Middle East are background for the film. The screenwriters connect these current events to findings of evolutionary psychology on human nature. Carol's scientist friend, whom she contacts for information on a suspicious skin sample she has found (the first sign of the infection), tells her, "Eighty percent of what we are is determined by our genetic expression." The film suggests that perhaps the assimilation might not be a bad thing if it changed our violent genetic tendencies as expressed by atrocities and violence worldwide shown repeatedly on television news and radio reports in the film, a chorus throughout. The Russian ambassador whom Carol meets at a dinner party gives us a lecture that might have been drawn from the findings of evolutionary psychology or perhaps John Lennon's song "Imagine": "Civilization is an illusion; a game of pretend. What is real is the fact that we are still animals driven by primal instincts. Civilization crumbles whenever we need it most. In the right situation, we are all capable of the most terrible crimes. Imagine a world where this was not so; imagine a world where every crisis did not result in new atrocities, where every newspaper is not full of war and violence. This is to imagine a world where human beings cease to be human" and do not succumb to the destructive primal narratives.

Before the assimilation, we hear of endless violence around the world. Then as the assimilation progresses, the media reports change. Peace has come and violence is nearly eliminated. But peace ends after Carol's develops a vaccine from Oliver's blood to cure those assimilated. At the conclusion, Carol and Dr. Galeano (her lover who saved her and Oliver) at breakfast with the radio telling of increased violence and war; and a look comes to Carol's face suggesting possible second thoughts about assimilation if it would end war and violence.

The assimilation narrative is pervasive in the science fiction–horror film. *The Host* (2013), based on Stephanie Meyer's young adult novel, gives the narrative a different spin. An alien race called Souls takes over humans and gains control. One of the aliens, Wanderer, enters the body of Melanie Strider (Saoirse Ronan), but Melanie retains some control, resulting in a conflict of Others and eventually a bonding. *The Faculty* (1998) is a run-of-the-mill teen horror movie with the usual cliché characters: bullies, cheerleaders, nerds and jocks. Students suspect that aliens have taken over their school's teachers through a protozoan infection brought by a master alien. The film at least has some amusing meta qualities with one character, goth girl Stokely (Clara DuVall), a science fiction expert, lecturing the other kids on *The Puppet Masters, Invasion of the Body Snatchers* and "Who Goes There?" as evidence of what's happening in their school. The 1994 film *The Puppet Masters* that *The Faculty* references is based on Robert Heinlein's 1951 novel of that name in which alien "slugs" invade people and ride their backs to control them, another form of assimilation. Heinlein's novel may have been a source for Finney's *Invasion of the Body Snatchers*, which was written just a few years later: both samples of the primal narrative of invasion through assimilation of the gene pool and the cultural backdrop of fear of Communist subversion.

Even the original *Star Trek* series used the assimilation narrative with an homage to the *Body Snatchers* films and perhaps Alfred Tennyson's poem "The Lotus Eaters." Tennyson alludes to the Lotus Eaters story in Homer's *Odyssey*. In "This Side of Paradise," a 1968 *Trek* episode, *Enterprise* crew members beam down to a planet inhabited by colonists where spores give perfect health and take away all tensions and ambitions. Mr. Spock is taken over by them and describes the spores to a horrified Capt. Kirk who has lost his crew, in language that seems directly drawn from Finney's novel and the first two *Body Snatchers* films (quoted above): "They drifted through space until they finally landed here." The crew has been assimilated, though not by any malign beings. Even the dour Mr. Spock falls in love with one of the colonists. But Capt. Kirk resists and frees his men from the spores' control. The final scene offers two views of the assimilation narrative and human nature. Dr. McCoy says, "That's the second time man's been thrown out of paradise." Kirk replies, "No, no, Bones. This time we walked out on our own. Maybe we weren't meant for paradise. Maybe we were meant to fight our way through. Struggle, claw our way up, scratch for every inch of the way. Maybe we can't stroll to the music of the lute. We must march to the sound of drums." But Mr. Spock gets the last word on the assimilation narrative when he says, "I have little to say about it, captain, except that for the first time in my life ... I was happy."

Dream a Little Meme with Me: The Zombie Meme and Its Origins

Zombie films are rooted in the same primal fear of assimilation as "Who Goes There?," *Body Snatchers* and their screen adaptations. Like them, they include a cultural spin that reflects their time. Exotic Voodoo folklore and the zombie have inspired a film narrative that has morphed into a cultural phenomenon, transcending the movies based on it. The zombie film is well-suited to whisper the primal fear of assimilation and loss of selfhood.

After *White Zombie* (1932), zombies from Voodoo mythology became an occasional presence in the horror film. But beginning in the 1960s, the zombie morphed into quite another figure in film and popular culture, one that has captured the popular imagination in a unique manner. Zombie films and TV series have proliferated. Anyone who has attended Comic Con, Dragon Con or any other science fiction–fantasy convention can attest to the hordes of fans shuffling along in zombie makeup and costume. Major League baseball teams schedule zombie nights with spectators coming dressed for the part. Zombie mania has spread throughout our culture. How can we explain this contagion?

An oft-repeated response to this conundrum is the influence of culture in creating the zombie apocalypse as a metaphor. Jeffrey Sconse's interpretation is fairly typical: "The zombie genre is really the story of two bodies in decay—the individual corpses of the undead and the social body as a whole."[6] But there is another answer, one that lies in the fields of memetics and evolutionary psychology. Findings from the fields point to primal dreams from our ancestors that whisper fear of assimilation and remain with us, influencing not only our behavior but bringing the pleasurable shiver of this narrative in the horror genre. Richard Matheson's 1954 novel *I Am Legend*, its three film adaptations and especially *Night of the Living Dead* have created an enduring meme rooted in those whispers.

In *The Selfish Gene*, Richard Dawkins coined the word *meme* as analogous to *gene* but a "unit of culture." It has spread like wildfire in academic discourse as well as in the popular media where it is used in so many contexts that it has almost lost its original meaning. "Examples of memes," he writes,

> are tunes, ideas, catchphrases, clothes fashions, ways of making pots or of building arches. Just as genes propagate themselves in the gene pool by leaping from body to body via sperms and eggs, so memes propagate themselves in the meme pool in leaping from brain to brain by a process which, in the broad sense, can be called imitation.... When you plant a fertile meme in my mind, you literally parasitize my brain, turning it into a vehicle for the meme's propagation in just the same way a virus might parasitize the genetic mechanism of a host cell.[7]

Dawkins finds that memes obey the laws of natural selection in ways analogous to genes. Like genes, memes are self-replicating and, as Dawkins writes, use humans as vehicles for their replication. His findings provide yet another avenue for primal traits criticism by connecting the study of adaptive behavior to a lively cultural phenomenon.

Evolutionary psychology would propose that the more powerful and enduring memes spring from whispers we inherit from our ancestors. To put the matter succinctly, long-lasting memes rise from genes: genetically adaptive predispositions spread by cultural transmission. It seems impossible to discuss enduring memes outside the context of evolutionary psychology. Ridley writes: "The ideas of which Dawkins was an early champion have changed biology beyond recognition. What was still—despite Darwin—essentially a descriptive science has become a study of function."[8]

Robert Auger observes that evolutionary psychologists distinguish between what they call "evoked" and "epidemiological" culture.[9] A textbook definition of the two would describe epidemiological culture as the product of learning from others—information spread through a population like a virus. Evoked culture, on the other hand, "is innate information that resides in human heads and is expressed contingently in different environments."[10] Memes may come from either, but what Auger designates as epidemiological culture may be influenced by evoked culture. Dawkins points out that memes may be ephemeral. "Some memes, like some genes, achieve brilliant short-term success in spreading rapidly, but do not last long in the meme pool. Popular songs and stiletto heels are examples."[11] But others, perhaps what we might trace to Auger's definition of evoked culture, flow from whispers of adaptive behavior that enabled our ancestors to survive and evolve. They resonate from the primal narratives that underpin much of our literature and mythology: narratives that contribute to the creation of culture.

Film is a ripe field for the generation of memes, with favorite actors, plots and quotations becoming imbedded in the collective human psyche. The familiar line "Play it again, Sam" from *Casablanca* is an example, which endures despite being a misquotation of "Play it, Sam" in the film. We find myriads of other examples in culture as in the ubiquitous "Kilroy was here" from World War II and urban folklore like the "man with a hook for a hand" story. David Dennett describes memes as the psychic equivalent of an invasion of the body snatchers.[12]

Memes, then, may spring from culture rather than the primal narratives, though in most cases evolutionary psychology's findings suggest that culture and genetic predisposition interact. Susan Blackmore likens the relationship of genes and culture to a dog on a leash, with genes being the leash and the dog being culture. The leash may expand and the dog pull hard against the leash, but the dog is always there. "Memetic evolution," she writes, "means that people *are* different. Their ability to imitate creates a second replicator that acts in its own interests and can produce behaviour that is memetically adaptive but biologically maladaptive.... The leash is sometimes very long, but the dog can never get away."[13]

The most powerful memes, then, spring from within. Brodie writes: "Meme evolution selects for the ideas, beliefs, attitudes and myths that we pay the most attention to and broadcast the loudest. And *without conscious intervention,* what we pay attention to and broadcast the loudest is determined by that complex web of feelings and drives, cravings and fears, that evolved to keep us alive and mating."[14] The zombie film is a prime example of a meme that has spread through the interaction of culture and primal narratives.

Voodoo in Film: *White Zombie,* Matheson's *I Am Legend* and Film Adaptations, *Night of the Living Dead, Maggie, World War Z* and *Warm Bodies*

Voodoo was alive and well in the U.S. from earliest times with the importation of African slaves who brought their religion with them. Cole Porter's 1929 song "You Do Something To Me" with its reference to the power of Voodoo shows that it also became part of popular culture. The zombie comes to us as baggage from this ancient religion, and the exotic quality of zombie folklore made it an ideal topic for the horror film. The very name "zombie" is inaccurate for describing the zombie film as it has evolved, however, as contemporary cinematic zombies are not the creation of Voodoo sorcerers.

Millions of people in Africa, Haiti, Central and South America and the United States practice Voodoo (also known as Vodoun) and Santeria, a sister religion, both of which combine Roman Catholicism and ancient African paths. In ecstatic Voodoo ceremonies overseen by a priest called a hougon, individuals are said to be "mounted" by spirits called loa, then going into a frenzy and speaking in the language of the loa. These supernatural beings are not gods but intermediaries, rather like saints in the Roman Catholic tradition and placed between the Supreme Creator, who exists far away from the material world, and humanity. Folklore about Voodoo and Santeria has it that the dead can be brought back to life by evil practitioners of magic to serve as slaves who are totally compliant to their masters.[15]

The success of Universal's *Dracula* (1931) guaranteed that more horror films would be made. *White Zombie,* an independent production, appeared in 1932, the first film to adapt Voodoo folklore. The film is set in Haiti, where Neil and Madeline, a young engaged couple, have come to visit Charles Beaumont, a plantation owner; and they are to be married there. The plot follows Madeline's transformation into a zombie by zombie master Murder (Bela Lugosi) at the behest of Beaumont, who wants her for himself.

Intermixed in the melodrama is a good deal of zombie lore, apparently drawn from William B. Seabrook's 1929 book *The Magic Island.* Seabrook claims to have witnessed zombies working in fields as slaves. A passage in the film echoes Seabrook: On the way to Beaumont's home, Neil and Madeline see a line of men shambling along, and their carriage driver says, "They are not men, monsieur, they are dead bodies ... Zombies! The living dead, corpses taken from their graves who are made to work in sugar mills and fields at night." The same lines appear almost verbatim in Seabrook's book. The film exploits other folklore about Voodoo, with Murder practicing Voodoo magic with wax dolls.

And so the zombie meme in film took root in modest fashion by enacting the primal narrative of assimilation. Murder turns humans into Other; and the focal threat is to the white woman, who would be seen as the carrier of the genetic heritage for most of the film audience of that day. In discussing the endurance of zombie folklore, Suzanne Goodney Lea writes that the attraction of the phenomenon as it comes from Voodoo culture is a desire to control and possess.[16] That desire is central to *White Zombie* and to other zombie films from the '30s and '40s, whether it be sexual or other forms of domination and exploitation. We see it in *Revolt of the Zombies* (1936), *King of the Zombies* (1941) and *Revenge of the Zombies* (1943), Saturday afternoon double-feature fare of this subgenre of the horror film.

I Walked with a Zombie (1943), a Val Lewton classic with a plot inspired by Charlotte Brontë's *Jane Eyre,* is the finest of the early zombie movies. Betsy Connell (Frances Dee) comes to a Caribbean island to care for the catatonic Jessica, wife of plantation owner Paul Holland (Lewton stalwart Tom Conway). The film adapts the usual Voodoo folklore with a hougan, a houmfort or temple, a Voodoo ceremony, much about zombies, Voodoo dolls and references to loas. Lewton and director Jacques Tourneur suggest, but do not quite affirm, that Jessica is a zombie, though the conclusion does leave the impression that she has been assimilated into one. But the film adapts Voodoo to show the contrast between the field workers, brought to the islands as slaves, with their culture and religion and the small white community of land owners, with the vast gulf between them. That gulf is symbolized by the figurehead of the ship that brought slaves to the island, "Ti-Misery" (St. Sebastian), pierced with arrows, in the courtyard of the Holland home.

The film demonstrates the contrast of cultures in many other ways, as in contrasting Mrs. Rand, who becomes a Voodoo priestess in order to get the natives to accept modern medicine, with Sabreur, a black native and Voodoo magician. The film plays on the power of Sabreur using Voodoo dolls to control the white Jessica, a racial conflict that would have incited horror in 1943. It achieves Lewton's brand of horror by creating an ambience of unease with light, shadows and sounds without showing any real violence, along with the racial conflict between the black and white communities.

Kyle Bishop points out that early zombie films reinforce the biases of a white, imperialist culture,[17] as is certainly the case with *I Walked with a Zombie* and many of these early zombie films. While not all use Voodoo as a frame, they share the same plot in which zombies are native people subjugated by Caucasians in foreign and exotic locations. But beneath the post-colonial critique imbedded in this plot lies something deeper and more enduring: the primal fear of the Other and assimilation, a narrative that inspired the zombie meme as we know it. Zombies fill the bill of Other but also one of Us who has been assimilated.

Though the cinematic Voodoo zombie was pretty much lost by the 1960s, another version of the zombie emerged. James Russell lists descriptions of 287 zombie or zombie-like films produced worldwide between *White Zombie* and the 2005 publication of his book *American Zombie Gothic*.[18] There has been a flood of them since, with the genre spilling over into television. Richard Matheson's novel *I Am Legend* provided the seed ground for the meme as we know it with a very different kind of zombie. Matheson introduced the central horror of the zombie apocalypse in his novel. Its primal narratives of assimilation as well as tribalism, territoriality and fear of the Other have rung bells in the popular consciousness to create the meme he helped to establish.

Early in *I Am Legend*, protagonist Robert Neville fails to convince officials that a disaster is about to happen. Matheson gives a reason for the rapid spread of the plague and his debt to Bram Stoker by having Neville quote *Dracula*: "The strength of the vampire is that no one will believe in him. Thank you Dr. Van Helsing."[19] Like Stoker's vampire, zombies infect victims who become Other, removed from our genetic heritage. Also, the zombie apocalypse can be interpreted as metaphor for Communist subversion in Matheson's novel and some zombie films.

A curious mix of zombie and vampire lore, the novel covers a three-year period following what might be described as the first fictional zombie apocalypse, which Matheson places in 1976. Neville is the last of his kind, a man immune to the plague (apparently because he was once infected with a light version that gave him antibodies) that has turned the population of the world into zombie vampires. He lives alone in a fortified house, his territory, stalked by zombies at night. He learns that the zombie-vampire condition results from a bacterial infection created from spores traveling by mosquito bites and wind-driven dust to infect all (including his wife and daughter) but him. Those infected rise from the dead, even digging their way out of the grave, as did his wife whom he thought he had killed because of her infection. Matheson raids Stoker's *Dracula* in creating his zombie-vampires: They dislike mirrors, have an insatiable thirst for blood and human flesh, are repelled by garlic, fear the cross, cannot stand daylight and are killed by being staked. As the novel progresses, Matheson provides more or less scientific reasons for all of these conditions. But as in the soon-to-be-created zombie meme, the infected mindlessly shamble about seeking prey. The novel stresses the fear of the Other narrative both through Neville's conflict with the zombies and with a group of survivors who have the zombie plague in their system but have found a drug to prevent total assimilation.

Matheson wrote *I Am Legend* before evolutionary psychology as we know it was part of public and very little of scientific discourse. But the work tunes into primal narratives that resonate as whispers from the adaptive behaviors and fears inherited from our primal ancestors. The zombies have taken the territory of the civilized world. They seek to invade Neville's personal territory, the house he has boarded up and defends with garlic and mirrors. Defending his territory, Neville kills without remorse, for the zombies are Other. And he is Other to the new people, another tribe, those who are changed but not assimilated. He is alienated, caught between. Neville has a final conversation with Ruth, a young woman from the unassimilated. It's not surprising that that the men from the new people are ruthless in hunting him, she says; "They're young. And they are killers—assigned killers, legal killers.... Men can learn to enjoy killing. That's an old story." Killing the Other without mercy, Matheson suggests, is part of the human condition. "As far as we know ... you're quite unique, you know. When you're gone, there won't be anyone else like you within our particular society." People are "terrified of you, Robert, they hate you. And they want your life."

Neville is unacceptable to those who do not share his immunity. "Robert Neville looked out over the new people of the earth. He knew he did not belong to them; he knew that, like the vampires, he was anathema and black terror to be destroyed.... I am legend": the last of his kind, an Other both to the zombies and the new people, to be cleansed from their tribe. Mathias Clasen describes the evolutionary whisper that creates the horror element of the novel and led to the meme that is enshrined in film: "Both the modern horror zombie's defining characteristics, the predation and the contagion, allow it to connect squarely with evolved defense mechanisms in human psychological architecture. We fear agents that have the will and the capacity to eat us, and we have strongly aversive reactions to cues of contagion."[20]

Three film iterations of Matheson's novel adapt the horror and pathos of the zombie assimilation narrative: *The Last Man on Earth* (1964) with Vincent Price, *The Omega Man* (1971) with Charlton Heston and *I Am Legend* (2007) with Will Smith. *The Last Man on Earth* follows Matheson's novel closely. He co-wrote the script but disliked the finished product enough to adopt a *nom de plume* for the credits. In *The Last Man on Earth*, biological warfare during a conflict with China causes the infection, killing most of the population except for Neville (who had developed a serum that was lost) and a few hidden survivors. The film mixes issues in the culture of the day and the fear of Communism as assimilation, along with other primal narratives. *The Omega Man* deviates a good deal from its source, with many of the differences reflecting the fear of apocalyptic war with China or Russia, another intersection of culture and primal narratives. The cult of mutants led by Matthias survived but are physically changed. They reflect another element of '70s culture in *Omega Man*. Fear of cults was in the air. Matthias' cult is called the Family, perhaps an allusion to the Manson Family whose five-week murder spree began in 1969. So we get multiple tribes of Others, the mutants and the survivors that Neville found, with Neville himself being alienated from both (as in the novel). Lisa, a survivor who leads him to her own group, says, "You don't belong.... Somehow you scare me more than Matthias." Everyone is eager to kill those outside their tribal group who are Other, and as in the other adaptations of *I Am Legend*, Neville's immunity to the assimilation has made him a genetic outsider.

Bearing the title of the novel, the 2007 adaptation *I Am Legend* does not follow the Matheson book closely but captures the spirit. As in the other films, Neville seems to be the sole survivor at the outset, except for his dog. Special effects improvement enable director Francis Lawrence to make New York look apocalyptically fallen, with escaped zoo animals running through the streets. The zombies are even more monstrous and Other in appearance. The apocalypse was caused by an accidentally released virus that is airborne or blood-borne, with only one percent of the world's population immune to it. Fears of the AIDS virus and the Ebola outbreak at the time of the film's release no doubt added to the horror of the apocalypse narrative. Also, the fear of a catastrophe caused by irresponsible research by government and corporations is now a horror genre fixture. As in Matheson's novel and the other film versions, Neville is barricaded in his apartment to avoid the mutant Darkseekers, the assimilated Others of the earlier films. Like *Omega Man*, *I Am Legend* offers hope for humanity.

In Matheson's novel and all three film adaptations, the template of the meme is a conflict of tribes: "Us" vs. "Them," zombies who would corrupt and destroy the human gene pool with the film and novel's hero along with the further complication of conflict between those who are somehow survivors. As is so often the case in the zombie meme, the humans in their tribes are in nearly as much danger from each other are they are from the zombies without. There are tribes within tribes, viewing each other as Other.

But in Matheson's book and the films it inspired, self-sacrifice is a common theme. Evolutionary psychology has much to say on the subject, from Dawkins' denial of the individual animal's sense of sacrifice for its group to Edward O. Wilson's description of eusociality. At any rate, we can feel vicarious pleasure in the survival of our species, though changed, at the conclusions of the films, made possible by the sacrifice of the hero.

Night of the Living Dead (1968) was born in a collaboration between George Romero and John Russo, who got together enough money to produce the film while using many friends as actors and production helpers. Romero usually gets credit for it, perhaps because of his success after he and Russo parted company over a disagreement on sequels. The film is not an adaptation of Matheson's novel, but Romero admits finding his inspiration for *Night of the Living Dead* in it. In an interview, he reported, "I read a book called *I Am Legend* by Richard Matheson and got very much into the socio-political thought-line that's present in it, although it doesn't really follow through with it."[21] His film, which seemed so insignificant at the time and at first received a very limited release, was influential in creating a powerful and enduring meme for what evolutionary psychologists might say was a very good reason. *Night of the Living Dead* tunes into important primal narratives. Made for a little over $100,000, the film grossed $112 million in the U.S. and much more on the international market, a huge box office take in 1968 dollars for a B movie. Romero and Russo did not share greatly in the film's financial success. They were amateur filmmakers by any standard, with little knowledge of the business side of the industry. They sold the rights to the film for a modest sum. But the popularity of *Night of the Living Dead* and of the horror film subgenre that it established showed that it touched something in viewers' psyches, sparking the meme as it evolved from its origins in zombie folklore through Matheson's novel and its adaptations.

Night of the Living Dead creates a microcosm of human nature. The opening sequence leads us to the farmhouse where Barbara (whose brother was assimilated by the newly risen in the opening scene), Ben, Tom, Judy,

Harry and Helen and their daughter Karen (who was bitten and is showing signs of turning) take refuge.

The film is rooted in four primal narratives. We get a struggle between what amounts to tribal groups: survivors against zombies and survivors against each other. The survivors occupy a territory, the house. They face assimilation by Others, whom Ben kills without compunction after he finds a rifle. As in multiple zombie films to follow, the survivors fight each other as well as the invading Other. In *Night of the Living Dead*, Ben and Harry enact the tribal leadership struggle. Ben's strategy is to barricade the house and wait for help. Harry insists on locking themselves in the basement. In the struggle for dominance as alpha male, Ben says, "Go the hell to the cellar. You be the boss down there. I'll be the boss up here." Barash points out that animal social groups will likely be led by a "dominant individual,"[22] a pattern common to human behavior that often involves conflict. The struggle for dominance within the group of survivors, a tribe in evolutionary psychology perspective fighting against assimilation, became a central element of the zombie meme in film as it has developed. And from the narrative perspective, of course, this dominance rivalry offers an approach to dramatic conflict.

In this as in other apocalypse films, the radio and television serve as a chorus, informing the people in the house and the viewer of events outside. The cause of zombie apocalypses is usually left rather vague. The radio announcer in this film says that no one knows the reason for the outbreak, but it might be radiation from a satellite returning from Venus. He also tells listeners to shoot the zombies in the head to kill them, an element in the formula for a multitude of zombie films to come. All of the inhabitants of the farmhouse perish, and the film offers a bit of social commentary when a white sheriff's deputy shoots Ben, an African American who is clearly not a zombie. The deputies seem to be having a good time killing and see a black man as just another Other.

Night of the Living Dead helped to create a template for the zombie apocalypse meme as it has spread. But not quite all of the meme is established here. Unlike Matheson's novel and other zombie films to follow, order seems to be restored, and at the fade there is hope: for civilization if not for human nature. The appearance of the zombies clearly identifies their otherness. As we see in so many horror films, appearance identifies otherness, and such is the case in the grotesqueness of the zombie. Desmond Morris writes of "badges" that identify people: skin color, ethnicity, religion and a host of other elements that may lead them to be seen as Us or Them. He writes, "It is a deep-seated in-group reaction" against those with badges other than our own that can cause a distrust or fear, and "the physical badge-wearers are there, literally ready-made to take the scapegoat role."[23] The zombies' visual and behavioral otherness are obvious badges, as is Ben's skin color.

Tony Williams notes that Romero's film introduced the grotesque imagery to be adopted for splatter films, with zombies snacking on the entrails of their victims. Thus we have the pleasure of seeing these Others killed, usually with gory head shots, with all our inhibitions against killing and ability to identify or sympathize with them as fellow humans removed, a strategy used in all the zombie movies to come. They eat human flesh and, as in Matheson's novel, "We" are assimilated into "Them" when they bite the living. In *Dracula,* "the blood is the life." Here it is the flesh craved by the Other, but the principle is the same. From an evolutionary psychology perspective, the genes are the life, making us what we are. The zombies' desire to eat brains is an interesting development of the meme because it is our highly developed brain that makes us unique in the animal kingdom and the organ that evolved to permit our adaptation and survival.

Some critics connect the power of the zombie meme to culture. Tony Williams is an example: "*Night of the Living Dead* not only represents an important and largely original development in both the zombie and gothic horror traditions, but the innovative film also establishes the zombie as a powerful psychological symbol for social and cultural anxieties and tensions."[24] Robin Wood calls it "the most uncompromising critique of contemporary America in American film."[25]

But there is something more than the influence of culture in the meme's power. In Matheson's creation and Romero's adaptation of it, the zombie meme exists as a combination of culture and the whisper of the primal narratives, good examples of Blackmore's dog and leash analogy.

In most zombie films to follow, the same narratives that captured the popular imagination in *Night of the Living Dead* underpin the plot. The source of the contagion varies. In the six-film *Resident Evil* franchise, the doughty Alice (Milla Jovovich) battles an evil corporation that created the virus through an A.I., another version of the Other. In *28 Days Later*, the contagion results from an animal rights group freeing chimps infected with "rage," a virus from a research lab. Sometimes, as in the long-running TV series *The Walking Dead*, the origin is a subject of speculation.

The source is also left uncertain in *World War Z* (2013). The film credits Max Brooks' 2006 novel *World War Z: An Oral History of the Zombie Wars,* but about all it has in common with the novel is zombies and the title. Brooks' version is based on interviews with survivors of the zombie wars after their conclusion and traces the outbreak to China. The film version follows retired United Nations investigator Gary Lane (Brad Pitt) in his quest to save humanity and his family, undertaking an odyssey to find the source of the infection and a cure to prevent assimilation.

Like all films of this subgenre, the plot strains probability. The zombies win far too easily, especially in the fall of Jerusalem, where they are fought with machine guns and rifles for the most part instead of heavier weaponry. But it has one element from the primal narratives that the more sensational zombie movies lack: a focus on family, with Lane desperate to save his wife, two children and an adopted son. While the film plays on fear of assimilation, as do all zombie films, it focuses on the hero's love for his family, taking the plot beyond the rather cold view of self-sacrifice described by Dawkins in developing an important narrative. Evolutionary psychologists credit our species' development of pair bonding and family loyalty as a central adaptation in our survival. We are evolved to respond favorably to a man defending his family, his personal genetic future.

In the plethora of zombie films, the formula supporting the meme usually remains the same, but it has been explored in a variety of dramatic approaches. The zombies may learn to move faster and even become a little sentient. In the 2017 film *The Cured*, a remedy restores most zombies. But they remain Other to those who were uninfected. The film offers a commentary on our distrust of anyone not specifically of our tribal group.

Some films explore the dramatic possibilities of interaction between the living and the undead. *Warm Bodies* (2013) is a love story about a zombie boy who takes the name R after eating the brains of a human girl's boyfriend. His meal starts him on a path to humanity and leads him to fall in love with the girl, Julie. In this *Romeo and Juliet* adaptation, with zombies and humans as tribes instead of Montagues and Capulets, we even get a balcony scene. *Maggie* (2015) adapts the zombie meme in a father-daughter love story. When Wade Vogel's daughter Maggie is bitten in a zombie outbreak, she is taken to a detention center where the infected are lumped with those who have already changed and are eventually euthanized. Wade (Arnold Schwarzenegger) insists on bringing her home, agreeing that when the time comes he will take the "third option" (killing her himself instead of having her quarantined), which he ultimately cannot do. The film has more dramatic interest than most in the genre, but the primal narratives remain the same, with the added interest of a father defending his child, his genetic future and his family, and being unable to kill her even though he knows it would be the right thing to do in defending his species.

The meme has also been adapted for the many zombie spoofs such as *Zombieland* (2009) and a host of made-for-TV and DVD releases with laughable titles like *Hot Wax Zombies on Wheels* (1999), *Zombie Shark* and *Zombie Strippers* (2008), as well as dark comedies such as *Shaun of the Dead* (2004). Burr Steers surely offended Janeites everywhere with his screen adaptation of Seth Grahame-Smith's comic novel *Pride and Prejudice and Zombies* (2016). But the primal narrative of assimilation persists even in comedy.

The zombie apocalypse meme no doubt reflects fears that arise from our culture and the possibility of society's collapse with the total disintegration of the social bonds that our evolution has created, a potential that seems ever more frightening in a world torn by tribal warfare and strife. These fears whisper to us from our primal dreams to create the primal screams of the horror genre. The zombie meme has taken root in a powerful way in relatively short time. An even more enduring meme has grown from Bram Stoker's novel *Dracula* and the multitude of films it has inspired.

Four
The Tribal Narrative

"Your girls that you all love, they are all mine already"

In their portrayal of the two groups of proto humans at the watering hole in *2001*, Kubrick and Clarke make a significant statement about human nature. Humanity, like most mammalian species, is social, territorial and tribal. And a tribal organization would have been optimal for defending territory against other tribes or predators. Charles Darwin recognized the evolutionary advantage: "There can be no doubt that a tribe including many members who, from possessing in a high degree the spirit of patriotism, fidelity, obedience, courage and sympathy, were always ready to aid one another, and to sacrifice themselves for the common good would be victorious over most other tribes; and this would be natural selection."[1] Kubrick and Clarke follow this basic premise of evolutionary psychology in making Moon Watcher's tribe the unit of defense against the predator and other tribes.

Evolutionary theory has established tribalism as essential to humanity's evolution, a hypothesis that seems rather self-evident considering the physical weakness of our species compared to so many predators and the need for mutual protection. Edward O. Wilson and evolutionary psychologists have expanded Darwin's remarks on tribalism. Wilson writes,

> To form groups, drawing visceral comfort and pride from familiar fellowship, and to defend the group enthusiastically against rival groups—these are among the absolute universals of human nature and hence of culture.... People must have a tribe.... The social world of each modern human is not a single tribe, but rather a system of interlocking tribes, among which it is often difficult to find a single compass.[2]

But in the modern world, as opposed to that of our primal ancestors, the nature of tribalism is different.

Sometimes tribes are easy to see, as in Native American tribal organization or that of Africans. Elsewhere, they can be seen in the proliferation of Christian denominations as tribes, gangs in cities and certainly in the ancient hatred shared by of Sunni and Shi'ite Muslims in the Middle East as well as the growing tribalism in American politics with animosity between left and right.

But tribalism can be more subtle. Our tendency to form tribal allegiances can be seen in sports fandom, with Yankees fans pitted against Red Sox enthusiasts. But throughout our culture, these mini-tribes overlap. A Yankees fan and Red Sox fan may play on the same church softball team, another tribe. Athletic teams of all kinds form intense tribal groups with hopes for the joys of victory. Matthew Alper writes, "Because of the strength and stability that came from the social adaptation, the group dynamic became the 'favored' evolutionary trend, particularly among vertebrates and most particularly among mammals."[3] Sebastian Junger chronicles stories of settlers in colonial America deserting to Native American tribes and never returning, while Native Americans almost never left to join settlers. He quotes Benjamin Franklin on the subject: "When an Indian child has been brought up among us, taught our language and habituated to our customs..., if he goes to see his relations and makes one Indian ramble with them, there is no persuading him ever to return."[4] He credits close tribal relations of the Native American culture as being seductive in comparison to the isolation and alienation of western society.

So humans' proclivity to form tribal allegiances as studied by evolutionary scientists suggests that we respond to primal narratives in film and fiction that portray a tribe, in the broad definition, with which we empathize in doing battle against an Other. Tribal plots in film cross genre boundaries from Westerns to war films to science fiction and horror, portraying male bonding with a group of warriors led by an alpha male fighting the Other. And in recent times, we see this narrative enacted with female bonding, yet another example of the effect of culture on primal narratives. The tribalism plot offers fertile seed ground for conflict between groups we could call tribes.

"I felt in my heart a wicked, burning desire that they would kiss me with those red lips": Bram Stoker's *Dracula* and Its Film Adaptations

In a frequently quoted passage, Hillary Clinton wrote, "It takes a village to raise a child." But in Bram Stoker's novel *Dracula* (1897) and its countless film adaptations, the narrative shows that it takes a tribe to kill a vampire.

Dracula offers an exciting example of the primal narrative of tribalism, with a sturdy band of defenders destroying an Other, an invader of our territory and a threat to our genetic heritage. Robin Fox finds "intense emotional attachment between males as having its roots in the pre-human group-living primates but coming to full flower in hominid evolution ... with the developments of hunting and warfare. Men hunting or fighting together had to develop a special kind of trust that went beyond simple friendship as might be expressed in grooming or proximity."[5] Stoker's novel adapts this narrative of a group of tribal warriors fighting a territorial invader. He follows the work of his predecessors in the vampire story and the origins of the gothic novel to create a meme that seems likely to be even more enduring than the zombie apocalypse.

Vampire legends go back to the beginnings of human history, with stories dating to ancient Greece, Rome and Egypt. Montague Summers, a devout Catholic and believer in all things occult, reports on dozens of vampire stories and writes with earnest credulity of one of them: "Of its authenticity and absolute fidelity," as he describes the vampire incident, "no doubt at all can be entertained."[6] J. Gordon Melton is a researcher of legends rather than a believer, and his *The Vampire Book: The Encyclopedia of the Undead* is a good source for background on the legends leading to the literary vampire.

Stoker adapted sources well established in his time both in legend and literature. He could have read Emily Gerard's book *The Land Beyond the Forest* (1851), which was popular in his day. Gerard's description of Romanian folklore offers a description of the vampire that parallels Stoker's creation and vampire books and films to follow.

> More decidedly evil is the *nosferatu*, or vampire, in which every Roumanian peasant believes as firmly as he does in heaven or hell. There are two sorts of vampires, living and dead. The living vampire is generally the illegitimate offspring of two illegitimate persons; but even a flawless pedigree will not insure anyone against the intrusion of a vampire into their family vault, since every person killed by a nosferatu becomes likewise a vampire after death, and will continue to suck the blood of other innocent persons till the spirit has been exorcised by opening the grave of the suspected person, and either driving a stake through the corpse, or else firing a pistol-shot into the coffin. To walk smoking round the grave on each anniversary of the death is also supposed to be effective in confining the vampire. In very obstinate cases of vampirism it is recommended to cut off the head, and replace it in the coffin with the mouth filled with garlic, or to extract the heart and burn it, strewing its ashes over the grave.[7]

She sums up much of the filmic vampires' nature and means of killing them. Augustin Calmet, an eighteenth-century priest and writer on the occult, wrote well-known books such as *Dissertation of Ghosts, Demons and Vampires* and *The Phantom World* that were still current in mid- to late nineteenth-century England. Scholars disagree on Stoker's exact sources but, in a conversation with the Transylvanian ambassador at a dinner party, he learned of Vlad Tepes, a fifteenth-century Transylvanian king called "The Impaler" because of his practice of impaling his enemies on stakes. This was the germ for his classic novel.[8]

Dracula did not spring into the canon of English literature without predecessors. James Malcolm Rymer and Thomas Peckett Prest's lurid potboiler *Varney the Vampire, the Feast of Blood* (1847) and John Polidori's *The Vampyre* (1819) are precursors, as are Samuel Taylor Coleridge's poem *Christabel* (1797 and 1800) and Sheridan Le Fanu's novella *Carmilla* (1872), an adaptation of Coleridge's poem. But Stoker, apparently influenced by lore in the works of Calmet and Gerard, added the element that has made the vampire one of literature's most powerful memes and one that would underpin the zombie film to come: vampirism as a means of transforming "Us" into "Them" and the corruption of the gene pool by assimilation.

The novel is in many respects the product and redirection of earlier gothic conventions in characters, setting and plot. The description of the Carpathian mountainous regions and of Castle Dracula is patently drawn from the sublime settings in works by eighteenth-century purveyors of the gothic romance. While it draws from that tradition, *Dracula* is also an unrivaled symphony of all the primal narratives. Its tale of tribal defense of territory and an invasion by an Other—a predator who preys on the novel's women, the source of our genetic heritage—has brought whispers of entertaining horror for readers since it was first published. It is one of the longest enduring novels (never out of print since its first publication) and the source of literally hundreds of film adaptations and sequels, revisionings and adaptations of the central vampire myth. *Dracula* is worth discussing in detail to establish how it has been interpreted and revisioned by filmmakers.

The opening chapters establish a territorial narrative with Jonathan Harker's journey to Count Dracula's castle, far away from the safety of Victorian England. Dracula is Other, not only in his status as undead but as a denizen of Eastern Europe, a place of longstanding unrest that would soon erupt into World War I. Stoker's vampire is well designed to incite the territorial fears of the xenophobic Victorian British. Robert Wasson observes that Dracula "represents those forces in Eastern Europe which seek to overthrow, through violence and subversion, the more progressive democratic civilization of the West."[9]

Stoker's innovative approach to narrative through journals, letters and newspaper accounts begins with Harker's diary. He writes in his journal of passing through the "Mittel Land," the area between civilization and the beginning of a land new to him and the territory of the Other. Those at the inn where he stays warn him, begging him to wait until St. George's Day is past. According to Gerard's *The Land Beyond the Forest*, occult forces are particularly strong on St. George's Day. The tension in these scenes raises the reader's unease as we empathize with the character. Harker is moving out of his own territory and into that of the Other, with the boundary marked in time by St. George's Day and in space by the Borgo Pass: a dividing line between the otherness represented by Dracula and the mundane world that the vampire plans to invade. Harker, writing in his journal, establishes the territorial geographic and spiritual divide: "[I]t seemed as though the mountain range had separated two atmospheres, and that now we had got into the thunderous one."[10]

The journey is laden with setting from the gothic sublime. Harker describes rugged mountain scenery and "great masses of greyness, which here and there bestrewed the trees, producing a peculiarly wierd [sic] and solemn effect" (8). And his description of Dracula's home could have come straight from the conventional Burkean sublime from many eighteenth-century gothics: "a vast ruined castle, from whose tall black windows came no ray of light, and whose broken battlements showed a jagged line against the moonlit sky" (14).

The castle and castle-like structures are basic settings for the horror genre and gothic romance, in both novel and film. Horace Walpole introduced the ruined castle as setting in *The Castle of Otranto*. But Charlotte Smith was the first to exploit and popularize the language of the Burkean sublime with the castle as fictional environment in her novel *Emmeline, or the Orphan of the Castle* (1788),[11] where the virginal Emmeline flees the overly ardent Delamere through Mowbray Castle's darkened passages. Stoker borrowed this language and passed it on to other novelists as well as filmmakers.

Dracula's castle is his home, his territory, and he cannot completely leave it. When he invades England, he takes boxes of earth from it with him so that he can sleep on it during the day, expanding his territory. When Jonathan arrives at Dracula's castle, Stoker invokes the ancient tradition of folklore, which held that evil spirits required consent to enter territory or consent from their victim to enter theirs. In "Christabel," Coleridge adapts this element of vampire lore in having his heroine forced to practically carry the seemingly fainting vampire Geraldine through the door of her father's castle. Le Fanu's *Carmilla* has a similar scene, as do many vampire films including *Let Me In* (2010). In *Dracula*, Van Helsing tells his friends, "[Dracula] may not enter anywhere at the first, unless there be someone of the household who bid him to come" (240). Stoker applies the same principle of the Other entering territory to those who arrive at his, bidding his victim to come in. When Jonathan arrives, Dracula says to his guest at the gate, "Enter freely and of your own will" (15). The territorial narrative underpins the scene. Harker must enter the Other's territory willingly. Also, later in the novel, Dracula gets an invitation from the insane Renfield, a go-between to enter Dr. Seward's sanitarium so that he can prey on Mina Harker: "Come in, lord and master, " Renfield murmurs (279).

Stoker establishes the novel's sexual tone, which would be central to most film versions, in the opening chapters set in Castle Dracula.[12] When Harker ventures out of his bedroom against his host's advice, he meets Dracula's brides, who are brimming with sexuality. Stoker describes them in powerfully erotic terms, as "voluptuous" and "both thrilling and repulsive." Jonathan, in his prone position with them bending over him, felt in his heart "a wicked, burning desire that they would kiss me with those red lips" (37). And when Dracula waves them away, the fair woman laughs with "ribald coquetry" and answers, "You yourself never love; you never love!" (39). Harker has strayed from his territory in coming to Transylvania and again from the territory the count established for him in his castle; he has entered a world beyond his ken and his kin group where his sexual identity and even his genetic link to humanity are threatened.

Dracula's voyage on the *Demeter* reverses Harker's straying into the territory of the Other with Dracula's invasion of England's territory. At this stage, the tribal warfare narrative begins. Dracula's preying first on Lucy Westenra and making her one with his kind and then on Mina demonstrates the primal fear of assimilation and corruption of the gene pool by an Other. Surely Stoker's name for Lucy Westenra is no accident, for Dracula represents an invasion of the West by the East, prompting Van Helsing and his fellow vampire hunters—Jonathan Harker, Quincy Morris, Lord Godalming and Dr. Seward—to enact the narrative of a tribe that must destroy the invader to maintain their kin group and prevent assimilation. As Van Helsing puts it, "But to fail here is not mere life or death. It is that we become as him" (237). Van Helsing describes his friends as God's holy warriors, "ministers of God's own wish: that the world, and men for whom His Son die, will not be given over to monsters" (320). Van Helsing sums up the necessity of success for these defenders of the gene pool: "He may be yet, if we fail, the father or furtherer of a new order of beings, whose road must lead through Death and Life" (301).

Dracula begins his quest soon after his arrival. He comes to Lucy in her bedroom like a lover, as he does when he vamps Mina. When the tribal Crew of Light corners him in his lair, he snarls, "Your girls that you all love are mine already" (306). Van Helsing tells his tribe of warriors protecting Mina that it is "your best and most holiest office" (331). But if she cannot be protected, she must not become Other. Mina tells the men, "There have been times when brave men have killed their wives and their womenkind, to keep them from falling into the hands of the enemy," and makes them swear to serve her in that way (331). Similar examples of the horror of corruption of the gene pool through rape occur throughout the history of literature and film. In D.W. Griffith's *Birth of a Nation*, Flora Cameron throws herself off a precipice to her death when threatened with rape by a black man; and Col. Cameron holds a gun to the head of his daughter Margaret when he fears they will be captured by marauding former slaves at the end of the film, prepared to kill his child to avoid the "fate worse than death." Evolutionary psychology would hold that these scenes' horror is not racial prejudice alone but also tribal and fear of assimilation by an Other narratives. These narratives are important factors in creating racism.

The novel dramatizes the tribal response to an Other, an evolutionary adaptive trait that favored the survival of our species. Van Helsing's crew has, in effect, become a tribe of warriors, with Van Helsing as alpha male referring to their meeting as a "council of war" (353). We respond with pleasure in identifying with this group of warriors with a common purpose because, as Lionel Tiger writes, "In both violent and aggressive action, male bonding is the predominant instrument of organization. Females tend to be excluded from aggressive organizations such as armies where violence may occur."[13] Tiger's comments reek with sexism from a twenty-first century perspective, but his point seems accurate to describe earlier sex roles and those of Stoker's time. Also, Tiger writes of the behavior that was adaptive for our earliest ancestors. Mina is not completely excluded from the battle, but like the female mountain sheep, she stands demurely to the side while the males battle for her. This perception of the female would change dramatically in the modern vampire film.

Stoker reasserts the vampire's otherness when Dr. Seward describes him as "panther-like" with "something so unhuman" about him. And to combat this otherness, Lord Godalming, Quincy Morris, Jonathan Harker and Dr. Seward function as a *posse comitatus* as they follow Mina's visions and track the vampire to Transylvania. Van Helsing exhorts his crew as they begin their quest to go out like "old knights of the cross" (320). They are a team, he tells them, "and we are all more strong together" (315), a version of the ancient hunting party. They begin with a "Council of War" (353) with each member taking his personal responsibility. They pursue Dracula, eventually cornering him and his Gypsy enablers and succeed in destroying him in his territory, which "is full of strangeness of the geologic and chemical world" (319). They go to war against the invader ultimately to save their species but more immediately to save Mina. She is, after all, as a female, the symbolic bearer of the genetic future of humankind.

Van Helsing and Mina have traveled separately to Castle Dracula, while the others pursue the Gypsies and Dracula's boxes. When Van Helsing finds Dracula's wives, he experiences all their "voluptuous" and "wanton" otherness. Though as a proper Victorian gentleman he says, "the very instinct of man in me, which calls one of my sex to love and to protect one of hers" (370), he finds their resting places and kills them with his phallic stakes. As they die, he sees "the repose in the first face, and the gladness that stole over it ere dissolution came" (370), demonstrating their return from Them to Us. Dracula dies similarly after the melodramatic battle between the Crew of Light and Dracula's Gypsy minions. Van Helsing reports that at "the moment of final dissolution there was in the face a look of peace" (377). Like his wives, Dracula has become Us at the moment of his death. With the death of the vampire,

Mina too is purified of the Other. Quincy Morris in his final words exclaims, "Now God be thanked that all has not been in vain! See! The snow is not more stainless than her forehead! The Curse has passed away!" (377–78). A primal traits perspective suggests that the reason the novel and its conclusion have enthralled generations of readers lies in the pleasure felt with the return of both Mina and the vampires from Other to Us.

Edward O. Wilson writes, "Finally, territories contain an 'invincible center.' The resident animal defends the territory far more vigorously than intruders attempt to usurp it, and as a result the defender usually wins. In a special sense, it has the 'moral advantage' over trespassers."[14] So at the primal level, we take satisfaction in this victory of those who defend our territory and invade that of the Other to end a threat. And we can admire the heroism of Quincy Morris in sacrificing his life to defend what Edward O. Wilson would call his social group or Richard Dawkins his genetic kin group. The novel's resonance from the primal narratives has firmly established *Dracula* and the vampire character in literary and film history as one of the most central of our tribal and territorial narratives, retold and adapted endlessly. Changes in culture would dramatically alter this version of the helpless female's rescue and the nature of the vampire as a character.

"I am Dracula…. I bid you welcome": *Nosferatu* and Tod Browning's *Dracula*

Matthew Alcock writes, "The interactive theory of development tells us that genes, as well as the environment, have something to do with the development of *all* the observable characteristics of organisms, including their behavioral traits."[15] The key words here are "as well as the environment," which today more than in prehistoric times means the cultural environment. Biologist Jay Gould has opposed the central concepts of sociobiology and evolutionary psychology as excessively determinist. But in his refutation, he rather concisely defines the extreme views of the field: "All these claims have a common underpinning in postulating a direct genetic basis for our most fundamental traits. If we are programmed to be what we are, then the traits are ineluctable. We may, at best, channel them, but we cannot change them, either by will, education or culture."[16] Clearly there is a middle way between the genetic determinism of the more extreme evolutionary psychologists and sociobiologists—perhaps a sort of straw man in Gould's scenario—and those who believe in unfettered free will. Most of them would hold that primal whispers continue to exist but are adapted through changes in culture. The popular arts are a powerful force in both stimulating and reflecting those changes. But as we see in the vampire film's evolution, despite dramatic revisions in the past 50 years, the tribal and defense-of-territory narratives continue to be central elements of the horror genre and the vampire film.

"I am Dracula" and "I bid you welcome": Bela Lugosi's opening lines in Tod Browning's film adaptation of Stoker's novel, with his smoky Central European accent and exotic dress and appearance, established the film image of the vampire as Other in a flood of movies to come. And so the filmic vampire has been with us from the 1931 production of *Dracula* to the present. The vampire character's amazing endurance and the various changes it has taken in different time periods demonstrate that the meme resonates deeply in our primal psyches. David Skal lists 39 stage productions featuring Dracula as a character and 203 theatrical films (American and foreign) as well as TV productions up to 2004.[17] And since then, there has been a plethora of films that adapt the vampire meme that Stoker established. The seismic shift in the portrayal of the vampire in film during the past 50 years mirrors the equally powerful shifts in culture.

The vampire remains a monster, totally Other, the invader, the threat to the gene pool from the beginnings of the genre. The vampire's bite equals the fierce drive to procreate, since he or she can transform Us to Them. The early vampire films, the spawn of Stoker's *Dracula,* capture that otherness. The visual medium in the multitude of vampire films adds new dimensions to this powerful *uber* narrative, altering or revisioning the novel in many ways.

The sublime mountain scenery and ruined castles captured in many of them visualize Stoker's descriptions as descended from the eighteenth-century gothic more graphically than prose can do. The film medium can arouse even more vividly the trepidation and pleasurable vicarious fear at scenes of unbridled nature and the ravages of time on ruined castles.

Visual signifiers identifying the vampire have developed through the many films, though specifics change from one to another. The appearance of the vampire on screen brands his otherness, paralleling the simplistic visual cue that we get from the outlaws in black hats and the good guys in white hats as signifiers in early Westerns or the shambling and decomposed appearance of zombies. The various actors who play Dracula are usually dressed to exhibit otherness, with the long cape and in some cases the high collar. That he cannot cast a reflection in mirrors again marks the vampire's inhumanity, and the visual trope of Dracula cowering before the power of the cross demonstrates his evil nature. Then there is the dramatic enfolding of the vampire's female victim in his voluminous cape. These visual indications of otherness are less powerful in the print medium. We have the band of heroes from Stoker's novel in the early Dracula films, with occasional shuffling of characters' roles, names and omissions of the novel's plot, who defend our territory and prevent the vampire from corrupting our gene pool and social group. But beginning in the 1970s, some filmmakers at first subtly and then radically altered the narratives. In a number of remarkable films, we see the vampire not as a ravenous monster, territorial invader and threat to the gene pool but as a rather heroic and romantic outcast.

German director F.W. Murnau created the first incarnation of the *Dracula* film with his 1922 *Nosferatu, a Symphony of Horror*.[18] Murnau plays fast and loose with the novel's plot and the names and roles of characters, probably because it was an unauthorized production and Murnau hoped to avoid copyright issues with the Stoker estate through the alterations. Dracula becomes Orlock, Jonathan Harker becomes Hutter and Mina becomes Ellen. These and other changes failed to impress the courts, and nearly all prints were recalled. The opening setting is the fictional city of Wisborg in Germany, but as in the novel the scene immediately shifts to Transylvania when the villainous Knock sends Hutter there, enabling Orlock to travel to Wisborg.

The primal narratives of the novel remain. Hutter's journey takes him through rugged Carpathian mountain scenery replete with the occasional jackal and ruined castles perched atop high peaks, an excellent setting for Murnau's expressionist style. Hutter gets warnings from peasants, as in the novel. But he perseveres and enters the territory of the vampire. Orlock's castle is the image of the sublime piles from gothic fiction, as is the building he purchases across the street from Ellen Hutter's Wisborg home. The opening establishes the territory of the Other with our hero straying from his own and the vampire's invasion of ours. Murnau quickly establishes the threat to the female when Orlock sees Ellen's picture in a locket and exclaims, with a wink and a nudge from the director, "Your wife has a beautiful neck." But Murnau omits the contagion resulting from the vampire's bite.

As would all directors of the early *Dracula* films, Murnau portrays Orlock's appearance as distinctly Other. Stoker establishes Count Dracula as "a tall old man, clean-shaven save for a long white moustache and clad in black from head to foot without a single speck of colour about him anywhere" (15). Murnau's film gives Orlock an even more distinctive appearance. His grotesque features brand him as Other from the first time we see him, a territorial invader, and obviously portrayed as a sexual threat from the moment he slavers over Ellen's picture. But unlike the Draculas to follow, Orlock is Other in an almost animalistic sense, with protruding fangs and distorted features. Murnau's arresting shots of Orlock's shadow as he climbs the stairs to Ellen's bedroom and his angular body framed by the curved doorway have entered film history. The bedroom scene in which he preys on Ellen, with the shadow of his hand grasping, is obviously loaded with sexual suggestion, the despoiling of one of Us, a woman, by one of Them. In all the early vampire film, the threat to a woman as the possessor of our genetic future is a central element of horror.

Ellen sacrifices herself by luring Orlock into her bedroom, where he is

Nosferatu: **The vampire Orlock (Max Schreck) is destroyed by sunlight through the sacrifice of Ellen Hutter (Greta Schroëder).**

eventually destroyed by sunlight. The various film adaptations vary in portraying the vampire's aversion to light. Stoker's Dracula is only weakened by it. But the addition of sunlight as a weapon in the plots makes Orlock even more powerfully a night invader who triggers whispers of the predators who stalked our ancestors; and the convention of death by sunlight carried over to innumerable other vampire films. But Murnau omits the defense of territory by tribal warriors, a narrative that has great appeal in Stoker's novel. That narrative would be central in the multitude of vampire films to follow.

British actor and producer Hamilton Deane acquired rights to produce a play based on *Dracula*, and it was first staged in London in 1927 with script by Deane and John Balderston. With a reworked script by Balderston, it opened in New York six months later with Hungarian actor Bela Lugosi (born Béla Ferenc Dezsō Blaskó) cast as Dracula. After a run of 241 performances, this version went on the road for another long run while a re-scripted version played at a larger theater in London. This stage adaptation's success attracted interest from Universal Studios, which bought the film rights from Mrs. Stoker. With some script doctoring by Louis Bromfield to the Deane-Balderston play, the film was produced and first screened in 1931 with Lugosi in the lead role.

The territorial narrative remains about the same as that of the novel with the work of a tribe of warriors against the Other. Jonathan Harker becomes Renfield in this adaptation of the novel, and as his coach rolls through the rugged Carpathian mountain landscape, one of the female passengers reads aloud from a tourist booklet: "Among the rugged peaks that frown down upon the Borgo Pass are found crumbling castles of a bygone age." As is the case in Stoker's novel, her description reflects language from eighteenth-century gothics, such as the sublime scenery and ruins described in the works of Eliza Parsons and Charles Maturin.[19] Dracula's castle is the cinematic equivalent with the addition of bats, rats and for some reason an armadillo seen as Renfield approaches the castle.

The film abounds with the novel's primal narratives presented visually. Renfield gets the same warnings about straying into the territory of the vampire. Then he gets a similar welcome to that given Harker in the novel, with Dracula offering his oft-quoted greeting, bringing his guest into his territory that he must enter willingly just as Dracula must be invited into his victims' territory when he reaches London. Director Tod Browning immediately reinforces Dracula's otherness when the vampire walks through the giant spider web. When wolves, the predators of our ancient ancestors, howl, Dracula exclaims, "Listen to them! Children of the night! What Music They Make!" As is the case with Max Schreck in *Nosferatu*, Lugosi's appearance, with long cape, high collar and Eastern European accent, marks him as the master of the territory into which Renfield has strayed. But this Dracula is not the animalistic monster from Murnau's film. Rather, Lugosi exudes male magnetism and power and more closely resembles Stoker's character. His leer as he wraps his prey into his cape was imitated by actors in many films, showing that he is making them his and either killing or assimilating them.

All of this comes smoking hot from Stoker's novel. In the film, Renfield is an interesting twist on the "Us-Them" conflict. He is a different character from that of the novel, but his transformation into a semi-vampire who subsists on insects and dreams of rats and other living things brings him to an internal sort of conflict. While he is enough Them to be the instrument of getting Dracula into the sanatorium, to which he must be invited, he is enough Us to feel the conflict of his betrayal and help Van Helsing, Dr. Seward and Harker—another stout tribe of territorial defenders to whom we can relate—hunt down and destroy the enemy.

Universal became the prime purveyor of horror film fare in the 1930s and '40s, profitably reincarnating Dracula through a variety of devices, as in *Dracula's Daughter* (1936), *Son of Dracula* (1943) and a host of ensemble monster double-feature films. Hammer Films in England exhumed Dracula in eight films starting with *Horror of Dracula* in 1957, the series ending near the demise of the company with *Legend of the Seven Golden Vampires* (1974).

Dracula: Count Dracula (Bela Lugosi) and his go-between Renfield (Dwight Frye).

Most featured Peter Cushing as Van Helsing and the redoubtable Christopher Lee as the vampire. Horrormeister Wes Craven began his own version of the Dracula narrative with *Dracula 2000* in the year of the title, and *Dracula 2: The Ascension* appeared three years later. Like most of the B movie vampire films, both hark back to the original vampire plot with Dracula as predator and tribal defenders doing battle with him. Craven changes the setting from haunted castle to modern-day London and to a spaceship in *Ascension*. But changes in culture have spawned new wrinkles on the ancient narratives of territory, tribes, assimilation and the figure of the vampire as Other.

The Postmodern Vampire: "A stranger in this breathing world, an erring spirit from another hurl'd"—*Blacula*, Dan Curtis and John Badham Adaptations

The narrative of the vampire as evil invader and Other to be battled by a crew of light has remained in the vampire film in movies like *Vampires*

(1998), *30 Days of Night* (2007), *The Lost Boys* (1987) and many another horror thriller. But a parallel track of films radically reimagines *Dracula* and the tribal narrative. Beginning in the 1970s, in some films Dracula has been transformed from predatory monster to a character who if not a hero is at least charismatic and attractive. Postmodern vampire films offer another example of the interaction of primal narratives with the transforming effect of culture. But beneath the changes, Dracula is still an Other who is a territorial invader; and the threat of assimilation remains, though altered.

Carol Senf writes that in our time, "changing attitudes toward authority and toward rebellion against authority have ... led to a more sympathetic treatment of the vampire."[20] John Cawelti's observations on literary formulas seem equally apt in explaining the cultural shift in the vampire film. He notes that literary formulas are cultural products and speculates about their function:

> Formula stories affirm existing interests and attitudes [of readers or viewers] by presenting an imaginary world that is aligned with these interests and attitudes.... Formulas enable the audience to explore in fantasy the boundary between the permitted and the forbidden and to experience in a carefully controlled way the possibility of stepping across this boundary.[21]

Cawelti's definition of formula as a cultural product raises the question of what influence primal narratives have in the creation of culture and literary formulas. Beginning in the 1960s, two versions of the vampire narrative coexisted that might be roughly compared to the contrast of cultural values between Archie Bunker and his mod son-in-law Michael (dubbed Meathead by Archie) in the long-running television comedy *All in the Family*. John Buktaman observes, "The best cyberpunk, tecno-surealism and postmodern textual praxis challenge conventional systems of meaning in disturbing ways, often from a position *within* (or aligned with) the commercial structures of mass culture."[22] He suggests that a new identity is being hammered out with cultural penetration of various forms of media, from novels to movies to games. The computer and the multiplicities of social media, he writes, create "terminal identities." But a primal traits critical perspective would suggest that something more timeless underpins and to at least some extent guides and interacts in the creation of culture. Joseph Carroll writes: "Evolutionists insist that genes constrain and direct human behavior. Cultural constructivists counter that culture, embodied in the arts, shapes human experience. Both these claims are true, but some evolutionists and some cultural constructivists have mistakenly regarded them as mutually exclusive."[23]

The late 1960s and the 1970s saw a sea change in western values. Young people found their voices as they protested the Vietnam War, racism and other issues, rocking university campuses with protests and creating their own culture, one that was soon co-opted by the entertainment media (with

TV shows like *The Mod Squad*) and by the fashion industry. This seismic shift in consciousness was apparent in films like *One Flew Over the Cuckoo's Nest* (1975), *Bonnie and Clyde* (1967), *Easy Rider* (1969) and a host of others that celebrate the outsider, the antihero who goes against prevailing values. Purveyors of the horror film quickly adapted to the changing views of the young, their most important target audience.

Blacula, a blaxploitation film released in 1972, signaled the impending changes in the vampire narrative. Eighteenth-century African Prince Mamuwalde (William Marshall) seeks Count Dracula's help in ending the slave trade. Instead, Dracula assimilates him to be a vampire and locks him in a coffin, which remained closed. It's finally opened in a museum in the present day (1972). The film establishes Blacula as a lover when he sees the comely Tina, who he believes is the reincarnation of Luva, his wife before Dracula converted him to a vampire. The plot of lovers reunited across time would appear in other vampire movies. *Blacula* scores high in the absurdity scale, but it is an early example of the postmodern vampire as evil but capable of all-consuming love, an outcast but somehow a character who inspires empathy.

Dan Curtis' 1973 made-for-TV adaptation of *Dracula* and the 1979 John Badham–directed *Dracula* (advertised with the promotional line "a love story") are two other examples of a fundamental shift in the vampire movie formula. Curtis and Badham each provide a quite different Dracula, a vampire capable of love. Starting in 1966, Curtis produced *Dark Shadows*, the long-running television gothic soap opera. His vampire Barnabas Collins, introduced in the series' second year, dramatized the latent sexuality of the vampire and stimulated the libido for an audience of women who followed the show.

Curtis' *Dracula* continues the cultural shift with its overt romanticism of the vampire figure. Curtis emphasizes the ambivalence we might feel for the vampire (played by Jack Palance) by suggesting that the Mina character is the reincarnation of Dracula's medieval love. Curtis' depiction of the count owes something to the Barnabas character from *Dark Shadows* but makes him even more sympathetic to viewers. True to the title, the film is closer to the novel's plot than most revisioning and, like Stoker's novel, is ultimately rooted in the primal narrative of tribalism and defense of territory; but the narrative has shifted to ambivalence in the portrayal of the vampire Other and of the tribal warriors.

As in other Dracula films, in Badham's *Dracula*, roles of the Stoker characters shift from that of their counterparts in the novel. The Mina Harker role transmigrates into Lucy Seward (Kate Nelligan), Dr. Seward's daughter. Rather than simply being possessed against her will by Dracula (Frank Langella), she falls in love with him. Van Helsing (Laurence Olivier doing his German accent), Jonathan Harker and Dr. Seward are killjoys who would spoil the lovers' future, a new approach to the portrayal of tribal warriors in the vampire narrative. When Van Helsing charges Lucy not to die "until this great evil which has fouled your life is true dead himself," she replies, "You dare try to confuse me, tormenting him who is the saddest, the kindest of all?" And instead of dying in agony, Dracula escapes after being hoisted into the sun, first apparently expiring but then hang-gliding as a bat-like apparition, a wild wolf howl ringing in the viewers' ears as Lucy smiles knowingly. Badham's film exemplifies Carol Senf's comment: "Most of the recent film versions ... portray Dracula as an attractive figure—far more attractive in every sense of the word than the vampire in folklore of earlier literary versions and far more attractive than his human adversaries."[24]

Not all filmic vampires were monsters prior to Curtis and Badham's revisionist tellings of the classic tale. In *The Vampire Film*, James Ursini and Alain Silver discuss a handful of titles predating these two films "whose roots go back to Lord Ruthven in Polidori's *The Vampyre* and Varney in *Varney the Vampire*. Like Ruthven and Varney, these figures are driven by a disease of mind and body; and no matter how assiduously they try to rid themselves of the curse of the undead, they are always unsuccessful."[25] The authors identify *House of Dracula* (1945), *The Vampire's Ghost* (1945) and *The Vampire* (1957) as films whose vampires are portrayed in a semi-sympathetic, albeit an unromantic fashion. The primal narratives of tribalism, territoriality and fear of the Other's contamination of the gene pool remain in these and the postmodern vampire films to follow, but shifts in culture have changed their focus. Van Helsing's warriors might be seen as the forces of conformity, warring against star-crossed lovers in some films.

Sex has always been a central element in vampire films. But the different portrayal of the vampire in a romantic role is only part of the cultural shift in adaptations of Stoker's character. The Byronic hero, an early version of the antihero from the nineteenth century, is a powerful influence not only on the new vampire film but on popular culture figures in other areas, George Gordon (1788–1824) became Lord Byron through a fortuitous series of deaths of those ahead of him for the title and was arguably the most popular poet of the Romantic Movement. His signature character type, called by scholars the Byronic Hero, appears with a variety of names in Byron's poems and has been reincarnated as a character type in countless works of literature and film, from the novels of the Brontë sisters to the works of Russian authors such as Alexander Pushkin in the nineteenth century to James Dean movies. Byron was influenced by writers from the eighteenth-century gothic tradition and their creation of the "hero villain," the powerful character from those novels who is a threat to heroines but is nonetheless a sexually compelling figure.

Julia Kristeva defines intertextuality as the interaction of texts: "Any text builds itself as a mosaic of quotations; any text is the absorption and transformation of another."[26] Influenced by Bakhtin's writings on heteroglossia and dialogism as well as Saussure's structuralism, Kristeva and other critics who analyze the interweaving of texts assume, as Jeanine Plottel and Hanna Charney put it, that every text "echoes another text unto infinity, weaving the fabric of culture itself."[27] We might define intertextual analysis as the discovery of meaning in the space between the lines in texts, bringing discourse that is imbedded in history and culture and surfacing in the creative process of authors. It seems unlikely that filmmakers who revision the Byronic Hero are directly influenced through acquaintance with Byron's poems. But the character type returns through intertextual echoes that reverberate in the cultural shift of the late twentieth century. The primal narratives of tribalism and protection of the gene pool as it is embodied in saving a woman remain, but they are dramatically changed.

Byron's hero has the same aura of sexuality and power as the evildoers of the hero-villain in early gothics, but he is redeemed by fidelity to one love of his life, which made him an attractive figure for readers. In "The Giaour," Byron describes him as "Undoomed for earth, unfit for heaven," a man superior to other men but one whose heart belongs to a beloved.

> He was a villain—ay—reproaches shower
> On him—but not the passion, nor its power,
> Which only proved, all other virtues gone,
> Not guilt itself could quench this loveliest one![28]

In "Lara," the poet describes him as "A Stranger in This Breathing World, /An Erring Spirit from Another Hurl'd."

This hero who appears over and over in Byron's poems (with different names) and the works of his imitators is wild, unrestrained by custom and capable of evil acts; but in his heart lives a pure love for one woman. The Badham and Curtis Dracula films have echoes of Byronism but the Byronic hero seems most fully portrayed in Francis Ford Coppola's *Bram Stoker's Dracula* (1992). The film's melodramatic tone matches Byron's poem, and it offers an excellent case study of changes in culture and its interaction with the primal narratives. In Coppola's adaptation of *Dracula*, the vampire takes on some qualities of the romantic rebel and inspires sympathy; but he is also a monster to be pursued and destroyed by our tribal warriors. From an evolutionary psychology perspective, we might see the romantic vampire as being both Us and Other rather than completely the latter. This approach offers the filmmaker an interesting conflict, which is, after all, the basic element of drama: the conflict the audience feels between support of the tribal defenders and sympathy for Dracula.

As in the multitude of other *Dracula* films, Coppola drew on the conventions of the early gothic in producing *Bram Stoker's Dracula*. One might even think that he and his screenwriters had read some recent criticism of Stoker's novel. Several scenes reflect specific critical interpretations. In the film, Dracula's ecstatic response when Mina puts her mouth to the wound in his chest suggests fellatio, as proposed by Christopher Bentley in 1972 in his article on the novel and later elaborated on by other critics. Also, the screen image of Dracula's wives kneeling over the recumbent and receptive Jonathan Harker in novel and film suggests fellatio and blood as a code word for semen, as described in Christopher Craft's interpretation of gender inversion in the novel.[29]

Yet Coppola and screenwriter James Hart have gone well beyond simply adapting *Dracula*, adding a great deal to the story in recasting the primal narrative of the Other and the tribal warriors who pursue him. The film alters the plot in ways that reflect changes in present-day gender relationships and the influence of culture on primal narratives. Coppola's Dracula, played by Gary Oldman, is a far cry from Stoker's evil vampire. A monster of a sort he remains, of course, and distinctively Other. However, Oldman brings to the role some of the ruined nobility, demonic majesty and cosmic melancholy of the Byronic Hero as well as that character's capacity for undying love. Like Byron's hero, he is Other but one who also reflects noble qualities of mind.

The film begins with Byronic posturing: the story of Dracula's transformation to vampire in the fifteenth century when he curses God after his wife Elisabeta is tricked into suicide by priests. "I shall arise from my own death to avenge her with all the powers of darkness. The blood is the life, and it shall be mine," he cries. Like Byron's hero, he has alienated himself from humankind to become Other. Then the film repeats the reincarnation theme that had appeared in *Blacula* and the Badham and Curtis films when during Jonathan Harker's visit to his castle 400 years after her death he recognizes Mina Harker (Winona Ryder) in a picture as the reborn Elisabeta. The film follows the general outline of the novel's plot, with changes in character that reflect shifts in culture. It repeatedly stresses Dracula's duality as both Us and Other, projecting in him the mixed qualities of the antihero, a distinct departure from the novel's primal narrative of otherness.

When Harker arrives in Transylvania, he sees Dracula as an old man, and the visual impression is decidedly unsympathetic. His skin is a pasty white, he appears forgetful at times and his hairstyle and dress, though the mode of his earlier day, projects a sort of decadent effeminacy to a modern viewer. Then when he arrives in England, at one point we see him as an incubus, a sexual night monster from medieval folklore, part man and part beast, mounting Lucy Westenra in the garden's maze. When Dracula later invades Mina's quarters at Dr. Seward's hospital, he confronts Van Helsing and his crew as a vaguely human figure with bat-like head, another visual manifestation of the monstrous otherness of the character.

But when Dracula seeks out Mina, we see him as a dandyish man about town. In this version, Coppola adds a touch of sympathy to the character absent in the aged Vlad in Transylvania or the incubus. When he and Mina meet, Dracula takes the young woman aside, saying, "I have crossed oceans of time to find you." He appears about to drink her blood, but controls himself. At that moment, the wolf that Dracula freed from the London zoo intrudes, causing a panic. But Dracula commands the wolf, and Mina actually pets the animal. The visual symbolism of the sequence establishes the wolf as Dracula's monstrous side. Mina's petting the creature shows her power in controlling it, and his memories of Elisabeta make him more Us. The Victorian dandy, then, represents Dracula's better nature.

The opposite of his Other nature is also apparent when Mina asks Dracula to make her his. "I want to be with you always," she breathes. "You cannot know what you ask me," he responds. "There is no life in this body."

But Mina insists, even after she learns that her "sweet prince" has murdered Lucy. When Dracula starts to give her his blood, however, he desists, crying, "No, I cannot let this be." He cannot let her "walk in the shadow of death through all eternity." He sighs, "I love you too much." But Mina insists on joining her lover in his deathless life and lifeless death. The film's Dracula is a far cry from Stoker's vampire.

Coppola's film reenacts the novel's portrayal of Stoker's tribal warriors' pursuit of the vampire, with its sensational conclusion. The change in the enactment of Dracula's death, though, reflects the shift in the tribal narrative. Our heroes corner the vampire and manage to wound him. But it is Mina who goes to him at the conclusion, when he asks her to release him. She stabs him through the heart and decapitates him, while we see a fresco of Vlad and Elisabeta ascending to Heaven. In this updating of the tribal narrative, our warriors succeed in defeating the invader, but only with the aid of a woman.

Bram Stoker's Dracula: Dracula (Gary Oldman) as Victorian dandy.

The film gives us a different female character from the novel's Mina

Harker and heroines of earlier films, a portrayal influenced by the cultural changes of the day and growth of the feminist critique. Buss writes, "Evolution has favored women who prefer men who possess attributes that confer benefits and who dislike men who possess attributes that impose costs. Each separate attribute constitutes one component of a man's value to a woman as a mate. Each of her preferences tracks one component."[30] Like many of the pronouncements from evolutionary psychologists, Buss' words seem quite sexist on the surface. But he speaks of adaptive patterns from primal ancestors. Culture has dramatically changed gender roles.

In this version of Stoker's tale, Mina reflects those changes. She is a more powerful presence than the character in other adaptations. Helen Fisher sums up what might seem to be the obvious when she summarizes her survey of over 800 men and women regarding their sexual attractions: "American women sought partners who offered financial security twice as frequently as men did.... In fact, women everywhere in the world are more attracted to partners with education, ambition, wealth, respect, status and position—the kinds of assets their prehistoric predecessors needed in a parenting partner."[31] From an evolutionary psychology perspective, in the society of our ancient ancestors such a man would be able to support and protect a woman and her children. But this desire for protection and stability, she suggests, is often overridden. It does not always quench spontaneous desire, as she puts it, that leads a woman to be infatuated by a powerful and charismatic man who might trigger love—or lust—even though he might not be a reliable parent and provider. Hence the attraction to the "bad boy."

The 1955 movie *Picnic* dramatizes the power of sexual attraction over stability, with nice girl Madge (Kim Novak), about to be married to a good man with resources, falling for ne'er-do-well and drifter Hal (William Holden). *Bram Stoker's Dracula* bends the narrative to make the Mina character attracted to the dominant male but strong enough to dispatch him.

Feminists can rightly point out the need for change in culture to free women from the condition of their ancestors. But women viewers and readers might still feel a response of pleasure—even though they would deplore such sex roles in real life—in the defense of a woman by tribal warriors and her attraction to a strong and dominating, if flawed, male. The *Dilbert* cartoon strip from April 10, 2009, offers an amusing commentary on evolutionary sexual attraction. In the first frame, Dilbert uses a pickup line in a bar and tells the young woman that he is employed, intelligent, doesn't live with a parent and would probably sire brilliant children. The girl looks agitated, her palms sweating and her breath quickening, and asks what's happening to her. Dilbert responds, 'It's a Darwinian thing." Millennia of adaptive behavior have created the girl's response, though culture has reshaped the narrative for modern women.

Tribal and Reluctant Vampires: The *Underworld* and *Blade* Franchises and *Interview with the Vampire*

Bram Stoker's novel provided the pattern not only for the various film adaptations of *Dracula* but for a multitude of other vampire narratives in film. Vampires in the Stoker tradition are lonely monsters. But what if there are tribes of vampires? We see the persistence of tribalism everywhere in human society. Stoker's novel dramatizes such a group of tribal warriors thwarting an invasion by an Other. Films adapt this narrative with portrayals ranging from the evil monsters of early adaptations to postmodern revisions. But the vampire film has fragmented into more complex forms of tribalism between new kinds of tribes and Others, a twist on a primal drive of humanity and a persistent narrative. Other film franchises, including *Underworld* and *Blade,* are examples of the adaptability of the vampire story and the tribalism narrative. If we respond to tribalism in films with characters who are human opposing the vampire as enemy Other, the narrative can carry over to the tribes within this Other as an added dimension of conflict.

Based on such a set of tribal conflicts, *Underworld* (2003) was panned by critics. Roger Ebert wrote, "This is a movie so paltry in its characters and shallow in its story that the war [between vampires and werewolves] seems to exist primarily to provide graphic visuals."[32] His comments are another example of the disconnect between critics and film audiences. *Underworld* was financially successful enough to spawn three sequels, *Underworld: Evolution* (2006), *Underworld: Awakening* (2012) and *Underworld: Blood Wars* (2016), as well as a prequel, *Underworld: Rise of the Lycans* (2009). The reverberations of tribal conflicts in the films have contributed to making the franchise popular, despite negative reviews.

The films develop a complicated legendarium that must be untangled to show the tribalism and hatred of the Other as well as family conflict that underpin them in creating viewer response to primal narratives. The backstory emerges in bits and pieces through the first two films, and *Rise of the Lycans* gives a more complete overview of the frame. The vampire tribe is composed of great houses within the greater tribe and multiple clans fighting a centuries-long battle against Lycans—werewolves. New information is scattered through the films. But we eventually learn that Alexander Corvinus was born immortal and had three sons: William, who was bitten by a wolf, making him a werewolf; Marcus, bitten by a bat, turning him into a vampire; and a third son who was not immortal but carried the gene to be passed down through his genetic progeny.

The films, then, are based on a central conflict between two tribes, lycans and vampires, who can be traced to the same family. The byzantine backstory, which takes place hundreds of years before *Underworld,* establishes the stress of tribal and family conflict in the *Underworld* universe. Selene (Kate Beckinsale) has become a "death dealer" in the centuries-old war against the Lycans. The film follows her relationship with a human, Michael Corwin, who carries the immortality gene and eventually becomes a hybrid vampire-werewolf and fathers a child with Selene. So we have the two species—tribes—introduced, each seeing the opponent as Other.

Tribal hatred in the films is implacable. When Michael asks Selene, "Why do you hate [lycans] so much?" she answers, "I've already told you. We're at war." No other reason is needed for her. Lycans are hated Others who must be destroyed, a sad refrain through human history that lives in our primal mind. The conflict may whisper vicarious pleasure for viewers even though culture has created values intended to prevent such slaughter, values that have too often been lost. *Underworld* establishes the total otherness of lycans and vampires in the fact that their blood does not mix. A lycan scientist explains, "At the cellular level, our species destroyed each other." But despite the tribal hatred between lycans and vampires, each group has its own internal conflicts.

The *Underworld* films take place in a fantasy world with a very sketchy frame. Just where the vampires get all the blood that they quaff in crystal goblets is never explained. And most of the battles between vampires and lycans seem out in the open without humans noticing. Clearly, much of the popularity of the films rests on the special effects violence as well as the presence of the shapely Beckinsale in her tight leather outfit. But despite the lack of detail in the films' fantasy frame, the conflicts between and within tribal adversaries of Others, their conflict with humanity, the family relationships and finally the entrance of another tribe, hybrids, have contributed to ensuring the films' popularity.

Reluctant vampires are another persistent theme in this subgenre of the horror film. They are in conflict with their own kind and their own nature, made Other against their wishes. This adaptation of the tribalism narrative offers additional opportunities for dramatic conflict and fits the postmodern ethos of alienation. Humans are tribal animals, and a character's internal conflict in being driven from his genetic tribe might whisper sympathy.

Anne Rice's 1976 novel *Interview with the Vampire* was adapted for the screen (1994) with a script by the author. Framed by an interview with a freelance writer in contemporary times, the film immediately flashes back to eighteenth-century New Orleans. Louis (Brad Pitt) has lost his wife and is despondent, seeking death. But when he is preyed on by Lestat (Tom Cruise) and is given the choice to die or be transformed, he reluctantly agrees to become a vampire, abandoning his own kind and tribe. And so begins a plot laden with conflict between Lestat and Louis and the internal conflict of the Louis character as he ruminates throughout the film on the ethics of his situation and the nature of good and evil. Lestat, on the other hand, has no problem with his state. "Evil is a point of view," he insists. "God kills indiscriminately, and so shall we. For no creature under God is as we are. None so like Him as ourselves." Critics have pointed out the homoerotic bond between Louis and Lestat and see Louis' angst rooted, as Jeffrey Weinstock notes, in Louis' "coming out story—his attempt to grapple with, understand, and come to terms with his 'powers,'" which symbolize his homosexuality.[33] Louis's conflict lies in his being taken from his genetic kin, a tribe, to become Other: and also, in Weinstock's interpretation, his conflict on becoming Other and one who is not only alienated as a vampire but gay.

Louis is a vampire with a human soul, we are told. He is lonely and guilt-ridden and trying to be a vegetarian vampire, feeding on animals. The primal appeal of his character lies in his being a combination of both Other and Us and, like some other postmodern vampires, a tribal outcast. To ease his loneliness, he adopts a child, Claudia, whom Lestat has turned to be a companion for him, giving him a family of sorts. Over the years, her mind matures to that of an adult but her body remains that of a child, and she is resentful of her state as Other, leading her to apparently kill Lestat (who turns up at the end of the film).

Neither Louis nor Claudia is satisfied with being outcasts. Both are alienated and reluctant vampires, and they desire to find their own vampire kind, their new tribe. This need culminates with their discovery of a community of vampires and a conflict with them. They cannot find their own kind of vampire and are torn between identities.

Blade (1998), based on a Marvel Comics character, is another postmodern reluctant vampire. In the plot frame, the title character (Wesley Snipes) was born immediately after his mother was bitten by a vampire, which somehow gives him special powers as a vampire half-blood, another alienated hybrid in the narrative. He is a "day walker" whom sunlight does not affect and who has the strength of the vampire with none of the weaknesses. Blade nurtures a burning desire to kill vampires to avenge his mother's death. Aided by Abraham Whistler (Kris Kristofferson), who provides a serum that keeps Blade's blood lust in check, he wars against the tribe of vampires that controls everything in his city and eventually does battle with Frost, a "turned" vampire who overthrows the vampire council of "born" vampires, those never turned but born to their condition. So from a primal traits perspective, we see two vampire tribes in conflict, with Blade as the outsider alienated from both.

The film adapts a familiar narrative in building on paranoia and fears of the hidden Other. Whistler says, "They've got their claws into everything: politics, finance, real estate. They already own half of downtown." They are aided by familiars, humans who collaborate with the vampires. The script gives the vampires a sketchy mythology, with a temple to the Blood God where the final battle takes place. And there are tribes within tribes, as Frost seeks to overthrow the old guard who want vampires to keep a low profile. Frost wants to enslave humanity.

In addition to the tribalism narrative, the *Blade* films focus on a cultural issue. Jeffrey Weinstock writes of its racial theme: "*Blade* is a thinly veiled allegory of American race relations in which vampires stand in for whites, and humans in general for racial minorities.... In this racial allegory the mulatto stands as the solutions to the race war."[34] This interpretation makes sense from a cultural perspective. But imbedded in the conflict on race in America is the narrative of tribalism and distrust of the Other, one that afflicts our time in race relationships. Brian Boyd sums up evolutionary psychologists' perspective on race: "Science itself shows us that despite differences strikingly visible to us, humans are genetically an unusually uniform species.... Aware of the ghastly consequences of racism in the twentieth century, modern evolutionary psychologists stress the 'psychic unity of mankind' and focus more on what human minds have in common than on differences."[35] But tribes evolve from culture, including those of race and ethnicity. We might earnestly desire better relationships cerebrally but also vicariously enjoy the films' tribal conflicts.

Blade was popular enough to establish a franchise. *Blade II*, directed by Benito del Toro, was released in 1992. *Blade Trinity* (2004) ended the series. The two films expand the legendarium and add to the paranoia with a band of "young vampire killers" aiding Blade and enhanced paranoia with the inclusion of humans secretly in league with vampire villains.

God Bless the Child: Child Vampires in Film

The threat to a child is one of the most moving narratives in the horror genre. Stephen King has populated his novels and the films from which they are adapted with a wide assortment of special children. Other examples of the endangered child abound: Hillary from *God Bless the Child* (1988) and Regan from *The Exorcist. Jurassic Park* and all of the sequels rely heavily on the threat to children. This powerful narrative of endangerment to the gene pool also turns up often in the vampire film and novel. One of the most powerful moments of horror in Stoker's *Dracula* comes when the vampire enters "as if lapped in a storm of fury" (38) to interrupt his wives from snacking on Jonathan Harker and carrying a bag with a child moaning, a gift to them. When the child's mother comes to the castle door begging for her child, Dracula calls his wolves to dispatch her.

"The Wurdulak" is one of three short pieces in the anthology film *Black Sabbath* (1963). An Italian production, it is a film that only ardent horror movie fans could love, but it has a truly affecting scene, depicting the doomed child. "The Wurdulak," starring Boris Karloff at his leering and grimacing best, is set in the Balkans, vampire country in film. He plays Gorka, the patriarch of a family, living with his sons Georgio and Pietro; Rika, Georgio's wife; Ivan, Georgio and Rika's son; and Danka, Gorka's daughter. The narrative point of view comes from a visitor, Vladimir Durfa, a traveler who stays with the family for the night. Gorka leaves to kill a robber who is probably a *wurdulak*, or vampire, and returns infected. The plot has him turning some of the family and then those turned preying on others. Despite the film's overblown sensationalism and insipid performances, its depiction of a family, the basic unit of our species, in dissolution and being taken from Us to Other must have powerful potential for horror. But even more affecting is the scene in which Ivan, the child, stands outside the cottage after being turned by the patriarch, crying to his mother, who has not been changed, pleading, "Mama, Mama, let me in" and "Mama, mama, mama, I'm cold." As we see in so many films and stories, the threatened child evokes a powerful response. But the quandary of the mother is equally moving. The vampire must be invited in. But Rika cannot keep from letting him in, even knowing what he is, only to be turned by her vampire child. The scene brings to mind Rosemary accepting her demonic child in *Rosemary's Baby*. A mother doing anything for her child is surely an important element in our evolutionary adaptation.

Claudia, the child vampire in *Interview with the Vampire*, is an unwilling vampire. The scene of her being incinerated by the sun when the Théâtre des Vampires lock her out elicits pathos. So too does the child vampire Abby (Chloë Grace Moritz) as well as Owen (Kodi Smit-McPhee) in *Let Me In* (2010), a remake of the Swedish film *Let the Right One In*. We have both the horror of middle school, with Owen unrelentingly bullied by three larger boys to the point that he wets himself, and Abby, who is doomed to vampirism. Thomas, Abby's dedicated caregiver (we never learn their exact relationship), murders to give her the blood she must have and ultimately sacrifices his life for her, the response of a parent to support a child that has made our evolution possible. And the terrible revenge that Abby enacts on Owens' bullies triggers the satisfying response of revenge inherited from our hunter-gatherer ancestors when action against those who brought harm to others was returned with violence in return. Revenge is especially sweet when performed against those who harm a child.

Vampires Are Us

Both a cultural studies and a primal traits critique suggest that the vampire meme is a signifier, both of changes in society and the endurance of pri-

Black Sabbath: Giorgio (Glauco Onorato), Rika (Rika Dialina) and their vampire child (actor unidentified) in this anthology film's segment "The Wurdulak."

mal narratives at its core, especially tribalism. The vampire is Other, and evolutionary psychology proposes that reverberations from the adaptive behavior of ancient ancestors speak to us of tribal organization, including for defense. The vampire film serves as an example of how the findings of evolutionary psychology can be a tool for understanding how both whispers from our evolutionary past and cultural imperatives bring us pleasure from the horror film. Tribalism is one of the most powerful of those whispers, and the vampire—be he Murnau's monster or Coppola's Byronic Dracula, who is "Unfit for Earth, Undoomed for Heaven"—signals the vicarious pleasures of our warriors' defense of our territory and genetic and social heritage, even though we find the narrative reshaped by culture in different time periods. Sex has always been implicit in the vampire narrative, be it symbolic rape as in *Dracula* and so many other films or the more romantic vampire in others. The powerful animal attraction of the romantic vampire's sex appeal leads to discussion of the mating narrative.

FIVE

The Mating Narrative in the Gothic Romance

"What Is This Thing Called Love?"

Cole Porter's song poses a question that has been asked through human history by poets and philosophers and now by evolutionary psychologists. Whatever it is, love has inspired great works of literature throughout history. In Homer's *The Iliad,* Paris and Helen fall into each other's arms and run away from home together. When Helen's husband Menelaus cries to his big brother, Agamemnon organizes an army and sails to Troy, resulting in a war lasting ten years and ultimately destroying the city.

The history of literature is filled with such stories of love at first sight. Shakespeare's Romeo lays eyes on Juliet, immediately abandons his love for the fair Rosaline and declares his passion for the young daughter of the Capulets, his family's archenemies, resulting in both their deaths as a result of tribal conflict. So it goes too when Dante Alighieri has his first glimpse of Beatrice Portinari, inspiring him to make his obsession for her central to *The Divine Comedy.* In *Paradise Lost,* Milton has Adam eat of the fruit in the garden because he cannot be parted from Eve and determines to be destroyed if she is. Literature and film fuel the belief in the "Power of Love," as described in the song of that title recorded by both Céline Dion and Huey Louis and the News, making it a central element of our culture, as it is central to our evolution.

Evolutionary psychologists take a scientific approach to discover the power of love. Their description of it is decidedly unromantic. Love in this perspective is the power that leads us to mate, and mating is all about the propagation of our species. While procreation is probably not on the lovers' minds when they are attracted to each other, as Dawkins and others insist, the power of love comes from our genes crying out to make them immortal. Helen Fisher's view is typical: "I have come to believe that romantic love is a universal human feeling, produced by specific chemicals and networks in the brain. *This fire in the mind is caused by elevated levels of either dopamine or norepinephrine or both, as well as decreased levels of serotonin* [italics are hers]."[1] Her comments lend ironic support for the often explained reason for romantic bonding as in "They have good chemistry."

This quite unromantic description of the power of love is, of course, uncomfortable to hear. But evolutionary psychology would posit that when all of the layers of culture are stripped away, Porter's song and the thousands of similar ones reflect feelings inspired by the whispers of our genes to procreate. It is a primal narrative that is at the heart of literature through the centuries, especially the romance and now its adaptation to film. But the stark view of mating that we get from evolutionary psychologists cannot diminish the powerful response inspired by this narrative as enacted in literature and film. And evolutionary psychology be damned, the narrative of two people in love and after conflict finding a relationship speaks to most of us because we have experienced it, or at least want to. We feel it and respond to the narrative in film, poetry and fiction. Exploring our nature is central to the study of evolutionary psychology. But understanding the forces that drive us doesn't keep us from feeling the mating narrative imbedded in songs and the vicarious enjoyment of seeing it enacted in film and fiction. The gothic romance is a niche of both the romance and horror film genres and offers an example for a primal traits critique in understanding the power of love and answering the question posed by Cole Porter's song.

"Someday My Prince Will Come"

This song, written by Larry Money and performed by Adriana Caselotti in Walt Disney's 1937 animated classic *Snow White and the Seven Dwarfs*, voices a primal dream that speaks to the whispers of the mating narrative as it is embodied in the romance and gothic romance. The romance genre comes in many forms, from medieval tales beginning in the thirteenth century such as *The Romance of the Rose*. *Le Mort d'Arthur* shows that the power of love caused the disaster created by the relationship of Lancelot and Guinevere. In the medieval tradition of courtly love, love's obsession is born when Cupid shoots his arrow in the lover's eye, making him or her hopelessly stricken with desire. The naughty boy shot the god Apollo with a gold arrow to make him love the nymph Daphne and the nymph with a lead one, making her hate the god. Love in these tales is so powerful that those who fall victim to Cupid are seen as not entirely responsible for their actions.

The romance tradition in the novel dates to the eighteenth century beginning with Samuel Richardson's *Pamela, or Virtue Rewarded* (1740), tales of love confounded but eventually rewarded. The gothic romance is a subgenre with more sensationalism, sometimes supernatural elements, a threatening ambience and more intense perils for the heroine. The genre's popularity brought women readers the thrills that Jane Austen's naïve heroine Catherine Morland in *Northanger Abbey*, a spoof of the gothic romance, enthused over in novels that were delightfully "horrid." The gothic romance has always been rooted in the mating narrative, the need for a woman to find her prince, leaving readers the vicarious joy of a successful union at the end. And from an evolutionary psychology perspective as opposed to a romantic one, such unions bring the continuation of the species, a plot in film and fiction that elicits whispers of approval from the primal narrative. In modern film versions of the genre, however, the man whom the woman thinks is her prince may be a villain instead.

The lives and potential for women have changed dramatically since the origin of the romance genre. Today, women can have sex lives without fear of pregnancy and have achieved far better, though not yet equal, status in the workplace. They can, and do, raise children without help from a mate. But in primitive times, a woman needed a man who would protect her and their offspring and provide for them. They could only hope that he would be a "prince," who would be kind and generous. Bruce Ellis sums up the dream embodied in the Disney song:

> Over evolutionary time, ancestral females who had psychological mechanisms that caused them to find males of high mate value more sexually attractive than males of low mate value, and acted on this attraction, would have out-reproduced females with opposite tastes. This differential reproduction would continue until such mechanisms became universal and species typical in women. This logic leads one to expect that a man's sexual attractiveness to women will be a function of traits that were correlated with high mate value in our natural environment: the environment of a Pleistocene hunter-gatherer. Natural selection should have designed evaluative psychological mechanisms (information-processing rules or algorithms) in women that assess such traits and give rise to sexual and romantic attraction in response to them.[2]

His words are stingingly insensitive to describe so delicate an emotion as love. But evolutionary psychology would hold that, stripped to its essence, this dream, that of Snow White for her prince, is the wish for a faithful helpmate and provider with ample resources. A primal traits critical approach suggests that this narrative is imbedded in the genetic heritage of half of our species and whispers to them through the plot of the romance. The other half may share the dream of finding a woman who would be an attractive sexual partner and good mother to their children. A man defending or saving a woman from a villain who would do her harm is a narrative that has been central to the romance genre from its beginnings.

It is easy to see the power of the mating narrative's whisper. Romance

Writers of America, the organization of romance authors, reported $1.37 billion in sales in 2006, over 26 percent of all book sales.[3] The gothic division of the romance genre is a powerful corner of this market. Readers and viewers may deplore the sexist elements of the mating narrative's whisper as enacted in the romance; and culture has changed sex roles. Women can ignore the whisper completely if they choose. Yet for many, perhaps most, it is there, however faintly or insistently, and triggers enjoyment of novels that enact the mating narrative in the gothic romance. The advent of the film medium has added a new dimension to the genre.

One day in my literature class, a young lady raised her hand and asked, "Dr. Fry, why are so many of these stories about sex?" Bidding for a cheap laugh, and of course getting it, I responded, "Well, Katy, sex isn't just important. Sex is everything." Despite my feeble attempt at levity, I had said something a bit profound from an evolutionary psychology perspective without knowing it at the time. Steven Pinker states this perspective of the mating narrative from an evolutionary psychology perspective: "Sexual desire is *not* people's strategy to propagate their genes. It is people's strategy to attain the pleasures of sex, and the pleasures of sex are the genes' strategy to propagate themselves.... People don't selfishly spread their genes; genes selfishly spread themselves."[4] Evolutionary biologists contend that our genes whisper to us to make them immortal, and romantic love is their strategy to achieve their immortality. Desmond Morris articulates a common assumption of evolutionary psychologists in support of my classroom attempt at humor when he writes, "It could be said that the advance of civilization has not so much molded modern sexual behavior, as that sexual behavior has molded the shape of civilization."[5]

These words are hard to hear for romantics. Our belief that the power of love is more than just sex and procreation comes from the mother's milk of our acculturation, and the romance adds to the creation of this belief. The twin strands of culture and evolutionary imperatives that create civilization are inextricably intertwined. The gothic romance subgenre in fiction and later as it was adapted in film offers an illustration of how they have interacted in pleasing their audience for centuries. The focus is the great human dance of mating, and evolutionary psychology proposes that when all the glamour that writers and filmmakers have created in making the romance a product of culture are peeled away, what remains is the central human drive for procreation of the species.

Humans are something of an anomaly in both the biology and the culture of the mating game. The vast majority of animal species have no choice in the matter of mating and procreation. Instinct and biology rule them. Most female mammals have estrous, evolution's way of getting their procreation processes going. The female emits a scent that lets males know that she's in a romantic mood. For some species, as we see in television nature documentaries, courtship is central to initiate mating. Male birds enact elaborate dances or display of plumage to get the attention of a potential paramour. The beautiful feathers of the peacock that would seem to be disadvantageous for survival are an example. The plumage makes the bird easy prey for predators. But for attracting available peahens that see his attire as evidence of a good genetic match, the plumage has species survival potential, what Dennis Dutton calls a "fitness indicator."[6] Animals experience the courtship process in a myriad of other ways.

Homo sapiens are different from most species in courtship, for females do not experience estrous, though Desmond Morris suggests that the use of perfume is a replacement for those scents from earliest humans with the response to it bubbling up from the primal mind. Humans' different evolutionary development has led to multitudes of courtship rituals. According to Geoffrey Miller, "Our minds evolved not just as survival machines, but as courtship machines."[7] The romance and gothic romance at one level portray courtship narratives that trigger vicarious enjoyment for readers and viewers.

From an evolutionary perspective, courtship is the prelude to procreation no matter what cultural overlay is applied. Relationships between the sexes range from polygamy (a man with multiple wives) to polyandry (a woman with more than one male partner) to polyamory (in which individuals have more than one partner with the consent of all, usually in a group). But evolutionary psychology suggests that the pair bond of man and woman has been the evolutionary gold standard, at least for long enough for the progeny to be relatively independent. Human children are dependent on parents for far longer than the offspring of other species, and it would have been difficult for a Paleolithic or Neolithic male without abundant resources to provide for children from a number of mates. While western civilization has developed monogamy as the required pattern for mating with laws against bigamy, throughout history men who could afford to do so have supported mistresses, another reflection of men's primal drive to procreate and spread genes as widely as possible.

And women have always enjoyed a walk on the wild side, as we see enacted throughout the history of literature. Christopher Wilbur and Lorne Campbell observe, "Women value the security of a long-term committed relationship while remaining watchful of opportunities to seek sexual involvement with genetically superior men when conception risk is higher."[8] But monogamy, at least for the short term until the children are self-sufficient, has become the norm through most of the world. We love the idea of lifelong love with a soul mate, but evolutionary psychologists insist that we were not evolved to be completely monogamous. The "seven year itch" would have been the time in primal societies that it took to get a child up and running, perhaps leading to couples finding other arrangements.

From the evolutionary perspective of mating and the successful transmission of genes, men and women have different needs. It is in men's best interest to spread their genes as far and wide as possible. Fisher writes, "Coitus is a man's ticket to posterity; if his partner gets pregnant she will send his DNA into the future. So although men often have no conscious interest in making babies, the evolutionary payoff seems to have been bred into the male psyche as an unconscious tendency to regard sexual intercourse as the essence of intimacy, affection and companionship."[9] Women, on the other hand, have a much greater investment. And this difference in men's and women's needs has fueled the Cinderella story.

It is the foundation of the narrative for women seeking Mr. Right. The story runs through the folklore of many cultures and deep into history: from ancient China, to the Charles Perrault version published in 1697, to the most recent cinematic adaptation in the 2015 Disney film. But culture shapes the story in different packages. *Pretty Woman* (1990) offers a Cinderella character who is a prostitute, and *Maid in Manhattan* (2001) connects the story to modern culture by making the character a single mother. The story of a young woman who is persecuted but succeeds in finding her prince whispers a happy ending to the dream of women to meet and be romanced by such a man. Hundreds of novels and now films have celebrated true love, consummated in marriage after complications; for in the romance, in the Bard's words, "the course of true love never did run smooth." Conflict is essential for fiction and film. And the dramatic conflict at the core of both the romance and gothic romance plotline lies in the mating narrative: the tale of a successful union of a woman with a kind and generous man but in many versions pursued by a man who wants her only for physical pleasure. *Bridget Jones' Diary* puts a modern cultural spin on this eternal story with the contrast of Mark Darcy (the use of Jane Austin's character's name from *Pride and Prejudice* must be intentional) as prince and Daniel Cleaver as rake. But here the romance heroine is quite willing to have sex with the rake soon after meeting him.

Diane Kruger, Marianne Fisher and Ian Jobling categorize the two central male figures in the romance from an evolutionary psychology perspective as "cads" and "dads." Cads are philanderers likely to sire many children. For a woman, she gets a "sexy son" who inherits cad qualities and begets grandchildren. Dads attract women "by showing their potential willingness to paternally invest in children; these men tend to be compassionate, kind, romantic and industrious."[10] This narrative persists in literature, from the contrast of Lancelot and Arthur in the Arthurian tales to the present. Dennis Dutton suggests that a response to such narratives bubbles up from primal sources: Adaptiveness derives from the capacity of the human mind to build a store of experience in terms of individual, concrete cases—not just the actual lived and self-described life experience of an individual but the narratives accumulated in memory that make up storytelling traditions.[11]

The gothic romance genre in fiction was born in the eighteenth century with the development of cheaper printing and the growth of a reading audience made up of middle and upper middle class women educated enough to read and with time and the inclination to do so. As we see in the vampire novel and film, writers developed a formula that persists into the present featuring ruined castles, wicked but strangely attractive villains, and multiple suitors for the heroine. The Cinderella plot running through these novels features a vulnerable orphan pursued by a man she dislikes and supported by one who shares her sensibilities and passion for nature. Multiple suitors pursue the heroine, no doubt a wish fulfillment for female readers. The authors of the gothic romance were children of the age of reason, and while they may suggest supernatural events, they are usually explained away in the earliest gothic romances. There are exceptions from writers such as M.G. Lewis and Charles Maturin, whose novels bring true gothic horror.

Men of the period usually scoffed at the romance. Eaton Stannard Barrett wrote an amusing satire of the genre in his novel *The Heroine* (1812). His character Cherry, a farmer's daughter, reads gothic romance novels and confuses art and life. Convincing herself that she must have been adopted and is an orphan, she renames herself Cherubina and sets off to have the adventures of a heroine. Barrett defines such a character—a heroine:

> A young lady, rather taller than usual, and often an orphan; at all events, possessed of the finest eyes in the world. Though her frame is so fragile, that a breath of wind might scatter it like chaff, it is sometimes stouter than a statue of cast iron. She blushes to the tips of her fingers, and when other girls would laugh, she faints. Besides, she has tears, sighs and half sighs, at command; lives a month on a mouthful, and is addicted to the pale consumption.[12]

Barrett captures the formula character for the peripatetic heroine portrayed in gothic romances of the period who moves from castle to picturesque cottage.

Despite Barrett's sexist and condescending portrayal of Cherry, in the early gothic romances the heroine is a strong and resourceful character, determined not to mate with a man she despises. Young women of the period who were often given arranged marriages could no doubt relate to the heroine of the romances. The novels are achingly melodramatic, but the heroine breaks out of the mold of feminine docility in seeking independence and a relationship with a loving and supportive man. Evolutionary biologists would say that such young women readers dreamed of the best possible match for resources, genetic compatibility and kindness; the popularity of the romance genre suggests that many still do.

"Nellie, I am Heathcliff": *Jane Eyre* and *Wuthering Heights*

The earliest gothic romances have not been adapted to film. But Charlotte Brontë's *Jane Eyre* and her sister Emily's *Wuthering Heights* have seen numerous adaptations. Novels by all three Brontë sisters appeared in 1847, which also saw Anne's novel *Agnes Gray*. All three wrote with male pen names: Charlotte as Currer Bell, Emily as Ellis Bell and Anne as Acton Bell. While women authors had been stalwarts in the developing fiction market of the eighteenth century, Victorian culture had changed, and women had difficulty getting their work accepted. Mary Ann Evans had to adopt the pen name George Eliot to have her novels published.

Jane Eyre is an evolution of the gothic romance formula from the preceding century and the Cinderella tradition. The novel enacts the timeless narrative of mating and procreation, clothed in the romantic allure that culture has evolved. Brontë's novel has inspired numerous film adaptations. The Internet Movie Database lists eight, not counting various television and stage versions. The 1943 film is the most powerful in catching the spirit of the work. A distinguished trio of screenwriters including Aldous Huxley, John Houseman and Robert Stevenson (who also directed the film) provide a truncated plot from the novel that omits Jane's experience with St. John Rivers and his sisters and the details of her inheritance. But the writers and director Stevenson play to the strengths of the actors: Joan Fontaine as Jane Eyre and Orson Welles as Rochester. Welles captures the Byronic passion of Brontë's hero. The film also features a trio of child actors who were future stars: Margaret O'Brien as Adèle, Rochester's illegitimate daughter with a French dancer; Peggy Ann Garner as the young Jane; and 11-year-old Elizabeth Taylor as the consumptive Helen Burns, Jane's best friend at the Lowood School.

Brontë does not describe Jane as the beautiful young woman from the gothic romance tradition. She is "plain Jane." But the author adopts many elements of the conventions and the narrative that inspired it. The mating narrative as enacted in *Jane Eyre* whispers to a primal response of women through the early history of our species. As evolutionary psychologists insist, women have had a much greater stake in mating than men. Karl Grammer observes, "Selecting a 'bad' mate could endanger the survival of the female's rare offspring. In consequence, females should be more choosy than males."[13] Hence, as a fantasy, Rochester is a model mate for a female reading audience of Brontë's day: He is kind, generous, and possessed of ample resources. Though the novel describes him as lacking in masculine good looks, he is undeniably sexy, a power that Welles captures in the film. His dalliance with a French dancer makes Rochester even more attractive from a sexual perspective. He has fathered a child, so he could (and did as we find at the end of the novel) provide children for Jane.

Jane Eyre is a stronger heroine than we see in earlier novels from the gothic romance tradition. As is so often the case for the heroine as described by Barrett, Jane is an orphan with the equivalent of Cinderella's cruel stepmother, her aunt Mrs. Reed. She stands up to her aunt's cruelty and that of Reed's abusive son before she is sent to Lowood, a school for girls, where she is the object of ire for the school's director, Mr. Brocklehurst. In both novel and film, she tells Dr. Rivers, the school apothecary, of her dream of wealth and "a lovely coach and four," a Cinderella dream. As a grownup, Jane has the strength of character to change her life and reject Brocklehurst's condescending offer of a teaching position after he tells her that she will never find other employment because, as he says in the film, "You have no talent, your appearance is insignificant."

She advertises for a position and gets one as governess to Adèle at Thornfield, Rochester's estate. The film and novel establish Thornfield as a rambling structure with turrets, a vaguely castle-like appearance derived from the early gothic tradition. The structure as described in the novel and envisioned in the film is the appropriate setting for a gothic romance. And it has suggestions of the supernatural with bumps in the night from Bertha, who escapes Grace Poole, her keeper, to enter Jane's bedroom and then set Rochester's room afire. The setting with the madwoman in the attic and her antics take the novel and film from the romance to the gothic romance tradition.

Jane's first meeting with Rochester sets the tenor of their relationship at the conclusion. While she is on a walk, he returns home, galloping his horse, and to avoid hitting her is thrown off. She has brought him, as it were, to his knees and is quick to try and help him: an early example of her nurturing nature. The scene parallels her role as helpmate to the blind Rochester at the conclusion. Her actions in saving him from the fire in his bedroom and the comparison of her warmth and sensitivity in caring for Adèle to the glamorous Blanche Ingraham, who has the "accomplishments" expected of upper class young women but little feeling for others, endear her to Rochester: qualities that would signal a good mate from a primal traits perspective.

As is often the case in the romance genre, Rochester as hero is a wealthy man who chooses a woman beneath him in social class, a Cinderella. Welles' lines in the film when he proposes to Jane are a powerful version of those from the romance genre as he expresses his feelings, words that echo a wish fulfillment of millennia of women who dream of a sensitive and kind mate with resources to be a good provider: "Sometimes," he murmurs, "I have this feeling about you, Jane. It's as if I had a string somewhere under my left rib tightly and inextricably knotted to a similar string situated in a corresponding corner of your little frame." The lines reflect Helen Fisher's belief that we are attracted to those with similar social attitudes and values as our own, and "genetic types gravitate toward one another; we tend to be attracted to people like ourselves."¹⁴ Although Jane matches Rochester's passion in her quiet way and is more assertive than other romance heroines of the period, she nonetheless reflects much of the Victorian cultural feminine ideal, a nurturing and self-sacrificing woman.

As is usually the case in the romance tradition, Jane has more than one proposal in the novel. But St. John Rivers (omitted in this film adaptation) appeals only to her sense of Christian duty, not to the warmth of passion she feels for Rochester. An evolutionary psychology perspective would suggest that her instinct perceives Rochester as not only a more romantic and sexually fulfilling partner with better resources but also a better genetic match. The film and novel enact the greater wish fulfillment for women of Brontë's time and through history that comes with the conclusion when Jane returns to Thornfield with the wealth and independence she has inherited to nurse the wounded and blind Rochester. She has truly brought him to his knees as she did when they first met and he was unhorsed.

Nancy Easterlin offers a feminist perspective on the novel and film. Rochester establishes a relationship of dominance that Jane resists. His desire for control is an evolved response and unconscious while she needs a sense of autonomy. Easterlin contrasts Jane's resistance to Rochester's domination with St. John and his dominance through religion in the novel, to which she nearly succumbs but does not: "From the Darwinian feminist perspective here, Brontë exposes the evolved male proprietary attitude toward women, reveals some of the specific culture ... in the nineteenth century, and illustrates its potential to individual pair bonding for both men and women."¹⁵ Joseph Carroll's comment on the Elizabeth Bennet–Darcy relationship in *Pride and Prejudice* applies also to *Jane Eyre*. Men want youth and beauty and women want resources, but "[t]he single most important criterion for registering personal quality in the novel is the degree in which both men and women rise above this base standard and require also qualities of excellence in character and in mind."¹⁶ Both male dominance and the female need for autonomy are evolved characteristics, he suggests.

Emily Brontë's *Wuthering Heights* is a romance and an emphatically gothic romance, but it is distinctly different from others of the genre. Except for a 1920 silent film, William Wyler's 1939 adaptation of the novel is the first. It offers a distinguished cast, with Laurence Olivier and Merle Oberon as Heathcliff and Catherine. As is the case with *Jane Eyre,* the script—by acclaimed writers Charles MacArthur, Ben Hecht and John Huston—prunes and changes Brontë's novel, leaving out the most emotionally intense scenes, such as Heathcliff exhuming Catherine's body. It omits entirely Brontë's reconciliation of opposites with the union of Hareton and the young Catherine at the end.

The 1992 adaptation, directed by Peter Kosminski, with Ralph Fiennes and Juliette Binoche, captures the intense romantic relationship and gothic setting far more effectively and completes Brontë's tale of passion run riot. As in Brontë's novel, the film establishes the opposites that underpin the story: the wild Wuthering Heights setting as opposed to the rather pastoral Grange; Heathcliff's unrestrained passion compared to Edgar Linton's civilized behavior; and savage moors where Catherine and Heathcliff wander in their youth with the cultivated and landscaped environment of the Grange. All of these threads are unified with the climactic marriage of Hinton and the young Catherine. The film establishes the gothic ambience of the novel. Wuthering Heights has a Burkean gothic look, complete with castle-like turrets. The timeless and wild moors where standing stones remain from ancient civilizations enhance the wildness of the Wuthering Heights setting. Lockwood's dream and contact with Catherine's ghost in the opening scene seal the novel and film as gothic romance. The contrast between the Heights and the Grange reflects the contrast of the sublime as Burke described it and as generations of writers adapted it, which arouses unease, and the beautiful, which inspires tranquility.

The film provides two approaches to the mating narrative, each magnified by the intensely romantic vision in Brontë's novel that makes it unique in the gothic romance with its otherworldly setting. David Barash and Judith Eve Lipton observe, "One way to make sense of female sexual and romantic preferences is that women have been selected to choose good, reliable providers and cooperators as their social mates, while also being on the lookout

***Wuthering Heights*: Heathcliffe (Ralph Fiennes) alone on the moor.**

for sexy studs to be the genetic fathers of their children, a pattern that has been around often enough to leave a distinct evolutionary footprint."[17] Finding a stable and generous mate is the central dream of the Cinderella story and the romance genre. Evolution might also favor a woman's desire for the man who titillates her sexually because he would be exciting to be with and from a primal traits perspective might also be a good genetic match for fathering a child.

The film offers both kinds of male lovers. After the death of Mr. Earnshaw when the drunken Hindley has turned Heathcliff into a servant and neglects Catherine, the two young people peek into a window at the Grange, an environment that is the antithesis of their lives at Wuthering Heights. To Heathcliff's discomfort, Catherine is dazzled by a lifestyle she had not imagined to exist. Edgar, a gentle soul, has the resources evolutionary psychologists say women have dreamed of through history. He is, from an evolutionary mating perspective, Mr. Right, Cinderella's prince. But Isabelle, Edgar's sister, chooses the opposite kind of mate, the sexy cad in the returned Heathcliff because he ignites "the fire in the mind." Catherine feels the attraction she has always had for Heathcliff, even though she manages to resist his pleas to run away with him.

The novel and film adaptations give us a twisted version of the conventional romance formula's plot of a woman who has her choice between more than one man, with Catherine torn between Heathcliff and Edgar, who represent the two needs women might feel. In the early gothics, one of the men was a "seducer" or a "rake," who is charismatic and dangerous and has designs on the heroine's virtue yet is somehow strangely attractive, while the other is the sensitive and caring male. Heathcliff, in his Byronic passion and the intensity of his love for Catherine, reflects the former choice. Each offers advantages from an evolutionary perspective.

Joseph Carroll observes that *Wuthering Heights* enacts these advantages:

> The prospective marriage of Hareton and Cathy invokes a romantic comedy norm in which individual interests fuse into a cooperative and reciprocally advantageous bond, but no such bond is perfect or permanent, and many are radically faulty. The conclusion of *Wuthering Heights* juxtaposes images of domestic harmony with images of emotional violence that reflect deep disruptions in the phase of human life history.[18]

Primal dreams from the gothic romance reflect the attraction of both types of men. In the past, women needed an Edgar, and the allure of this kind of man persists today. But the attraction to the bad boy is a story that runs through the annals of literature and film. Heathcliff is such a character, destroying poor Isabelle who is attracted to him as a moth to the flame, as is Catherine. But he is redeemed by the Byronic intensity of his love for Catherine. In his essay on the novel, David Cecil writes, "Any character may be superficially attracted to those whose characters and values they admire [as

Catherine to Edgar]. But their deeper feelings are only roused for someone for whom they feel a sense of affinity that comes from the fact that they are both expressions of the same process. Catherine does not 'like' Heathcliff but she loves him with all the strength of her being."[19] He describes the two kinds of lovers that evolution might make attractive for a woman: the good provider and the man who exudes sexuality and passion that override her better judgment.

The Kominski film enacts a scene from the novel when Nellie asks Catherine what she likes about Edgar. "He is young, and he will be rich," she replies, a good answer for a mating decision. And she later adds, "My love for Linton is like the foliage in the woods. Time will change it as winter changes the trees. I love Heathcliff. He's like the eternal rocks beneath, a source of literal visible delight.... Nellie, I *am* Heathcliff." The lines articulate the decision for women in the mating narrative: one choice for stability and a reliable mate and father for their children; the other for a man who ignites the chemical cascade that may have evolutionary advantage for the species but might bring unhappiness for the woman, as is the case for Isabella and the quandary of Catherine in *Wuthering Heights*. We can label the novel and its film adaptations as a gothic and a romance, but it rises above the genre's formula with the passion it enacts.

"Torn Between Two Lovers": The *Twilight* Films and *Rebecca*

Mary MacGregor's song reflects a modern version of an old narrative that is enacted over and over in the romance and the gothic version in which a woman is torn between two men. It is a central conflict in Stephanie Meyer's *Twilight* novels and the film adaptations. *Twilight*'s undeniable appeal to readers and viewers derives from tribal and territorial narratives in the vampire tradition. But they are at their core gothic romances rooted in the mating narrative with a focus on finding Mr. Right, even if he happens to be a vampire—or maybe a werewolf.

Twilight combines the conventional teen romance with a vampire story when 17-year-old Bella (Kristen Stewart) moves to the small town of Forks, Washington, to live with her father, the chief of police. She locks eyes with Edward Cullen (Robert Pattinson), a soulful and pale young man, on her first day of school; and love blooms, a staple scene from the romance tradition. He is strangely reluctant but eventually reveals that he is a vampire and part of a family of vegetarian vampires (they consume only animal blood). The novels' and films' focus on the territorial conflict of the Cullens as vampires and the Quileute Indians as shape shifters; the conflict of Edward with the

Quileute boy Jacob for Bella's favor; and conflicts between the Cullen family and evil vampires.

Bella's place in the love triangle with Jacob and Edward is an old refrain in the romance narrative, a woman—or girl in this case—desired by more than one suitor. If the vampire and tribal narratives are stripped away, the film is a very conventional romance, with a young woman put in distress, pursued by a villain who has designs on her virtue (supplanted here by a vampire who stalks her) and supported by a hero who has sensitive feelings. Edward shares her interests, lets her set the pace of their relationship and defends her. Bella's choice between two men who love her is a wish fulfillment for women from the dawning of the romance genre in fiction that seems to persist today for many readers and viewers.

Bella is such a conventional heroine. As in the traditional romance, she is more or less helpless without the hero. Edward saves her repeatedly. That defenselessness seems part of her attraction. Edward confesses to her, "I feel very protective of you," and "You're like my own personal brand of heroin." Such sentiments reflect the primal imperative of protecting the female as the source of the next generation and continuation of the gene pool. He is the sort of dominant and sensitive male who might trigger primal response to an audience of romance readers. The Cullenses are obviously wealthy, and one hardly needs evolutionary psychology to tell us that a man's resources are a factor in making a male like Edward attractive to women.

The relationship between Bella and Edward in acting out the mating narrative might also bring vicarious pleasure for many male viewers or readers of the novels. Fisher writes, "Men feel manly when they rescue a damsel in distress. No doubt millions of years of protecting and providing for women has bred into the male brain this tendency to choose women they feel they need to save."[20] The "wounded bird" heroine, as Fisher calls a female who attracts men's protective instinct, may trigger male primal response at some level. But the power of this element of the narrative—a woman's dream of a man who cares and protects— has made the romance a popular genre from the beginning of the novel to its adaptation in film.

Bella reflects the evolved whispers of the mating narrative that are central to the romance and gothic romance genres' appeal. She clings to Edward as the only possible mate for her. Fisher notes, "Women have evolved brain mechanisms to make them exceedingly possessive when a mate threatens to withdraw resources or emotional support or abandon the relationship for another."[21] In Fanny Burney's *Cecilia* (1782), one of the most influential of the early romances, the heroine runs mad in the streets when she loses her lover, a scene that became *de rigueur* in the romance. Bella is such a character, hysterical and nearly suicidal when Edward tries to break off the relationship for her sake. Male characters in the romance genre may be similarly affected by the loss of a loved one. In Johann Wolfgang von Goethe's 1774 novel *The Sorrows of Young Werther,* a powerful influence on young romantics of the period, the hero commits suicide because Charlotte, the woman he adores and who is married to another, sends him away. A generation of young men wore yellow waistcoats, favored by Werther in the novel, to honor the character's intense feelings. Edward enacts a Werther moment when he decides to commit suicide by sunlight because he cannot have Bella but is rescued when she rushes to save him. The mating narrative is completed in the final film when Bella bears a child, another hybrid that blends Others as in *Blade* and *Underworld.*

Daphne du Maurier (1907–1989) set the tone for the revival of the gothic romance, novels whose covers show a castle-like building in the background with a young woman in the foreground looking distressed. *Rebecca,* her first successful novel, appeared in 1938. It was followed by Alfred Hitchcock's film adaptation two years later, his first U.S. production at a time when Britain was enduring Nazi bombing of its cities and in peril of invasion. Rather than a woman torn between two lovers, *Rebecca* tells the story of a man torn between the memory of a faithless wife and the naive young woman he marries.

Like so many others of the gothic romance genre, *Rebecca* enacts a version of the Cinderella story and with mild thrills. The film's heroine (Joan Fontaine) is a young woman who has lost her parents. We get no name for her until she becomes Mrs. de Winter. As in the romance tradition and like Jane Eyre, she is an orphan and a paid companion for a wealthy woman traveling in France, an equivalent of Cinderella's cruel stepmother. Then she happens to meet Maxim de Winter (Laurence Olivier), a wealthy Englishman, who she thinks is about to throw himself off a cliff. When she insists that he stop (he was not actually suicidal), he takes notice of her and love blooms. He proposes marriage after he has known her for only a few days.

And so the film establishes the heroine as the vulnerable orphan of the romance tradition who has met her prince. Du Maurier's updating of the gothic romance, as reflected in Hitchcock's film, enacts the essentials of the mating narrative. De Winter is an appropriate hero for a romance, owner of a large estate in Cornwall and Manderley, a grand mansion there. He is older than the woman he marries by 20 years, and evolutionary biologists say women tend to be attracted to men older than they because of their experience and the likelihood that they will have more resources than their younger counterparts. Men such as de Winter and Charlotte Brontë's Rochester trigger the primal whisper of approval from readers and viewers.

Mrs. de Winter is the sort of woman to whom, evolutionary psychologists suggest, men are likely to be attracted, as we see throughout the romance genre. Of course, most men are not thinking of offspring when they are beguiled by a woman and want to have sex with her. But evolutionary psychologists posit that their genes push them toward women who would be good candidates to bear children. Helen Fisher writes,

> Evolutionary psychologists now believe that men subconsciously also prefer youth and beauty because it gives them reproductive payoffs.... So these scientists theorize that across our long hunting-gathering past, those males who chose youthful, healthy, exuberant partners had more children. Those robust babies lived—and passed along to contemporary men this male bias for youthful, good-looking women.[22]

So it is understandable that de Winter would be drawn to such a young woman, not because he is intent on having children but because in the primal mind his genes call out to him. She is a perfect contrast to his first wife Rebecca, who, as we learn, was certainly not a wonderful candidate for motherhood: She was an unscrupulous and greedy adulteress.

Everyone belittles or patronizes the new Mrs. de Winter. When her employer, Mrs. Van Hooper, learns she is marrying de Winter, she says, "You haven't the faintest idea how to be a great lady." But it is this innocence in contrast to Rebecca to which de Winter is drawn. He shows his attraction to her youth and inexperience when, after she tries to take on a more sophisticated role as hostess, he says, "Pity you had to grow up." Later, when she dresses in a sleek evening gown for a dinner party and gets a more sophisticated hairdo, he is shocked and says, "What have you done to yourself?" Her guilelessness is characteristic of the romance heroine, which, we eventually learn, makes her the opposite of Rebecca. She is also the model for women who have interested a sizable part of the male gender through the millennia.

Hitchcock builds enough suspense for the film to be categorized as gothic romance, with the mad Mrs. Danvers, who had been obsessively in love with Rebecca, saying, "I can almost hear her quick, light step in all of the rooms of the house.... Do you think the dead can come back to watch the living?" She then tries to get the new Mrs. de Winter to leap from the window onto the rocks below Rebecca's room. The film is set on the shore of Cornwall with many scenes of crashing waves below Manderley, the kind of gothic ambience endemic to the genre.

Cads and Dads in the Gothic Romance: *Suspicion, Dragonwyck, Gaslight* and *Crimson Peak*

Billie Holiday's song "My Man" tells of a persistent and often harmful dream that whispers in the minds of many women. The woman in the song is in love with a very bad man. It identifies her man as a philanderer who beats her and does not contribute to her support. Why would a woman be attracted to such a man? Or stay with him? From an evolutionary and very anti-romantic perspective, a primal whisper might come to women to stick with a man who is the father of their children, or at least the prospective father, rather than risk losing emotional and financial support. Barry Schwartz sums up the mating narrative:

> Males and females have different interests. The female produces the egg and has a huge investment in it, for pregnancy and child rearing. The male has a gazillion sperm and would like to spread them far and wide for his genetic immortality. So the two have different strategies. The female has to choose a male who will stick around and offer support. The male wants her for the night. So she's choosy and wants courtship so she can observe whether he is responsible and has resources and tenderness.[23]

Schwartz states only a primal response, and obviously culture has molded a variety of romantic versions of relationships. But in the gothic romance, women, once they have committed to a man, may put up with his bad behavior to protect their investment.

In many novels and films, a woman finds herself in the control of a bad man, but one to whom she has invested herself such as described in "My Man." Alfred Hitchcock's film *Suspicion* (1941), an adaptation of Francis Iles' 1932 novel *Before the Fact*, is a classic example of this narrative. It lacks a gothic setting, but it has enough thrills and suspense with the suggestion of a controlling male who might harm the heroine to be classified as a gothic romance.

Diane Waldman defines the central plotline for the gothic romance film of the 1930s and '40s: "A young, inexperienced woman meets a handsome older man to whom she is alternatively attracted and repelled. After a whirlwind courtship she marries him."[24] Also, as in the romance formula through the ages, she is more often than not a vulnerable orphan. The version of the gothic romance Waldman describes omits supernatural incidents. But the prospect of a woman being in the power of a man who has emotional and financial power over her and might mean her harm is scary enough to enter films of the type into the gothic category. Walter Allen sums up this version of the romance in his book *The English Novel* when he describes the plot of eighteenth-century romances for women readers as "a mouse's eye view of cats." And no doubt, cats are quite frightening to mice.

Waldman's characterization describes *Suspicion*. Lina Laidlaw (Joan Fontaine in an Academy Award–winning performance) meets ne'er-do-well Johnnie Asgarth (Cary Grant) on a train where they share a compartment. The scene includes a shot of the train going through a tunnel, a standard sexual trope and a Hitchcock favorite. Lina is shy and introverted, dressed plainly and with thick-lens glasses. He is her opposite, a handsome extrovert. When the conductor arrives to punch tickets, Asgarth is short of money to pay his fare in this first class compartment when his ticket is for third class and has to borrow change from her. Later, when he sees her at a fox hunt astride a horse and prettied up, he is smitten. When he flirts more aggressively, she says, "I don't understand men like you. I always feel you are laughing at me." A conflict of opposites is conventional in the romance, so we have the shy heroine at first repelled but then attracted to the sexy Johnny. He sweeps her off her feet and persuades her to elope, defying her father's wishes. The rest of the plot develops "suspicion" of the rascally Asgarth, whom Lina comes to suspect not only of larceny but murder.

Suspicion enacts a classic situation. Lina's parents have decided she will be a spinster because of her shyness. She is like Charlotte Brontë's Plain Jane, a favorite character in the romance tradition. But in this ancient story of a man striking love's spark in a woman, or as evolutionary psychologists might put it awakening the call of her genes to procreate, she is inextricably attached to her man. He is not the prince of the fairy tale. He is, in fact, Mr. Wrong. The film softens Iles' story. In the novel, Johnnie is not just a thief and a liar but a compulsive philanderer and apparently a murderer: perhaps killing Lina at the conclusion with untraceable poison, though Iles leaves that uncertain and the film omits this possibility. The novel is an even more powerful morality tale of what happens when a woman who stands by her man comes to grief, with both film and novel enacting this version of the mating narrative.

The story of a woman who commits herself to a bad man goes far back in literary history. In Samuel Richardson's eighteenth-century novel *Clarissa*, the title character elopes with the rascally Lovelace, leading to her imprisonment and rape. Dennis Dutton suggests that stories such as this have adaptive value: "Adaptiveness derives from the capacity of the human mind to build a store of experience in terms of individual, concrete cases—not just the actual lived and self-described life experience of an individual but the narratives accumulated in memory that makes up storytelling traditions."[25] Lina's experience as described in *Suspicion* is such a narrative.

Diane Waldman's description of the gothic romance also fits *Dragonwyck* (1946), based on an Anya Seton novel. The film and novel blend a little historical fact with a gothic romance formula. The anti-rent movement of early nineteenth-century New York forms part of the background for the novel. Patroons, feudal landowners, controlled great estates, renting to farmers for money and a share of crops. Nicholas Van Ryn (Vincent Price), a patroon, is the wealthy older man from the gothic romance as Waldman describes the character. He invites Miranda Wells (Gene Tierney), the daughter of a puritanical farmer in Connecticut, to stay at Dragonwyck, the manor house of the Van Ryn family, to be a guest and companion for his eight-year-old daughter Katrina, who soon disappears in the film's plot. Miranda is the formula character of the genre, a naive young woman who comes under the influence of an older and powerful man who woos and marries her. But as the film plays out, Van Ryn is the opposite of a benign Rochester. He seems to have married Miranda only to beget a son after the death of his barren wife, who dies under suspicious circumstances. *Dragonwyck* has enough supernatural shivers to qualify it as gothic. The ghost of Van Ryn's great grandmother, who had hated Dragonwyck and felt trapped there, haunts the place; and occasionally those of the Van Ryn bloodline can hear her ghost sing and play the harpsichord at times of family stress. Dragonwyck itself is cut from whole cloth of the traditional gothic structure, down to a forbidden tower that Miranda finds at the end of the film.

As in many another work from the romance genre, the heroine has multiple suitors. The local physician, Dr. Turner, supports the local farmers in their protest against the patroon system and offers an antithesis to the hubris of Van Ryn, who sits on a sort of throne like a medieval lord when his tenants come to pay their rent. Turner is smitten with Miranda. But she prefers this older and wealthy man who fits the pattern of males to whom women in earlier times, and often in the present, would be attracted, one with resources and power. And from the evolutionary psychology viewpoint, both are doing what their genes would tell them to do: Miranda to find a mate with resources to support her and possible children and Van Ryn to pass his genes on to a son who would inherit his estate. But he dominates her after their marriage and loses interest in her after their son dies soon after he is born. As in Nancy Easterlin's analysis of *Jane Eyre*, Van Ryn demands dominance and Miranda seeks autonomy, which she eventually finds.

Gaslight (1944) enacts the same narrative of a woman who is attracted to the wrong man, one who dominates her. In the backstory, singer Alice Alquist is murdered in a robbery attempt, a crime witnessed by a child, her niece Paula who has blocked the memory out. The murderer is never caught. Paula (Ingrid Bergman) tries to become a singer herself when she grows up but lacks her aunt's talent. Her piano accompanist, Gregory Anton (Charles Boyer), who had murdered the aunt and managed to avoid being caught, persuades her to elope, and so begins a plot similar to others in this narrative: a woman who chooses the wrong mate, a hyper-dominant male. The film establishes the folly of her elopement when she says, "I don't know you, I don't know anything about you." But as in other films of the gothic romance tradition, sexual chemistry leads her astray.

Elopement is portrayed as an error for women in the romance genre from its beginning. Marriages among the wealthy or even the upper middle class were usually arranged with financial goals in mind, and a standard villain in British novels tries to persuade young women with a "fortune"—money or a potential inheritance—to elope to Gretna Green in Scotland, where they could marry without posting banns. In *Pride and Prejudice*, Jane Austen includes a disastrous elopement when Lydia Bennet runs away with

Dragonwyck: The patron, Nicolas Van Ryn (Vincent Price), demands homage from his renters.

the charming but unscrupulous Wickham, who had tried the same tactic with Georgiana Darcy.

Anton attempts to drive Paula mad, persuading her that she loses things and forgets her actions. This story has also been an ingredient of the romance genre from its inception. Mary Wollstonecraft's 1798 novel *Maria, or the Wrongs of Women*, unfinished and published posthumously by her husband William Godwin, tells a story that must have been not uncommon in her time: that of an inconvenient wife imprisoned in a mental asylum by a husband to get her out of the way and get her fortune. That is the plot of *Gaslight*. Gregory, an assumed name for Sergius Bauer who is really Alice Alquist's murderer, persuades Paula to elope and move into her aunt's house so that he can search for the jewels he had failed to find when he killed her, at the same time attempting to drive Paula mad so that he can institutionalize her and control her fortune.

Gaslight enacts the formula and captures the ambience for the gothic romance. London's streets are always foggy. The Alquist house has the forbidden room that appears over and over in the genre, this time where Gregory searches for the jewels. Director George Cukor focuses on the gaslight fixtures of the house, returning to them repeatedly to establish its threatening ambience. The flames rise and lower as Gregory tries to convince Paula she is going mad. When she tells him she hears noises from the deserted room above, sounds that contribute to the spooky atmosphere, Gregory tells her that she is delusional, though we learn that they emanate from his searches for the jewels there. The maid, played by a young Angela Lansbury in her first film, acts out the role of a controlling servant, the same kind of threatening presence with her spiteful comments to Paula that we get in *Rebecca* from Mrs. Danvers. Paula is the vulnerable orphan, a conventional role in the romance tradition. Her lack of friends and advisors leads her to an elopement with the bad man of the mating narrative. The film ends with Scotland Yard inspector Brian Cameron (Joseph Cotten), who had been part of the investigation of Alice Agular's murder, gradually realizing Anton's plot and foiling it.

The version of the mating narrative in *Gaslight* has long had appeal to a feminine audience of the romance genre. The story of a powerful man controlling a vulnerable woman and bringing her harm has been enacted throughout human history, in life as well as in literature, and speaks from the accumulated experience of millennia. Viewers get the vicarious satisfaction in seeing a false prince in this version of the mating narrative, a cad in the cads and dads dichotomy, humiliated at the end, when Paula first hints to Gregory that she might help free him and then enacts a version of abandonment rage revenge. Brian Boyd links the universally favorable response to revenge to instinctual behavior:

> Revenge elicits intense emotions, from gnawing curiosity to moralistic anger to acute apprehension as the rewards and risks of retribution loom. Until it is satisfied, moral anger can preoccupy us like little else.... Since we became human long before we invented legal institutions to break cycles of offense and retaliation, the urge to avenge affronts and injuries remains deep in our psyche.[26]

So at the fade, the bad mate has been punished, and the mating narrative ends happily with Cameron, Paula's savior, the knight in shining armor and protector character in the genre, becoming the right mate when they seem drawn together.

Guillermo del Toro's *Crimson Peak* (2015) adapts the gothic romance as it has developed in film and fiction but offers an interesting revision of the mating. Del Toro has done other adaptations of the horror genre: the werewolf in *The Wolf Man*, 2010; the vampire narrative in Blade 2, 2002, and *The*

Strain novels (*The Strain*, 2009, *The Fall*, 2010 and *The Night Eternal*, 2012), produced as a TV miniseries. He also adapted fantasy with *Pan's Labyrinth* (2006) and the Satanic film in *Hell Boy* (2004), in all of these films supplying a twist that either revisions or in some way massages the genre. *The Shape of Water* (2017) recasts the 1954 film *Creature from the Black Lagoon*. But this film's twist is that the creature is captured and persecuted while the unrequited love of the monster for the woman in the '50s version is fully requited in this one. It ends with a nod to the 1984 film *Splash*.

Gaslight: Paula Alquist (Ingrid Bergman, not shown here) gets her revenge against her husband Gregory Anton (Charles Boyer).

Del Toro has clearly studied the gothic romance. The heroine is cut from the cloth of those from *Suspicion*, *Gaslight* and other films of the genre but revised to match changes in culture. Edith Cushing (Mia Wasikowska), a wealthy young woman in late nineteenth-century New York, is unable to resist the emotional fire started by Thomas Sharpe (Tom Huddleston), a poverty-stricken English baronet who has come to America with his sister Lucile (Jessica Chastain) to find investors in his scheme to harvest red clay for brickmaking on his English estate. The conventional fortune hunter of the genre, Sharpe (and his sister) murder Edith's father, leaving her an orphan in the romance tradition. They lure her to his dilapidated manor house, Allerdale, in remote Yorkshire. It is there that the formula for the gothic romance is enacted, with an important twist.

Allerdale Hall is reminiscent of the eighteenth-century and Victorian gothic romances in setting. The structure is a pattern from the ruined castle, or manor house in this case, from the genre. The roof is open to rain and snow. There are secret rooms, and throughout the film, we see ghosts. In the opening voiceover, Edith says, "Ghosts are real. This much I know," followed by a scene with Lucille's deceased mother whispering to her when she was a child to "Beware of Crimson Peak" (the location of Allerdale Hall). Then at

Allerdale, Edith sees ghosts of Thomas' wives, whom he had married for their money to support his enterprise, and finally those of Thomas and Lucille at the end, all oozing ectoplasm. The closing voiceover from Edith on ghosts and why they exist would fit well in a spiritualist book.

As in so many gothic romances in film and fiction, the heroine is in peril in this ruined manor, gradually picking up clues from ghosts that haunt it. They finally lead her to an attic (another hidden or forbidden room from the gothic romance genre) where she finds evidence of Thomas' other wives who were murdered for their money. The Sharpes' plan the same for Edith with slow poison. As is common in the romance tradition, Edith has multiple suitors. Safe, secure Alan McMichael (Charlie Hunnam), a New York physician, loves her and suspects foul play in her father's death; and he eventually learns the truth about the Sharpes. In the romance and mating tradition, he represents the mate who would be Mr. Right from an evolutionary perspective.

But it is Thomas who has lighted the mating fire for Edith, and he clearly knows how. He says all the right things for a lover from the perspective of the mating narrative. When he woos her in New York, he murmurs, "A link exists between your heart and mine, and should that link be broken, either by distance or time, my heart would cease to beat and I would die." The lines echo Heathcliff's to Catherine in *Wuthering Heights* and Rochester's to Jane in *Jane Eyre* as quoted above.

His protestations of love are a ruse, of course, and one he has practiced in the past. But this is a romance, and Thomas falls in love with Edith, to the distress of his sister Lucille with whom he has an incestuous relationship. So when Alan goes to Yorkshire to save Edith and is himself wounded, we have a battle between two strong women in the blood red snow. It is here that del Toro revises the gothic romance mating narrative. He said in an interview, "I sort of wanted to actualize the genre a little and make the female role the central role."[27] Speaking from his Victorian perspective, Charles Darwin wrote: "Man is more courageous, pugnacious, and energetic than woman, and has a more inventive genius. Woman seems to differ from man ... chiefly in her tenderness and less selfishness."[28] His was an age when women were enjoined, in the words of the title of Martha Vicinus' book, to *Suffer and Be Still*. Times have changed.

Though the "suffer and be still" injunction may linger in the whispers from the primal mind for many women in the developed world (and speaks more loudly in Third World countries), culture has quieted it, or at least redirected it. But the whisper may still be there for many viewers and readers. We empathize with a character such as Edith who wants to stand by her man, as shown when she lures Thomas away from the Hall to consummate their marriage and win his love in a nearby hotel. So while del Toro certainly tweaks the mating narrative and conventions, much remains. We have Alan McMichael, clearly the dad in the cads and dads dichotomy from the romance tradition, longing for Edith and coming to Yorkshire from New York to save her. And then we have Thomas Sharpe, the cad, dangerous and sexy, not a good bet as a provider and protector: a story we see in other bad mating choices in the genre, as in life.

Like heroines in other gothic romances, Edith chooses passion over safety and eventually actually earns the love of this scoundrel, to his peril. But in the end she is with McMichael, the safer choice from a mating perspective. Yet it is she who saves the man who tries to save her rather than the resolution we normally find in the gothic romance, a conclusion that reflects the transforming effect of culture. The term has been defined in many ways, but Steven Pinker's seems appropriate to see the changes in the romance formula. It is phenomena that "arise as people pool and accumulate their discoveries, and as they institute conventions to coordinate their labors and adjudicate their conflicts,"[29] and it revises and reshapes primal narratives, just as primal narratives influence the creation of culture.

The film also enacts a different and twisted branch of mating, the lifelong incestuous pairing of Thomas and Lucille. Most evolutionary biologists agree that incest is counterproductive for evolution. Dennis Dutton writes, "Incest avoidance is an instinct that humans share with other sexually reproducing animals, including all of the other primates.... But with humans there is also a cultural packaging for incest avoidance."[30] The plight of Oedipus in Sophocles' tragedy is an early example of incest avoidance in literature. But even this twisted version of mating has its rules, and jealousy is a fundamental trait of our species to which the mad and obsessive Lucille responds. The green-eyed monster drives both male and female behavior, and though Lucille's kind of love for her brother has been condemned through the centuries in most cultures and is counterproductive from an evolutionary perspective, she feels the same whisper of abandonment rage that women have felt through evolutionary history when a mate and his resources are taken away.

David Barash and Judith Lipton give the scientific definition of love from an evolutionary psychology perspective: "To begin with, love is neither more nor less than a mechanism, a means to an end rather than an end in itself, a device that evolved by natural selection to facilitate breeding, the transfer of genes into the future."[31] But it would be hard to convince centuries of poets and lovers that this definition is adequate. The Bard has Helena express her love of Demetrius for all his faults in *A Midsummer Night's Dream* when she murmurs, "Love looks not with the eyes, but with the mind, and therefore is wing'ed Cupid painted black." It is no doubt important to understand our primal drives. And maybe what we think of as love really is an illusion.

The Temptations song "Just My Imagination" tells of a man who sees a pretty girl from his window and creates a fantasy scenario in which they date, get married and have a comfortable home with children. But at the end, the song concludes that the scenario only exists in his imagination. So maybe the mating rituals our culture has created are just products of our collective imagination. But if so, love is an illusion that not only underpins the gothic romance but one that enriches our lives and inspires us with the hope of finding a true and lifelong bond with a loved one.

Six
The Predator Narrative

"All the better to eat you with."

In Charles Perrault's telling of the folktale, this is the response Red Riding Hood gets from the Big Bad Wolf after she comments on what big teeth he has. Perrault offers a moral to the story, warning young ladies to stay away from strange men who might eat them up, not in a literal but rather in a figurative way. But the tale as it has come through the ages in its various versions from a variety of cultures also touches on a primal fear: being hunted and eaten by a predator.

Again we return to the opening sequence of *2001: A Space Odyssey*. Both Clarke's novel and the film underscore the proto humans' defenselessness in the face of a predator that is more successfully evolved for survival than they, that will kill and eat them. In the novel, the cat preys on the tribe in their cave home at night, carrying off members at will. In the first chapter, Clarke describes the cat invading while other tribe members not only cannot help but cannot imagine doing so. Clarke describes the man apes huddled in fear: "In the caves, between spells of fitful dozing and fearful waiting were being born the nightmares of generations yet to be" (10). Then after the work of the monolith, when the cat enters the cave, they attack it as a tribe with clubs, and "the implacable hunter was now the victim and was trying desperately to escape" (21). The novel underscores a dual narrative in the horror film from the findings of evolutionary psychology: *Homo sapiens* as both hunter and the hunted.

In addition to becoming predators themselves in feeding on the tapirs, the proto humans have learned to fight other predators. And most significantly for our evolutionary adaptation, they have developed social behavior as a survival trait in uniting as a team against a more powerful enemy. Evolutionary psychologists propose that this fear of predators, a species against which we are defenseless as individuals, must be deeply ingrained in our genetic memory as, in Clarke's words, "nightmares of generations yet to be." But like *2001*'s man apes, we have evolved adaptive traits to defend ourselves with our highly developed brain, unique to the animal kingdom, which enables us to make tools and weapons, think creatively to solve problems and develop tribal loyalty. We have evolved into the hunter rather than the hunted, though in Africa and India predators still kill and eat hundreds of people each year. And one occasionally hears of such attacks in the United States.

Evolutionary scientists have debated whether humans evolved as prey or predator. C.K. Brain wrote a book with a title that establishes a frequently asked question, *Do We Owe Our Intelligence to a Predator Past,* and he suggests predator avoidance would have been a significant factor in the evolution of the brain, since those members of the species with the intelligence to avoid the predator would have passed on their genes. Donna Hart and Robert Sussman agree with this theory, noting that "predation may well have been one of the prime stimulations to that increase of brain and even to our need to stay in groups and be a social animal. *Not* getting killed is a powerful force to deal with each day."[1] A tribal organization would have been critical to species survival. So a primal traits critical approach suggests that the whisper from the experience of our Paleolithic and Neolithic ancestors who were hunted, killed and eaten by predators and who learned to fight against them for survival lingers and can bring pleasurable vicarious fear in the predator narrative of the horror film. While *Homo sapiens* may have been prey in our evolutionary past rather than hunters, the narrative of hunting is a later development that burns in the primal mind along with fear of the predator.

As in the vampire film, where it takes a tribe to kill a vampire, cooperation is central in stories from the predator narrative. Reg Morrison's description of tribalism reflects the common findings of evolutionary psychology: "The urge to belong to a tribe remains incomparably seductive and thoroughly immune to rational accounting. Not only does it bestow a satisfying sense of identity and tribal exclusivity, but it also lights a bonfire of belief and self-righteousness."[2] The premises of evolutionary psychology propose that the narrative of a tribal band cooperating to face a predator is deeply imbedded in the human psyche. Vampires and zombies are predators of a type. But the films *Predator* and *Alien* with their sequels and fusions (*Jaws, Anaconda* and werewolf movies) are rooted in the same narrative of predation portrayed in the tribal struggle with the great cat in Clarke's novel. With the exception of the *Predator* aliens, who are trophy hunters in much the same sense that has come to be the case for *Homo sapiens* since we became the dominant species, predators eat our flesh. Whispers from the hunting pack, evolutionary psychologists speculate, reverberate from our genetic heritage, and the narrative of the hunter is matched by the whispers of being hunted by predators and fighting back as a tribe. The predator and hunting narrative in film could hardly be more clearly established than in the 1987 John McTiernan–directed, testosterone-drenched *Predator* and its sequels and spinoffs.

"There's something out there waiting for us, and it ain't no man."

These lines from *Predator* reflect the primal fear of being stalked by a powerful predator. The film's narrative is rooted in a substrata of tribal and invasion themes: humans' invasion of another group's territory to hunt them down and kill them and then an alien Predator who hunts the humans. The opening sequence shows Dutch Schaefer (Arnold Schwarzenegger), the leader of an elite Special Forces unit, arriving by helicopter with a very phallic-looking cigar clenched in his mouth at full erection. In a meeting with his commanding officer, he is tasked to undertake a mission with an old friend, George Dillon (Carl Weathers), now a CIA agent and also smoking a cigar. They immediately have to establish male dominance with an arm-wrestling match, including more close-ups of biceps. The scene reflects the timeless male competition for determining an alpha and creating bonding. The interaction of Schaefer's five-man crew establishes them firmly as a male hunting group, tribal warriors. Blain, one of Schaefer's men (played by Jesse Ventura before his Minnesota gubernatorial days), adds to the testosterone atmosphere, offering chewing tobacco to his mates and assuring them that it will "make you a goddamn sexual predator, like me." From the evolutionary psychology perspective of human behavior, they are bonded as a male hunting pack.

They are assigned to rescue survivors of a helicopter crash who are held by a rebel group in South America. But then they become prey to an alien, the Predator, a trophy-hunter killing for sport. Like many aliens in science fiction, the Predator reflects an essentially human quality: our tradition of hunting and in more recent times hunting for trophies rather than food. It is a formidable enemy because of its camouflage that renders it nearly invisible and its assortment of weaponry. The men are at first vaguely aware that they are being stalked. Poncho, a Native American, fingers his spirit bag and says, "There's something out there waiting for us, and it ain't no man." As they are picked off, Blain says, "He's killing us one at a time," to which Dutch replies, "Like a hunter," which it truly is, a situation well-suited to excite pleasurable shivers from our primal past as prey being stalked. The film ends with a new level of machismo, a *mano-a-alien* battle when only Dutch is left.

Like other successful film franchises, *Predator* established a legendarium, with characters or character types and plot situations that appear through the series. In this first of the franchise, the Predator is a creature of honor, a pattern that would be followed in the sequels. When it has Dutch cornered, it takes off its helmet for individual combat, only to lose the battle to our species' cunning, an ending that offers vicarious satisfaction at the victory of our warrior over his enemy. As in so many films based in the predator narrative, the human uses the adaptive gift of intelligence to compensate for physical inferiority. This narrative from the horror film reflects H. Clarke Barrett's comment about human adaptability as hunter and hunted: "Until very recently, attacks by formidable alien beasts [non human but skilled predators] were a real and constant possibility in everyday life.... Selection to be aware of these creatures, of their thoughts, plans and intentions, as well as a strategic intelligence to take advantage of this awareness, would have been strong."[3] In other words, predation may have been a major factor in developing the human brain and intelligence.

The *Predator* sequels and spinoffs add to the legendarium on the nature of the Predators and further develop their physical and psychic makeup. Unlike many aliens in science fiction, they seem to have no desire to conquer Earth, only to hunt worthy opponents. *Predator 2* continues their portrayal as hunters when they stalk prey in New York, drawn to a fire fight in the opening scenes between drug gangs and the NYPD. The hero is tough cop Mike Harrignan (Danny Glover), the leader of a squad of detectives. When the Predator kills his men, he wants vengeance. The FBI is aware of the incidents from the first film and sends in a heavily armed team to dispatch the invader. Keyes (Gary Busey), the head agent, tells Harrigan that they are "other-world life forms, a fucking alien ... drawn by heat and conflict. He's on safari." When the FBI fails, Harrigan faces off with the Predator in a vast underground complex the aliens use as a staging area and defeats him, again with humanity's superior intelligence. The final scene reinforces the first film's portrayal of the Predators' honor and respect for a winning adversary when a group of them appears and spares Harrigan after his victory, even giving him a trophy for it: a weapon, of course. Our evolutionary adaptation gives us fear of these aliens as predators but our culture might add a bit of admiration for their honor.

Predators (2010), the third film, builds on the Predator legendarium as hunters, with a group of carefully chosen humans being abducted and dropped to an alien world where they will be stalked by the Predators. The film develops a new level of conflict with two different species of Predators who hunt each other while both hunt humans. This and other *Predator* films offer an interesting twist on the prey and predator narrative. W.S. Laughlin called hunting "the master behavior pattern of the human species" and considers it "a way of life, not merely a means of obtaining food."[4] The films make Predators quite like us in many ways, including their own Other narrative.

Predators is rooted in this similarity. *Homo Sapiens*' evolutionary development as hunters has deep roots in evolutionary history. In the third in the franchise, the alien predators prove to have the typically human trait of seeing some of their own kind as Other to be hunted. This narrative offers additional potential for dramatic conflict. But some of the reaction to that conflict comes from the whispers of our primal ancestors not only of fear of the predator but of the excitement of fighting against others of our own kind, as do the Predators. The amalgam of Predators and Aliens in future films only reinforces this kind of species and interspecies conflict and enacts the predator and prey narratives. And as Donna Hart and Robert Sussman describe the narrative, "Remnants of those predator-prey interactions still occur.... They occur psychologically every time we feel the primitive chill up our spines because one of our species has succumbed to a predator."[5]

In Space, No One Can Hear You Scream.

That was the promo tag line for director Ridley Scott's 1979 science fiction horror film *Alien*. It projects a future with intergalactic space travel to enact the predation narrative and establish a legendarium for sequels. The crew of the *Nostromo* (the ship's name an homage to the Joseph Conrad novel) respond to a distress signal and unwittingly take on a passenger, an insectile alien whose life cycle makes it a predator by necessity. It needs a living victim for the continuation of its species as well as food.

Kane, the crew member infected, is brought aboard against the orders of Ripley (Sigourney Weaver), the officer in charge, because of infection protocol. After Kane gives birth to the Alien offspring that bursts through his chest in one of the memorable scenes in the science fiction–horror genre, it hunts the crew through the spaceship. It is an environment a little like the haunted house ambience but set in space with an alien predator stalking instead of some supernatural being. As in so many horror films, the characters enact the "go and look" response to a strange noise, evoking horror in viewers who know they are doomed if they open that door.

John Carpenter introduced a twist on the "Don't open that door" scene in *Halloween*, when one of the characters goes through the house looking for whoever made a noise. He opens the door, with the audience expecting to see Michael Myers leap out with his knife, but he is not there. The boy turns away, relieved, and that's when the slasher burst out but from another place. This kind of scene has been endlessly imitated in B horror movies, and it is repeated in *Alien*. But the film adapts it to the predator narrative, with the setting on the ship as a hunting ground where the predator stalks its prey. Mathias Clasen suggests a universal evolved audience response to feel vicarious fear from such scenes: "the human fear system evolved to be hyper sensitive to cues of danger.... In other words, in terms of survival, it is much better to react fearfully toward an ambiguous cue that might indicate danger, such as a rustling in the leaves during a twilight stroll in the woods, than it is to disregard such a cue."[6]

Like other films adapting this narrative, the horror element of *Alien* is based on whispers from our evolutionary past of being stalked by a predator. But as is so often the case in the predator film narrative, humans win because of their most important evolutionary adaptation: their superior intelligence and use of tools. Ship's officer and survivor Ripley demonstrates the human evolutionary gift of intelligence and tool-making in her confrontation with the Alien queen. Bruce Kavin observes, "The *Alien* movies set the best of humanity against the worst the stars have to offer, and they show that we have to lose part of ourselves in the fight, because it is a serious one."[7]

Evolutionary psychologists believe that the original hunting pack was all male, an approach we have seen in the films discussed here. The *Alien* series provides another example of how culture has created a new kind of hero who is "the best of humanity": a strong woman. She is opposed by an Alien who has something in common with her, as is shown throughout the series: Both are female and react as mothers (as does Ripley in *Aliens*). The Alien hunts for the best of evolutionary reasons: to reproduce and pass along its genes, the same prime directive that drives so much human action.

The heartless corporation Weyland-Yutani is to blame for the deaths of the crew members. In the horror film, corporations and shadowy government agencies are often the villain of choice. From a primal traits perspective, loyalty to tribe instilled into us through evolution leads us to see the corporation that sacrifices members of our own species, our own tribe in effect, as evil and betrayers of tribal and species loyalty. In *Alien*, Weyland-Yutani directed the ship to the planet with a secret agenda: to capture an Alien and return with it. Ash, who turns out to be an android, programmed by the mega corporation to bring the alien home with the crew as expendable, describes it: "You still don't understand what you're dealing with..., a perfect organism. Its structural perfection is matched only by its hostility. I admire its purity, untroubled by conscience, by culture, remorse or delusions of morality." It is a splendidly evolved predator; and Ripley responds, "All I can think of is [the corporation] must've wanted the alien for their weapons division."

In the 1987 sequel *Aliens*, Ripley is persuaded to accompany a tough-as-nails Marine detachment to a planet that has been out of communication. The predictable happens when the newly arrived Marines and Ripley are hunted by the Alien predators in the same fashion as we saw in the original film: for food and to be used as incubators for the queen's eggs. The horror of the situation rises from seeing those we empathize with, being stalked through the colonists' structure as prey, as were the *Nostromo* crew members. We get another contest between two dominant females, Ripley and the Alien queen. Ripley finds a girl child, Newt, who somehow survived the colonists' extermination (all of them used to hatch eggs by the queen). Ripley becomes a surrogate mother to Newt.

We get another primal conflict in the confrontation of the two mothers fighting for a genetic future when Ripley, Newt and what's left of the mangled android Bishop manage get to the ship, without knowing that the queen has stowed away on the lander. When the queen threatens Newt, Ripley dons the cargo loader machine to do battle, saying, "Get away from her, you bitch" and eventually pushes the queen to a hatch, expelling her into outer space. As in the final scene of *Alien*, humanity uses its superbly adapted brain to create a weapon to defend against and defeat a more powerful adversary. Ripley responds to the primal drive of a mother protecting a child, a situation that should bring whispers of pleasure from our genetic heritage. Joseph Carroll places a mother protecting a child as a central evolutionary behavior: "Literary authors can nonetheless count on readers to feel the weight and value of maternal care. This is part of the common frame of reference, not for just any culture but for all cultures."[8]

Alien[3] (1992) and *Alien Resurrection* (1997) continue the conflict of dominant females, with the redoubtable Ripley facing off with Alien queens and even giving birth to a hybrid after she is infected. She throws herself into a furnace on the prison planet where she has landed after her escape in *Aliens* because she is infected. When the Alien bursts from her chest, she looks at it not with hatred but with something like a mother's tenderness for a child. Those who follow Dawkins' approach to evolution might point out that her self-sacrifice is for the survival of her own gene pool, like the bird that puts itself at risk to save others. But the scene is complicated by the instinctive response on Ripley's face of a mother to even a monstrous child. Just as Dracula was resurrected repeatedly, so it goes with Ripley in *Alien: Resurrection*.

The United Systems Military is determined to have an Alien to adapt as a weapon. The film is set 200 years after the events of *Alien*[3]. In an improbable scenario, the Weyland-Yutani corporation makes a clone of Ripley from her DNA kept on file with the Alien queen still inside her, eventually surgically removing it to breed more Aliens. The film is more of the same, with the Aliens escaping and stalking. But the confluence of powerful females continues when Ripley and Call (Winona Ryder), an android, manage to destroy the Alien queen and escape to Earth, both Other to humanity. In the last scene, when they are near to landing on Earth, Cal asks what they will do now. Ripley answers, "I'm a stranger there myself." Both are alienated outsiders in the postmodern tradition, and they are successful women warriors.

Evolutionary psychologists emphasize what seems obvious even to casual observation: Humanity is an intensely social species. So we enjoy stories that focus on bonding. Tiger writes:

> Bonding is a process the outcome of which involves specific individuals recognizing other individuals as directly and distinctly relevant to themselves. Thus, was the male-male bond as important for hunting purposes as the male-female bond was for reproductive purposes, and this is the basis of the division of labor by sex. In other words, there would be a definite genetic advantage to those males who insisted on hunting in all-male groups, and a disadvantage to those who hunted with females in the group.[9]

Tiger's assessment seems strikingly sexist. But in fairness, he describes human behavior from eons ago, not as it is today. As the *Alien* films demonstrate, however, culture has changed gender roles. Male buddy stories and bromances have been standard fare in literature and film from the beginning, with Gilgamesh and Enkidu in *Gigamesh*, Achilles and Patroclus in *The Iliad*, then Sherlock Holmes and Watson, the Lone Ranger and Tonto and Batman and Robin continuing the ancient tradition. Clearly, this narrative whispers pleasure from the adaptive behavior of our ancestors; back then, those who relied on each other were more likely to survive than those who did not. Only in the twentieth century has that tradition of bonding as exclusively for males in literature and film been broken with women buddies in the movies *Thelma and Louise* (1991), *9 to 5* (1980), *Beaches* (1988), *Steel Magnolias* (1989) and of course *Wonder Woman* (2017) and her fellow woman warriors. The popularity of these landmark films that dramatize female bonding is yet another demonstration of the power of culture in reshaping primal narratives while maintaining their core. Robert Boyd points out something about human nature but connects it to evolutionary imperatives: "People have innate peer social motivations, and these feelings are elicited by roles of common group membership,"[10] be it male or female. Films like the ones in the *Alien* series specifically demonstrate the culturally evolved role of the woman warrior and female bonding in battling a predator.

If the *Predator* and *Alien* films did well at the box office, why not have a marriage of true monsters? The idea worked for Universal in the 1930s and '40s. So *AVP: Alien vs. Predator* (2004) established yet a third franchise from the originals, expanding on the legendarium underpinning the two. In the first, we get an amalgam of Erich von Däniken and Mayan myth that fuses the *Predator* and *Alien* franchises.

The film gives us another intrepid heroine, Alexa (Sanaa Lathan), an environmental engineer persuaded by a wealthy industrialist to join an expedition to investigate an intense heat source under an island in Antarctica. They discover a tunnel into the depths of the ice where they find a complex built by the Predators where they breed Aliens to use for their hunts as part of an initiation ritual. But it becomes a place where the expedition is hunted by the two forms of predator, one that hunts for sport and the other for species survival. In what seems to be a Mayan pyramid, they accidentally awaken an Alien queen that starts laying eggs to produce offspring, with members of the expedition as incubators. The horror of the film begins with the escape of Aliens, leading to battles with Predators while human are stalked by both species.

The film rests firmly on the predation narrative. The expedition members wander through labyrinthine passages, rather like the settings of the *Alien* films. It continues the portrayal of the Predators as hunters with their own sense of honor. We see one of them marking his helmet with the acid from an Alien kill. Another marks Alex after she dispatches one and causes the Alien queen to be cast into the freezing depths: a nod to the initiation ritual from Faulkner's story "The Bear," a literary allusion to another story of a successful hunter. As in *Predator* and *Predator 2*, the Predators admire courage and a worthy adversary; so after the site has been destroyed and all the aliens killed, they leave Alex behind, giving her one of their spear weapons, another case of an appropriate gift from a Predator, as in *Predator 2*. It has been good hunting for the Predators, to which our primal whispers might relate. While they inspire vicarious horror as hunters of human, they also elicit some sympathy for their code of honor.

The franchise has continued with *AVPR: Alien vs Predator—Requiem* (2007), with the two aliens species meeting for conflict in a small American town. *Prometheus* (2012) offers a prequel view explaining the origins of humanity and the original Aliens. *Alien: Covenant*, a sort of sequel to the *Prometheus* prequel, appeared in 2017. Clearly, the two franchises have brought the sublime shiver of vicarious horror very successfully through stirring ancestral memories of hunting and being hunted by beings with superior evolutionary strength. Hans Kruuk observes that predation "is likely to have had signal influence in the evolution of our behavior and our reactions to predators."[11] The *Alien* and *Predator* franchises success with a popular audience lies in their exploitation of our instinctual horror at being hunted. But they also celebrate humanity's gift, a powerful intelligence and capacity for group action.

"I see a bad moon rising": Werewolves as Tragic Victims and Predators

Credence Clearwater Revival and songwriter John Fogerty catch the spirit of the werewolf film in their song "Bad Moon Rising," the theme music of *An American Werewolf in London*. Cinematic werewolves are predators, of course. Many films adapt a similar narrative to inspire horror, such as the vampire and zombie movies: fear of being stalked by a predator and of loss of self and transformation into Other. So werewolf films give us characters like those that some vampire films portray: one who embodies the pathos of a man (or woman) who is pure at heart but becomes a wolf against his or her will when the full moon is bright. This version of the predator narrative differs from that of the zombie and vampire films in that zombies may be unfortunate enough to be changed but are unrepentantly evil in their conditions; and while some cinematic vampires may be reluctant, they are always vampires. Unlike vampires and zombies, werewolves in their wolf form are not of our species, are flesh-eating predators but are otherwise still Us after the moon sets. Like vampires and zombies, their bite can assimilate and change the nature of the victim.

The werewolf predator narrative in film may owe homage to Robert Louis Stevenson's 1886 novella *The Strange Case of Dr. Jekyll and Mr. Hyde*. Like the werewolf, Jekyll has a dual nature, a sort of shape shifter. But unlike them, his transformation into a monster comes from his own free will, a result of his experiments; and when he has made the choice too often, Jekyll cannot change his state. The werewolf also has a dual nature, but in most instances, it is created against the person's will. Both the werewolf and Jekyll-Hyde are a mixture of Us and Other.

Montague Summers describes the werewolf:

> A werewolf is a human being, man, woman, or child (more often the first), who either voluntarily or involuntarily changes or is metamorphosed into the apparent shape of a wolf, and who is then possessed of all the characteristics, the foul appetites, ferocity, cunning, the brute strength and swiftness of that animal. In by far the greater majority of instances, the werewolf to himself as well as to those who behold him seems completely to have assumed the furry lupine form.[12]

Summers includes lurid tales of werewolf attacks through history and describes two types: the lycanthrope, who is an innocent victim, and the true werewolf, a devotee of Satan. The classification rather neatly describes the two forms of this predator in film.

The werewolf as predator should strike chords in the primal whispers of our ancestors who were hunted by wolves. A truly terrifying passage in Willa Cather's novel *My Antonia* (1918) offers a pattern for the age-old fear of this predator: Pavel, who has emigrated from Russia, tells of an incident he had experienced there. A pack of wolves follows a group of people leaving a wedding in horse-drawn sleighs. Pavel and his friend have the bride and groom in their sleigh. Terrified, they throw bride and groom off to lighten the load and stop the wolves' pursuit. The view of the wolf has softened in recent years from its early image. Now zoologists and environmentalists consider them to be a useful part of the food chain, though those who raise sheep might demure from this view. But Cather's story reflects an ancient fear of a dangerous predator that stalked our ancestors. Whispers of that fear have created the pleasant horror of the werewolf movie. Alistair Graham observes that stories of humans being eaten by a predator triggers ancient memories: "One of civilization's imperative taboos is against cannibalism: little else arouses such fear and loathing. And we do not distinguish, emotionally, between a human eating a human and an animal eating a human."[13]

Summers and other scholars find evidence of the werewolf legend far back in history, with tales of man beasts or shape shifters in Greek, Roman and Indian myth. The beast may change by culture, with weretigers in India, for instance. Chantal Bourgault du Courdray traces the history,[14] noting that the legend heated up during the witch craze beginning in the fifteenth century. The werewolf enters fiction in the nineteenth century in thrillers like George W.M. Reynolds' *Wagner the Were-Wolf* (1809) and Charles Maturin's *The Albigenses* (1824) as well as penny dreadfuls, all enlarging the folklore base of the narrative. In the U.S., Guy Endore's novel *The Werewolf of Paris* was a 1933 bestseller in. Du Courdray observes that around two-thirds of films featuring werewolves "have relied on the narrative structure established in the 1930s and 1940s in which a respectable, white, heterosexual man is accidentally afflicted with lycanthropy, suffering trauma as a result."[15]

"Even a man who is pure in heart...": *WereWolf of London, The Wolf Man, An American Werewolf in London, An American Werewolf in Paris, The Howling* and *Wolfen*

The popularity of Guy Endore's novel *The Werewolf of Paris* may have inspired the 1935 film *WereWolf of London,* the first werewolf movie, with Henry Hull starring as London botanist Wilfred Glendon. While in Tibet searching for the mariphasa plant, he is bitten by a werewolf. Back in London, he is warned by Dr. Yogami (played by Warner Oland, taking a break from the Charlie Chan series) that he could become a werewolf and that the flower of the mariphasa plant could allow him to avoid the metamorphosis. Glendon later finds that Yogami has been stealing them because he too is a werewolf. Chaos ensues when he is unable to resist the transformation and kills repeatedly, finally shot and killed at the end after dispatching Yogami. Much of the horror of the film lies in a predator stalking his human prey. But it also focuses on the powerful fear of assimilation, as Glendon's condition results from the werewolf's bite. It transforms him from Us to a predator who kills his own kind. In films, the werewolf in wolf form becomes a sort of cannibal, one who eats other humans, even though in most cases such actions are against the will of the person transformed.

The Fredric March *Dr. Jekyll and Mr. Hyde* had been released in 1931, and the similarity of plots between it and *WereWolf of London*, along with the release date being in the depth of the Depression, may have cut into the film's box office take. By 1941, the date of *The Wolf Man*'s release, the writings of Sigmund Freud were much read and discussed in the intellectual community. Freud's tripartite division of the psyche into id, ego and superego offers one critical perspective for analysis of the werewolf predator narrative. The id (the pleasure-seeking and irrational element), the superego (which incorporates the rules and morality of society) and the ego (the mediator between the two) neatly sum up Larry Talbot's condition in *The Wolf Man*, as well as many werewolf characters to follow. A Freudian interpretation would note that Talbot's transformation suggests the release of the id, and his guilt when he discovers his condition is the superego. Freud's theories have been discredited, but they are a useful plot frame for writers and no doubt many intentionally adapted them. But something deeper underlies the plot, echoing from primal narratives.

A late addition to the Universal Horrors, the film is set in a Hollywood version of Wales where some people speak with a British accent and some with an American one, as does Larry Talbot (Lon Chaney, Jr.). He returns home after being estranged from his wealthy father Sir John Talbot. In an opening scene, Sir John tells Larry, "Even a man who is pure in heart and says his prayers by night, may become a wolf when the wolfbane blooms and the autumn moon is bright," a memorable line in film history that comes not from folklore but the imagination of screenwriter Curt Siodmak. The lines are repeated three more times as foreshadowing, lastly by the old Gypsy woman, the most often remembered repetition.

Near a gypsy encampment, Talbot fights and kills a werewolf using his cane with a silver wolf's head handle.[16] But he is bitten and, of course, cursed, becoming Other, assimilated and doomed to be a predator of his own kind. The findings of evolutionary psychology regarding gene kinship would explain why we react with horror from the primal mind at one of Us being alienated from his species as well as to our horror of being hunted by such a predator.

Larry Talbot is a version of Summers' lycanthrope category, an innocent who is assimilated against his will. He is now marked with a pentagram on his hand and is able to see the sign on his next victim. He is hunted by a team, another tribal warrior group, and his own father eventually slays Talbot while his son in his werewolf form. Another character, Frank Andrews, sets the tone for describing Summers' lycanthrope character and the werewolf film in general when he says of Talbot, "There's something very tragic about that man." And so there is from the perspective of whispers from the adaptive experiences of the human race, inspiring our empathy for one who has lost connection to his own genetic kind against his will as well as our horror of being stalked by a man-eating predator. Larry Talbot was exhumed four times

The Wolf Man: The Wolf Man (Lon Chaney, Jr.) attacks the grave digger (Forrest Harvey).

by Universal for *Frankenstein Meets the Wolf Man* (1943), *House of Frankenstein* (1944), *House of Dracula* (1945) and *Abbott and Costello Meet Frankenstein* (1948), always the reluctant Other who has lost connection to his own kind. The 2010 adaptation, *The Wolfman,* gives a different spin with a different father-and-son relationship, a sort of reversal of the timeless story of a man finding his father.

An American Werewolf in London (1981) and *An American Werewolf in Paris* (1997) have similar storylines and different settings and actors but some plot connections, since the second alludes to the first. Both are examples of Summers' lycanthrope character, and both model the central narrative of one of Us becoming an unwilling predator. Their writers channel the horror narrative of *The Wolf Man*, a character's loss of tribal identity and kin group to become Other and a predator on his own kind. The two films mix horror with a kind of offbeat humor and love stories.

In the first film, two young Americans, David Kessler and Jack Goodman (David Naughton and Griffith Dunne), are on a walking tour of the moors in Northern England where a werewolf attacks them, leading to Jack's death and David's infection. After David is taken to a London hospital, his nurse Alex (Anne-Marie Dunne) falls in love with him and takes him to her apartment to be her lover. Jack's reanimated spirit returns at odd intervals like Marley's Ghost to insist that Jack, who doesn't believe in lycanthropy or ghosts, must kill himself to prevent harm to others. Jack is the conventional disbeliever who has to be convinced of the supernatural. But he changes, killing several people; and when he finally accepts his situation, he feels remorse from the human side of the dual nature. Like many of his kind in film, he is the tragic outcast, transformed against his will to Other.

An American Werewolf in Paris follows a similar plotline, with the exception that the hero's love interest, Serafine (Julie Delpy), is a werewolf, one of the few female lycanthropes in film and the daughter of Jack and Alex from the original. The plot is a bit more complicated than that of *An American Werewolf in London*. While Andy McDermott (Tom Everett Scott) and his two friends are in Paris for a ramble, he meets and is obsessed with Serafine. Eventually, the three boys visit the Club de la Lune, where a society of werewolves attracts tourists in order to attack for their prandial pleasure. These werewolves have a serum that allows them to change at will, without waiting for the full moon. Andy is bitten and changed. As in *American Werewolf in London*, we get a love relationship in which the girl tries to save her man, which she eventually does after pitched battles with the Club de la Lune werewolf society.

The young lovers find a way to rid themselves of lycanthropy in a tacked-on happy ending. From a primal traits perspective, they have returned to their own kin group and fulfill the mating narrative as well. Also, the werewolf society and their attack whisper the horror of being pursued by the wolf pack: predators, as described in *My Antonia*. And both *American Werewolf* films reflect the pathos of the lycanthrope, the innocent victim transformed to Other and desperate to remain "Us." The film contrasts the character with the evil werewolf such as the Club de le Lune pack in *American Werewolf in Paris*. Du Courdray equates the metamorphosis of the young heroes in these two films to "a form of adult initiation and bravado," coded as excessive masculinity.[17] His description sums up the story of the boys on vacation. While Du Courdray's description is accurate enough regarding the young men in the films, these and other werewolf films inspire horror not just from their cultural implications but fear of the predator and alienation from the human kin group.

The heroine of *The Howling* (1981) is another innocent victim in the werewolf film, and another female lycanthrope. TV reporter Karen White goes to a resort called The Colony for a rest. It turns out to be home to a pack of werewolves, and not of the sort to feel guilty about their condition. Karen herself is bitten. She escapes with the help of Chris, a friend who visits with a pistol and silver bullets, and they burn the place. To prove that werewolves exist, Karen allows herself to change on-camera during her newscast, and is killed by Chris with a silver bullet.

Joe Dante directed *The Howling,* and it has become a sort of cult classic of the horror film, for good reason from an evolutionary psychology perspective. Dante's visual effects in creating the werewolves make them true monsters and convincing predators. The film's dark ambience contributes to the fear of being stalked and changed. These are evil werewolves, with only Karen feeling guilt about her condition. So the predator narrative in the film mixes satisfaction at the slaying of the evil werewolves as predators and Other with empathy for the pathos of Karen's condition brought through no fault of her own.

Some filmic werewolves, such as the club members in *American Werewolf in Paris* and the Colony residents in *The Howling,* feel no guilt for their state. It seems significant that both the Colony and the Club de le Lune are cults, Others hidden within our midst. Such is also the case in *Wolfen,* released in 1981, the same year as *The Howling* and *An American Werewolf in London,* apparently the year of the werewolf in film. One of the most interesting werewolf movies, *Wolfen* adapts the hunter and predator narratives as well as tribalism and the hidden Other in its horror elements. It opens with a ceremonial groundbreaking for an urban development in a ruined area of New York, initiated by developer Christian Van der Veer. He, his wife and his bodyguard are torn apart after a stop at Battery Park on the way home. Dewey Wilson (Albert Finney), a retired police captain, is called into the investigation and is assisted by police psychologist Rebecca Neff (Diane Venora). After the deaths of homeless people in the ruins of the city, Wilson and Neff determine that Van der Veer and others were stalked and killed by werewolves, shapechangers from the Mohawk American Indian tribe. They are workers on the "high iron" of bridges because they do not fear heights and were instrumental in building the Twin Towers.

After Dewey suspects and finally confirms that the killings are done by Native Americans, he interrogates Eddie Holt, an Indian activist, who gives him apocryphal answers about the power of the spirit to change the body. But the primary revelation comes after Wilson's friend Whittington is killed and a shattered Dewey goes to the Wigwam, an American Indian bar. Holt and an elderly Indian lecture him: "For 20,000 years, Wilson ... the skins and the wolves, great hunting nations, lived together, nature in balance. Then the slaughter came. The smartest ones, they went underground, into the new wilderness, your cities, into the great slum area, the graveyard of your fucking species." The slums, he says, are their hunting ground. Van der Veer and his development threatened their territory, where they clean up what they call "the human garbage," homeless people.

The skin walkers are simply a different species, a predator within human society. They are more highly—or at least differently—evolved, with acute senses of smell, touch and sight. They are more than a tribe but "other nations" as Dewey learns: Others and predators. Dewey muses, "Family, hunting territory.... They kill to protect their hunting ground." Dewey and Rebecca, after their survival, are happy to blame terrorists for Van der Veer's death and leave the shape changers free to roam and prey. We are left with mixed feelings in our post–Aquarian culture where we have discovered guilt for the treatment of Native Americans and have accepted that white civilization took their territory and destroyed the natural world in which the skin walkers of the film had lived for thousands of years. Van der Veer's development symbolizes the damage we have done. So we are left conflicted, with some sympathy for the skin walkers even though they are Other and killers, another example of the impact of culture on primal narratives. They are content with their condition as predators, which is a natural state to them, unlike werewolf characters who are victims.

Wolfen is a model for the predator and hunting narratives in the horror film with its almost Burkean *mise en scène*, an urban sublime. Ruins have always been the setting of choice since the beginning of the gothic, with dilapidated castles and abbeys as settings in early gothic fiction and in present-day horror with houses that look rather like them. Here we have urban ruins with piles of rubble, where buildings have been cleared for redevelopment. And the focal point is a gutted church, something close to the ruined abbey from the early gothic novels. The film's subjective camera from the werewolf perspective and thermal imagery make a powerful setting for the predators' hunts.

Cat People (1942) is not a werewolf film, but it is one of the best of the shape-changer genre and another with a woman as such a character. We usually identify a director or perhaps actors as being the source of a film's artistic success. Producers are the bean counters for a film project, but Val Lewton is an exception. Joel Siegel writes: "It is generally nonsensical to speak of producers as creators when in all but a few cases, they were the enemies of creation. Lewton was one of the exceptions who though credited only as a producer was unarguably the artistic creator and prime mover of his films."[18] He was hired by RKO to emulate the success of Universal's horror film money machine, and management dictated outrageous titles to Lewton without supplying scripts and told him to make a film that matched them. The first title was dreamed up by a studio executive to be a film about a werecat that they wanted called *Cat People*, a title the studio hoped would connect potential viewers' minds with the successful *The Wolf Man* released the year before. Lewton's biographers record his frustration but also his success in filling in the concept to guide gifted writer DeWitt Bodeen and director Jacques Tourneur in making a film classic of *Cat People*.

The film focuses on Irena (Simone Simon), a Serbian immigrant who believes that she is part of a cursed lineage from her homeland: women who turn into great cats if they are sexually aroused. When she falls in love with Oliver Reed (Kent Smith) and marries him, she keeps delaying intimacy, causing Oliver in frustration to become closer with a workplace colleague, Alice (Jane Randolph). Irena's jealousy turns her into her inner predator, leading her to stalk Alice. Then when Dr. Judd (Tom Conway), the psychiatrist Oliver has insisted she see, makes sexual advances, she turns and rends him.

The artistry in the film lies in its use of light and shadow and symbolic images with Freudian overtones. The multi-level plot is on the surface a moody and effective thriller. On another level, the film develops a theme of sexual repression through Freudian imagery. The parallels are so obvious that Lewton and Bodeen must have been well acquainted with Freud's writings. Irena's trips to the zoo to contemplate the black leopard suggest her own caged sexuality. We see Freudian sexual images of keys, keyholes and knives in her dreams. In their apartment, she has a statue of King John of Serbia holding a phallic-looking sword over his head piercing a huge cat and we see a picture Irena draws of the black leopard pierced by a similarly phallic-looking knife. The last scene in which she goes to a nearby zoo to release a leopard suggests the final dissolution of her mind after her sexual self was released in the episode with Dr. Judd.

Cat People's imagery and cinematography substitute suggestion for actual violence and combine to illustrate Irena's split personality and psychic destruction. But on yet another level, the film's appeal is similar to the visceral and pleasurable fear of the predator with Irena in cat form stalking Alice, her rival. Lewton's genius was to create horror without actually showing the monster or bloodshed. In a memorable scene, we see Alice in the pool of the building where she lives with Irena's stalking her. We see only shadows on the darkened wall and low rumblings from Irena in cat form as Alice screams for help. Much of the understated horror of the film comes from Alice being hunted, scenes well adapted to trigger primal response. In another scene, Alice walks alone on a dark street, hearing noises and fearful. Then as she looks desperately over her shoulder, we hear a loud noise, and we expect Irena to pounce. But the sound comes from a bus pulling to a stop. This kind of scene has been adapted in other forms and called a "bus" in many horror films. *Final Destination* (2000), for instance, has multiple homages to Lewton. One of the characters is named Valarie Lewton. We get an ironic twist on a bus scene when a character narrowly misses being hit by a car, and just as we think he is saved, he is smashed by a bus. The bus and pool scenes in *Cat People* demonstrate what Mathias Clasen calls an evolutionary response exploited by many a horror film: "The most basic, universally, genetically hardwired fears are the fears of sudden, loud noises and of looming objects."[19]

Most viewers at the time probably did not recognize the sophisticated pattern of imagery in *Cat People*, but it did good box office and may have saved RKO from bankruptcy. The film has charmed succeeding generations of viewers and critics to become a classic, not just of the horror genre but as an enduring work of film art. Beneath the surface monster movie plot, the Freudian overtones, the sophisticated pattern of imagery and moody cinematography lies the narrative of the predator. Irena's repressed sexuality reflects also her dual nature in the werewolf tradition, both predator and one of Us. She longs to suppress her predator nature and be a wife to Oliver but cannot do so. Even a movie audience unable to understand the patterns of symbolism and allusion gets the sublime shiver from seeing a predator preying on our own genetic family. While Lewton and his film crew may have intentionally tapped into Freud as a plot frame, the film's horror comes from a visceral response to Irena's condition and great scenes enacting Alice being stalked by an unseen predator.

Forty years later, director Paul Schrader's *Cat People* remake featured an updated Irena (Nastassja Kinski) and Oliver (John Heard). This version is a revisioning with similar characters but lacks the visual power and pathos of the original. And the theme shifts from the Lewton film's portrayal of a woman's sexual conflict to outright misogyny when Irena is "tamed" by Oliver, and we see her in her predator form caged at a zoo and being petted by her lover.

Fins and Teeth: *Jaws, Deep Blue Sea* and *Open Water*

In Stephen Crane's short story "The Open Boat," the tiny dinghy with the five men stranded at sea after their ship sinks is a metaphor for his view of the human condition from the perspective of American naturalism: a struggle to survive in nature that is indifferent or even hostile. They are buffeted by wind and wave, and when they get close to a shore, they know that the heavy surf will swamp their boat if they try to land. In the midst of their agonies, a shark swims by to check them out. "But the thing did not then leave the vicinity of the boat. Ahead or astern ... fled the long sparkling streak and then was to be heard the *whirr* of the dark fin. The speed and the power of the thing was greatly to be admired. It cut the water like a gigantic and keen projectile."[20] Crane's story reflects what would be the findings of evolutionary psychology: that humanity is one more species in nature and the shark would be as happy to eat the men as it would a tuna.

Steven Spielberg adapted Peter Benchley's 1971 novel for the film *Jaws* (1975), a tale of men at sea in a battle against a giant shark, one of nature's most feared predators. *Jaws* has created a meme of sorts, as dozens of shark movies have spawned from it. *Jaws, Deep Blue Sea* and *Open Water* are three of the more interesting in this narrative from a primal traits perspective. All three seem rooted in the theme of literary works. *Jaws*, for instance has frequent nods to Herman Melville's classic novel *Moby Dick*.

The shark in *Jaws* is well-suited to arouse the ancient fear of being eaten by predators. Spielberg intensifies this horror element of the film through an understated approach. We don't actually see the shark in great detail until the final section and the fight between it and the men on the *Orca*, an approach that enhances the power of the film and builds suspense. In a comparison of surprise and suspense, Alfred Hitchcock observes that when a man puts a bomb under a table and soon it explodes, we experience surprise. But if we see a man put a bomb under a table and are told that it will explode in 15 minutes, we feel suspense because the characters don't realize their danger.[21]

Spielberg builds suspense in this manner in *Jaws* by letting us know that a predator, a great white shark, as we soon learn, is snacking on swimmers and boaters in the waters outside the fictional New England resort community of Amity Island. The tension builds with a sort of prolonged foreplay as the audience and eventually the city fathers of Amity gradually accept the presence of a great white without seeing it. Police Chief Martin Brody (Roy Scheider) understands the threat and knows that the beach should be closed to tourists. But business is business, as we get the standard film conflict of profit trumping human safety: a conflict that reflects our inborn response to threats against community and tribal protection.

All this boils down to a culmination of the suspense when Brody, oceanographer Matt Hooper (Richard Dreyfuss) and Ahab-like Quint (Robert Shaw) sail out in the latter's fishing boat *Orca* to do battle. The three have their conflicts in the film, especially a class conflict between Quint and Hooper. The film mercifully omits Brody's wife's ruminations in the novel on her regrets at marrying for love and losing her place in society's upper echelons as well as her brief assignation with Hooper, which Brody suspects. Character conflicts in the film disappear when Brodie confronts the shark while throwing chum overboard. It rises immediately in front of him, and he says in a stunned voice says, "You're gonna need a bigger boat."

Both film and novel describe the shark as a force of nature, indifferent to humanity as is the one that swims by to check out the boat in Crane's story, and a magnificent predator. In the film, Hooper describes him to the mayor: "What we are dealing with here is a perfect engine, an eating machine. It's really a miracle of evolution. All this machine does is swim and eat and make little sharks. And that's all." Then after the hunt has begun, in a rambling five-minute soliloquy, Quint describes in terrifying detail his experience in the water after the U.S.S. *Indianapolis* was torpedoed by a Japanese submarine on the way to Leyte after delivering to Tinian the atomic bomb that destroyed

Jaws: Sheriff Brody (Roy Scheider) has seen the shark and tells his boat mates they're "gonna need a bigger boat."

Hiroshima. He describes the sharks' attacks on survivors: "Sometimes that shark, he looks right into you, right into your eyes. You know a thing about a shark? He's got lifeless eyes, black eyes like a doll's eyes. When he comes at you, he doesn't seem to be living, until he bites you. You hear that terrible high-pitched screaming. The ocean turns red." The monologue and the ensuing battle reflect the horror of being at the mercy of the predator with insufficient tools to fight it, as were Moon Walker and his band when stalked by the great cat.

The three men enact the timeless story of a primeval group of warriors hunting a highly evolved predator and being hunted by it. They are isolated in the ocean, a metaphor for savage nature. Film and novel portray a microcosm for one of humanity's most enduring narratives with a plot well designed to stir whispers of vicarious horror from our genetic heritage. The predator is a monster of its type and seems to be almost intelligent in hunting the *Orca*, a malignant force like Melville's white whale.

Our hunters win despite losses in both novel and film versions of *Jaws*. It is Brody, an everyman hero and protector of his community, who defeats the predator using intelligence, our chief survival trait, and tools: a vintage World War II M-1 rifle and a scuba air tank, linear descendants of Moon Walker's bone as weapon. In an interview, Peter Benchley gave an explanation for the film's power that seems taken from the findings of evolutionary psychology: "We do not just fear our predators, we are transfixed by them. We are prone to weave stories and fables and chat endlessly about them. Fascination breeds preparedness and preparedness survival."[22] Like most financially successful films, *Jaws* inspired a franchise, with three sequels: *Jaws 2* (1978), *Jaws 3-D* (1983) and *Jaws: The Revenge* (1987).

Deep Blue Sea (1999) is another version of the shark as predator narrative. As *Jaws* seems indebted to *Moby Dick*, *Deep Blue Sea* references Mary Shelley's gothic novel *Frankenstein*, the original story of a man who takes science too far in altering nature and a narrative often revisited in film and fiction. *Deep Blue Sea* is set in an underwater laboratory, Aquatica, where researchers experiment on sharks for medical breakthroughs. The vast structure offers yet another setting rather like the conventional haunted house–castle in the gothic tradition where humans are stalked and preyed on by the supernatural or in the various settings of the *Alien* and *Predator* films.

Here the predators are not quite natural, but neither are they supernatural. Dr. Susan McAlester (Saffron Burrows), the Frankenstein figure, has altered the subject sharks' brains to create a serum that would cure Alzheimer's, breaking scientific protocol in the process. She has, like Mary Shelley's character, created monsters: four mako sharks, giving enhanced strength and intelligence to already powerful predators. Another scientist, Dr. Whitlock, establishes sharks' evolutionary credibility as a predator in foreshadowing the film's conclusion: "Sharks are one of the oldest creatures on the planet from a time when the world was just flesh and teeth."

When asked what she has done to the sharks, McAlester responds, "Their brains weren't large enough for sufficient amounts of the protein. So we violated the Harvard Compact ... to increase their brain mass.... As a side effect, the sharks got smarter." And these enhanced predators find a way to seek prey from the only source available: the humans in Aquatica as they plot to escape. When Carter (Thomas Jane), the "shark wrangler" who tags the fish, finds out what McAlester has done, he says: "You've taken God's oldest killing machine and given it a will and a desire. What you've done is knocked us to the bottom of the goddamn food chain." They are predators that are not only far more powerful than humans but have been engineered to share our survival trait, intelligence, while they retain the hunger that evolution has given them. "They've been herding us," Carter says when a storm destroys the upper platform and traps everyone below, "to get us where they want us: to flood the facilities.... That's what an 800-pound mako thinks about: freedom, about the deep blue sea."

Mary Shelley may have tuned into an evolutionary adaptation with her Frankenstein character. We might expect that those who resisted engaging in hazardous experiments with unknown consequences might be more likely to survive than those who tried them and failed, bringing an instinctual response to the narrative of the intellectual overreacher. So in this fictional situation, we might see the folly of McAlester creating enhanced predators that consume her and all of the other scientists as a bit of poetic justice. As in *2001: A Space Odyssey*, however, where we see Moonwalker's brain envision a solution to starvation and defense, human intelligence, our most important survival tool, overcomes the final shark. Carter and Preacher, the cook, manage to destroy it before it can breach the fences surrounding the compound and reach the deep blue with a harpoon and explosive, tools in the tradition of Moonwalker's animal bone. Evolutionary psychology suggests a positive primal response to the victory of our warriors. The scientists, intellectual overreachers, on the other hand, perish.

If *Jaws* references *Moby Dick* and *Deep Blue Sea* nods to *Frankenstein*, *Open Water* (2003) channels "The Open Boat," though the two characters in the film are adrift without even a dinghy like the one in Crane's story. But this young couple are in the same situation: stranded beyond help and at the whim of nature. Daniel (Daniel Travis) and Susan (Blanchard Ryan) leave their overly busy lives for a vacation in the Caribbean. They book a tour to go diving, and are somehow left behind by the tourist boat. So like the five men in Crane's story, they are left in hostile nature, floating in their wetsuits and air tanks with sharks closing in and poisonous jellyfish around them. Instead of trying to attract the attention of people on an island as do the men in Crane's story, in this version of the predator narrative, the couple futilely wave at passing boats that don't see them. The horror of the film (supposedly based on a true story) comes from our inherited fear of our helplessness in facing predators without tools of defense that our evolutionary adaptation has enabled us to develop. Unlike the narrative in *Jaws* and *Deep Blue Sea*, they have no weapons with which to fight sharks. The film's concept was adapted to two more with *Open Water* films with similar plots of abandonment at sea at the mercy of nature.

The success of *Jaws* in adapting a narrative that triggers vicarious fear with whispers from our primal ancestors spawned a veritable industry of shark films. Dozens of made-for-DVD and -TV movies, with catchy titles such as *Sharktapus*, *Megashark versus Giant Octopus*, *Trailer Park Shark* and the campy *Sharknado* with its three sequels, have graced TV screens and sold DVDs. The shark meme has even been adapted in children's animated films as in *Finding Nemo* (2003) and *Shark Tale* (2004) with vegetarian sharks as well as the fins and teeth monsters.

Man Eaters in the Horror Film: *The Ghost and the Darkness* and *Anaconda*

The Maroon 5 song "Just like Animals" describes the sexual hunt rather than flesh eating predators, though psychologists might find a good many parallels. Evolutionary psychologists posit that along with gathering, preying on animals was an integral element in the survival of our primal ancestors, making us a species of omnivores. But humans were also hunted by fierce carnivores, and evolutionary psychology holds that whispers of their adaptation to these predators must remain in our genetic memory from the time, as one of the characters in *Deep Blue* says, "when the world was just flesh and teeth." So in addition to shark movies, we see dozens of other films that trigger the whisper of being hunted and eaten by a predator.

The Ghost and the Darkness (1996) is an especially good example of a truly frightening horror film rooted in the predator narrative: being hunted by man-eating lions. These mighty animals have come to be seen differently since they are endangered as a species and most humans are not prey for them. Perhaps we can afford a sentimental and romantic view of large predators once we are not likely to be hunted by them, as we see them sympathetically portrayed in nature documentaries on television or Alex the lion in the animated film *Madagascar* (2005). But as Donna Hart and Robert Sussman observe, "We had millions of years during which we were vulnerable lip-smacking delicacies. We've had only a flick of an eye during which we have exerted some dominion over the predators."[23] Still, in many parts of the world, predators are a constant danger, especially tigers in India and crocodiles in both India and Africa.

The Ghost and the Darkness is set in the late nineteenth century with British Lieutenant Colonel John Patterson (Val Kilmer), an engineer, leaving his pregnant wife in London to build a railroad bridge in Kenya, a project that is underwritten by British financier Sir Robert Beaumont. Director Stephen Hopkins and screenwriter William Goldman give an unabashed postcolonial spin to the story when Beaumont tells Patterson, "We're in a race, colonel, and the prize is nothing less than the continent of Africa." They are, he says, "building the railroad for the glorious purpose of saving Africa from the Africans."

The camp doctor articulates this post-colonial theme, the voice of cynicism about the real purpose of the bridge. He tells Patterson that it is "only being built to protect the ivory trade—make rich men richer." Patterson finds problems with the workers: Hindus, Muslims and native Africans who detest each other and do not work together well, a tribal narrative enacted in the film. The real trouble begins when man-eating lions begin to carry off workers. Patterson has to become a hunter to deal with the predators preying on his workers. He kills one, but two more attack the camp with almost supernatural intensity. When Patterson finally has one in his sights, he is hypnotized by the creature's eyes and cannot pull the trigger. Samuel, his African foreman who provides voiceover through the film, triggers our whispers of such predators when he says, "There is nothing like the fear a man-eater brings. They own the night and kill so quickly." The raw horror of the situation is driven home when they find the remains of one of the men the lions have taken: They "licked his skin off so they could drink his blood." Samuel adds ominously, "Lions don't do that." The terrified workers call the lions the Ghost and the Darkness.

But humans are hunters too, and the film develops both hunter and predator narratives. When famed American hunter Charles Remington (Michael Douglas), hired in desperation by Beaumont, arrives with his Maasai lion hunters, things get even worse. After a lion takes Remington, Patterson finally kills the last lion in a frantic battle in which he saves his life with his rifle, another evolutionary development of Moon Walker's bone as weapon, prevailing over a seemingly indomitable and, in the context of the film, possibly supernatural predator.

The post-colonial theme continues to the end. In voiceover, Samuel reports that "some thought they were not lions at all but the spirits of dead medicine men come back to spread madness. For others they were devils, sent to stop the white men from owning the world." The film is in part a commentary on the Europeans' exploitation of Africa, taking the land and territory from a native people. The narrative of white civilization's right to expand territory played well in film up to the 1960s, as in the cavalry-and-Indian film. The influence of culture has changed it with films like *Little Big Man* (1970) and *Dances with Wolves* (1990). But the true horror of *The Ghost and the Darkness* lies in the primal horror of being stalked and our flesh eaten. Donna Hart and Robert Sussman report that these two lions killed, and presumably ate, 135 people in 1897–98. The film's end credits tell us that the events portrayed were based on real incidents and that stuffed versions of the lions can be seen in a diorama at the Field Museum in Chicago. Such predation on humans by lions is hardly unusual. Hans Kruuk reports that one animal killed 84 people in Uganda while a tiger killed 436 in early twentieth century India.[24] If such predation was common in relatively modern times, our Paleolithic and Neolithic ancestors' experiences would have been horrific and would whisper vicarious horror of attack by such predators.

A great many people fear snakes, which perhaps accounts for the numerous horror films that focus on them as predator. Edward. O. Wilson and others have noted the prevalence of serpent aversion. Arne Ohman and Susan Mineka suggest that this aversion springs from a primal origin: "The high prevalence of snake fear in humans as well as in our primate relatives suggests that it is a result of an ancient evolutionary history. Genetic variability might explain why not all individuals show fear of snakes."[25] It might be argued that the serpent in Genesis offers a remnant of this fear. Our simian ancestors who lived in trees would be especially good prey for snakes, the thinking goes. Emily Dickinson's poem about the "narrow fellow in the grass" that inspires a "zero in the bone" describes the feelings of many regarding snakes. So serpent aversion has been adapted for the horror genre in dozens of low budget films such as *The Snake Woman* (1961), *Ssssss* (1973), *Fangs* (1974) and more recently in *Snakes on a Plane* (2006) and then *Snakes on a Train* in the same year. The snake pit sequence in the first Indiana Jones film *Raiders of the Lost Ark* (1981) is an especially memorable example of a scene that plays on serpent aversion.

Anaconda (1997) is another adaptation of this ancient fear. In some respects, *Anaconda* references *Jaws* in pitting a group of humans against a seemingly indomitable predator. Six anthropologists, led by Prof. Cale (Eric Stoltz), hire a boat to travel up the remote reaches of the Amazon to make a documentary about the legendary Shirishama Indians. Along the way, they find snake hunter Paul Serone (Jon Voight), stranded when his boat is damaged, and grudgingly take him along. Serone claims he is leading them to the Shirishama village, but instead uses them to try and capture a giant anaconda, another example of putting money ahead of group welfare.

The script establishes the power of the serpent as predator. Serone describes anacondas in words reminiscent of Hooper and Quint's descriptions of the great white shark in *Jaws*: "Anacondas are a perfect killing machine. They have heat sensors.... They strike, wrap around you, hold you tighter than your true love, and you get the privilege of hearing your bones break before the power of the embrace causes your veins to explode." The film further demonizes the serpent with Serone telling the others that they like killing. After eating, they "regurgitate their prey in order to kill and eat again."

A barometer of a film's appeal is the number of spinoffs and sequels it generates. Critics may have disliked *Anaconda*, but it was popular enough to establish a franchise, with three more films: *Anacondas: Hunt for the Blood Orchid* (2004), *Anaconda III* (2008) and *Anacondas: Trail of Blood* (2009), the latter two made for television and DVD sales.

Other man-eaters in film abound. *Lake Placid* (1999) and its three sequels have monster crocodiles emerging from a Maine lake, where crocodiles no more belong than do great white sharks off the coast of New England. The film's plot establishes a sort of tribal group with a conservation officer (Bill Pullman) as alpha male, a museum anthropologist (Bridget Fonda), the local sheriff and a professional crocodile hunter battling the man-eating monster. Three sequels have been produced with a fourth in the works at this writing. Donna Hart and Robert Sussman detail the crocodile's place as predator of primates. They also tell of an incident from World War II: When Japanese soldiers were being driven back by British troops in Burma, they retreated into a mangrove swamp, waiting for evacuation. But British ships prevented the Japanese from rescuing their troops. Of the 1000 soldiers who entered the swamp, 20 survived. The remainder were taken by crocodiles.[26] The *Anaconda* and *Lake Placid* franchises were popular enough to not only inspire sequels but a made-for-TV meeting of snake and crocodile, *Lake Placid vs. Anaconda* (2015). *Tremors* (1990) has giant worms spring up from the earth to gulp down unsuspecting humans. The *Tremors* flesh-eating predator plot inspired five sequels, all for DVD and cable release.

Yuval Noah Harari's comment about our nature explains much of why primal narratives whisper to us and make fear of the predator an enduring story in film:

> Our eating habits, our conflicts and our sexuality are all the result of the way our hunter-gatherer minds interact with our current post-industrial environment with its megacities, aeroplanes, telephones and computers.... To understand why, evolutionary psychologists argue, we need to delve into the hunter-gatherer world that shaped us, the world that we subconsciously still inhabit.[27]

And it can be a very scary place, as it is in films adapting the predator narrative.

SEVEN

The Other Narrative: Ghosts, Slashers, Witches and Robots as Other

In the Book of Judges, Jēpthah and the Gileadites defeat the Ephraimites in a great battle. When the Ephraimites who survive try to cross the River Jordan to return home, victorious Gileadites ask each if he is an Ephraimite. When they say "no," they are asked to say the word "shibboleth." If an Ephraimite soldier could not pronounce the word correctly, "they seized him and slew him," because he was unmasked and perceived as Other. Forty thousand Ephraimites were slaughtered.

Findings from evolutionary psychology lead us to see the power of narratives such as territoriality, tribalism, mating, assimilation and fear of the predator that inspire vicarious thrills in the horror film as emanating from the experiences of our primal ancestors. Central to them all is the distrust or hatred of those perceived as Other, as exemplified in the story of the Gileadites and Ephraimites. Steven Pinker describes the idea that the mind, like the body, "consists of multiple individual organs or 'modules' engineered by natural selection to maximize the reproductive fitness of our Upper Paleolithic ancestors and reflecting that design more or less directly in their current operations"[1] As demonstrated in preceding chapters, this whisper from hundreds of thousands of years of evolution continues to inspire horror in film.

The perception of otherness comes in a kaleidoscope of forms throughout recorded history. Racism is one of the most devastating. William Allman observes,

> [R]acism is not part of our evolved psychology. Rather, our Stone Age mind is tripping over something that is more fundamentally "us" vs. "them." ... Early humans spent most of their lives interacting with a very few people, all of whom looked and talked just as they did—and for whom strangers and members of neighboring groups were "scarce." When the "shadow of the future" is small—that is, when it is unlikely you will

ever meet that person again—it is unlikely that cooperation will flourish. Thus, our evolved psyches regard anyone who is not part of our intimate group as a "them." Skin color is just one of many "us/them."[2]

Evolutionary psychology would hold that this fear and capacity for hatred of the Other—who does not look like us, use our language, has a different religion or ideology or appears threatening in some way—is central to the vicarious thrills of the horror genre as well as the devastating conflicts we see around the world. Jack Morgan describes this response in film or literature and life: "The material for some *other* to do with us what it will, is one of primordial reach, one wherein we are violated from within and without and appropriated into the system and agenda of the predator."[3]

The paranoia and fear of the Other runs through all of the primal narratives in film, entwined with them. But some film types offer more focused and complicated adaptations of the Us-Them narrative. Indeed, the horror genre is a house of many mansions, and the ghost film, the more recent development of the slasher film, the ancient fear of the witch and humans' interaction with robots and computers reside there. They are rooted in the horror of contact with the Other in a more complex manner than its appearance in films centered more narrowly on the other narratives discussed in this book.

"I see dead people": The Ghost as Other

Tales of departed spirits recur in folklore and literature through thousands of years. The question of life after death has haunted, so to speak, our species. In the midst of his trials, Job asks our most troubling question: "If a man dies, will he live again?" (14:14). Tales of encounters with the departed are usually quite frightening in literature, be the spirit benign or hostile. The cemetery is always described as a scary place. As Robert Blair describes it in his long 1746 poem "The Grave," it is "the mansions of the dead," where spirits "roused from their slumber/In grim array the specters rose."[4] When Shakespeare's Hamlet meets his father's ghost on the ramparts of Elsinore Castle, he shouts, "Angels and Ministers of Grace defend us! Be thou a spirit of health or goblin damned.... I will speak to thee."[5] The lines suggest two versions of the ghost in film and literature, benign and hostile. Plots include the ghost with a mission who still seems one of us but is transformed to Other and remains behind to fulfill its purpose; the vengeful ghost seeking justice; the evil ghost; and the malevolent possessed house.

The tradition and beliefs from spiritualism are central to the ghost film and have been an important source for movies about encounters with the departed. The roots of spiritualism can be traced to the illuminist tradition of the eighteenth century but more specifically to the writing of Emanuel

Swedenborg (1688–1772). A gifted scientist, he experienced a "spiritual awakening" in 1744, claiming to have spoken to angels and to the spirits of the dead. In his book *Heavenly Doctrine,* he wrote, "Man is so created as to live simultaneously in the natural world and in the spiritual world. Thus he has an internal and external nature or mind; by the former living in the spiritual world, by the latter in the natural world."[6] The mild-mannered Swedenborg was a scholar and a mystic, not an evangelist; but his many books describing his exploration of the spirit world attracted a wide following and even a religion called Swedenborgianism that has survived the centuries. According to their website, the Swedenborgian Church of North America currently boasts congregations in the U.S., and there are many more congregations in Great Britain, Europe and Canada.

Hosts of others have claimed contact with the dead, such as the Fox sisters in 1840s New England with "table rapping," messages from the departed, supposedly sent through the tapping of table legs (they were convincingly discredited during their lifetime). Interest in spiritualism spiked during and after the American Civil War, when millions of lives were lost and the bereaved longed to contact loved ones through professional mediums: those who claimed a gift for speaking with the dead. No doubt the findings of Darwin, which undermined traditional religious doctrine, contributed to a need to believe that the souls of lost loved ones had found peace in a happier place. Celebrity mediums achieved notoriety in the nineteenth century.

Two approaches developed. Spiritists followed the teachings of Andrew Karnac. His philosophy centered on reincarnation leading to spiritual perfection, while spiritualists denied rebirth and insisted that the departed remained permanently in a different dimension. Spiritualism has become the dominant approach. The widespread interest in spiritualism and spiritism in the nineteenth century led philosopher-psychologist William James and his colleagues in the British Psychical Research Association and its American counterpart to conduct a scientific investigation of mediumship both in Great Britain and the U.S.

In her excellent study of James' work *Ghost Hunters,* Deborah Bloom uses letters and journals from James and other Association members to trace their findings. They easily unmasked almost all mediums as fakes. But even blindfolded and in a dark room, Daniel Dunglas Home (excoriated by Robert Browning in his poem "Mr. Sludge the Medium") could tell anonymous visitors facts about their lives that James and his colleagues were convinced he could not have known. They could neither prove nor disprove his authenticity. Sir Arthur Conan Doyle believed that the game was afoot in terms of contact with the dead, and many other important people of the day, including the poet Elizabeth Barrett Browning, were firm believers.

Interest again spiked during and after World War I with the deaths of millions of young men on the battlefield as well as more millions who died of influenza. Interest died down as the twentieth century progressed, but today there many spiritualist churches in the U.S., Canada and Great Britain and three organizations: the National Spiritualist Association of Churches, the National Spiritualist Alliance and the International Spiritualist Federation. The growth of the New Age has both influenced spiritualist beliefs and spread them. Filmmakers and novelists have long mined spiritualists' beliefs and practices for plots because ghosts have always been pretty scary in an entertaining way. They are Other in both sympathetic and threatening roles.

Most spiritualist churches are Christian, and except for "readings" given to members of the congregation by a panel of mediums, their services resemble those of mainstream protestant denominations. Spiritualists don't believe that ghosts can harm people, but they do assume that some spirits are wicked and that there is danger in contacting them. There is much discussion in spiritualist literature of ectoplasm (the viscous substance formed, they say, by the manifestation of a ghost), levitation, appearance of spirits at séances, mechanical writing, ability to interfere with electricity, scents from perfume used by the deceased in life, crisis visitations to a loved one through dreams or apparitions at the moment of death and changes in temperature when the dead are present. Recently, spiritualists have harnessed technology, claiming to contact the dead by capturing voices on tape recorders left running, so called electronic voice projection. EVP, as it is called, was adapted in the film *White Noise* (2005). All of this lore is common property of the ghost movie genre, and it creates levels of otherness and unease or horror, depending on the film, in the ghost movie.

While belief in ghosts is part of human history, spiritualism has fueled it. *A Rumor of Angels* (2000), a close adaptation of Grace Boylan's 1918 book *Thy Son Liveth: Messages from a Soldier to His Mother,* is based on spiritualist lore. The film describes the experience of a mother whose son was killed in Vietnam who communicates with her through Morse code, describing his life after death in language spiritualists would recognize: "The soul leaves the body as the school boy jumps out of the school door, with joy. There is no horror in death." These lines from the film are lifted directly from Boylan's book.

Not all ghost movies are true horror films, but tales of ghosts and the supernatural have always been frightening and disturbing. Mathias Clasen quotes C.S. Lewis from *The Problem of Pain*, who observes that a tiger inspires fear and so do ghosts but of a different kind: "No one is primarily afraid of what a ghost may do to him, but of the mere fact that it is a ghost. It is 'uncanny' rather than dangerous, and the special kind of fear it excites may be called Dread.... They make us doubt our beliefs and even sanity."[7] After all, they signal our own mortality and the assimilation of death into something Other. In an amusing passage from Henry Fielding's 1749 novel *Tom Jones, a Found-*

ling, Tom takes his servant and sidekick Partridge to a performance of *Hamlet*, a scene captured in Tony Richardson's 1963 film adaptation. When the ghost appears on stage, Partridge is terrified. "His knees knocked against each other" and even though Tom explains the difference between art and life, Partridge cries, "Nay, you may call me a Coward if you will, but if that little Man there upon the Stage is not frightened, I never saw any man frightened in my life."[8] Partridge's fear, even of a fictional ghost, is at the heart of the titillation in all ghost movies, even those in which we can identify with the ghost as Us but not part of our species any longer and assimilated into another form.

"I think I can go now. Just needed to help someone and I did." The Ghost with a Mission: *The Ghost and Mrs. Muir, The Uninvited, Ghost* and *The Sixth Sense*

The theme of benign contact with the other side underpins the plot in many movies, including spiritualist romances. In *The Ghost and Mrs. Muir* (1947), Lucy Muir (Gene Tierney), a recently widowed woman, moves with her daughter and a maid to a cottage by the sea that she has been warned against because it is reputedly haunted. There she confronts the spirit of Captain Gregg (Rex Harrison), who had died there a few years earlier. When she refuses to be frightened by him, they gradually form a relationship—the sort of doomed love plot common to the romance genre—that could only be consummated many years later when Lucy dies as an old woman and the captain is there to greet her soul. While the encounter with a ghost is titillating, the film is really a twist on the romance and not a true horror film. The captain was once one of Us, though assimilated, and inspires empathy in being both Us and Other.

The romantic ghost appears in many other films, often with a mission to complete before the soul can rest. Spiritualist lore underpins this plot. Spiritualist writer George Anderson observes, "Sometimes a soul will linger temporarily on the earth if some issues of their lifetime have not been completely resolved, or they might visit regularly if there is a particular affinity for a loved one or location."[9] An often used plotline in the ghost film has a departed spirit remaining to protect a loved one. Sylvia Browne, the most prolific author of sensational spiritualist books, writes that a "ghost is created when, at death, the spirit either sees the tunnel and turns away or refuses to acknowledge the tunnel in the first place, with the result that it gets caught outside of its body, between our dimension and the ... Other Side"[10]: in effect, different territories.

Ghost (1990) is an example. On a date with his fiancée Molly Jenson (Demi Moore), Sam Wheat (Patrick Swayze) is murdered in an apparent street crime. He rejects going into the light, an allusion to Raymond Moody's books about near death experiences beginning with *Life After Life* (1975). Moody interviewed dozens of people who claimed to have died, usually on the operating table, but were brought back to life. They recorded being out of their body, floating above, seeing a light that led to a tunnel at the end of which they met departed friends and relatives but were sent back. Details from Moody's books have been adapted for use in many a ghost movie.

The film dramatizes Moody's findings through Sam's experience in another spiritualist romance. He stays behind for love and ends up protecting Molly. In the spiritualist tradition, he gets help from a medium, Oda Mae Brown, who goes from a fake to a legitimate link to the spirit world, leaving her amusingly terrified. He meets other ghosts, some of whom are just waiting for the light and others who are trapped for reasons described in spiritualist literature such as suicide. Spiritualists are divided on whether ghosts can manipulate physical objects, but a trapped ghost teaches Sam how to do so. And we get a conclusion that demonstrates the fear that ghosts have always inspired when he gets revenge by terrifying his murderer and the one who hired him, causing their deaths. As in *Ghost,* visitors from the spirit world as they have been portrayed throughout history are frightening as Other and inspire a primal fear of our own mortality.

Spiritualists are divided on the presence of evil ghosts. Sylvia Browne opines that those who reject God on Earth become malign spirits, "Earth's sociopaths, remorseless and amoral, valuing no life but their own." According to Browne, those who have led good lives go through the "right door" into the light and the Other Side. Those who have led evil lives may remain here before being sent to "an abyss of dark, Godless, empty, joyless all-encompassing nothingness," reincarnated until they get it right.[11] The scene from *Ghost* when black, screaming specters appear to drag Sam's murderers to Hell fits her description. Other romantic ghost movies portray spirits who remain behind to help loved ones they neglected in life, including *Always* (1990, a remake of *A Guy Named Joe* (1943) with forest fires instead of World War II bomber raids) and *What Dreams May Come* (1998).

The Sixth Sense (1999), M. Night Shyamalan's first hit film, is surely the classic of the ghost with a mission plot. Katherine Fowkes observes that "ghostly haunting has been transformed by Hollywood into a dilemma of poor gender relations, often blamed upon distant or absent husbands and fathers."[12] Fowkes' comment fits the theme of *The Sixth Sense.* Child psychologist Malcolm Crowe (Bruce Willis) treats a disturbed child, Cole Sear (a pun on "seer" of ghosts), who finally confesses in the most memorable line of the film, "I see dead people." As the unbeliever character common to films that adapt the supernatural, Crowe must eventually learn that the child does indeed see the departed, with the result that he confronts a mistake from his past that haunts him and eventually his own status as one of the departed whom Cole sees. In films that exploit this plot derived from spiritualism, a man confronts his mistakes in the afterlife and tries to make amends. We can identify and sympathize with the ghost as Us, transformed to a different state of being to become Other while retaining our moral imperatives and capacity for love. And he is confronted with leaving his territory and entering another state. Crowe is a pattern ghost with a mission, saying to his sleeping wife when he finally realizes his state, "I think I can go now. Just needed to help someone and I did." *The Sixth Sense* has some scary scenes, when ghosts demanding Cole's help attack him. But beyond the usual unease ghosts bring as symbols of our mortality, most ghost-with-a-mission films are not true horror films. That is to be found in movies that focus on an evil ghost preying on the living.

The Uninvited (1944) is a classic of the gothic romance and a different approach to the ghost-with-a-mission plot. Brother and sister Roderick and Pamela Fitzgerald (Ray Milland and Ruth Hussey) buy a house on the Welsh coast that looks like a prototype for the haunted house. Love blooms when Roderick meets Stella Meredith (Gail Russell in her first role), who seems strangely drawn to the house. The film provides plenty of the thrills from the

The Sixth Sense: Cole Sear (Haley Joel Osment) tells Dr. Crowe (Bruce Willis), "I see dead people."

gothic romance. When Stella visits the Fitzgeralds, she is possessed by a ghost that tries to lead her to throw herself into the sea. We get much of the standard spiritualist plot material: strange wailing, a Ouija board of sorts for a séance, the perfume of the departed, temperature changes, flowers suddenly wilting and spiritual possession of Stella. The film develops another protective mother story, as we eventually learn that two ghosts inhabit the house: one her father's wife, supposedly Stella's mother, who is trying to kill her, and the other his Gypsy mistress, her true mother who struggles to save her (the ghost with a mission). In addition to the mating narrative from the romance of Roderick and Stella, we have another mother, a ghost, fighting to save her child.

"An evil old house, the kind that people call haunted": *The Haunting, The Legend of Hell House, The Shining, Burnt Offerings* and *1408*

Movies based on a malevolent house are true horror films in the ghost movie subgenre. Dale Bailey takes a cultural criticism approach when he observes that the haunted house film symbolizes what has failed in the American dream.[13] But a primal traits critique would suggest that there is something more powerful in this version of the horror film. In Horace Walpole's 1764 novel *The Castle of Otranto*, a gigantic helmet falls from the sky to crush the son of Manfred, the master of the place, its plumes periodically waving, and then a figure walks out of a portrait and a statue oozes blood. Dozens of imitations would follow beginning in the 1790s. In the nineteenth century, the ruined castle or abbey from the gothic mode as we see it portrayed in Dracula's castle morphed into the haunted house. The setting has been adapted so often in literature and film that we might speculate that it reflects something from a primal response: mutability and the inevitability of decay.

So the haunted castle plot was transformed into the sentient house in the horror genre beginning with Edgar Allan Poe's "The Fall of the House of Usher." In this classic story, the house itself is a malign Other. Mad Roderick Usher explains the sentience of the house to the narrator: "The condition of the sentience had been here, he imagined, fulfilled in the method of collocation of these stones—in the order of their arrangement, as well as in that of the many fungi which overspread them."[14] Poe identifies Roderick and his sister Madeline as the last remnants of a "house," or family, that is somehow intertwined with the structure itself; and it eventually possesses Madeline. Its collapse into the tarn symbolizes the death of Roderick and his sister, the last of their house, as the structure falls.

The sentient house story adapts a different protagonist-antagonist approach from other horror films. Most portray an identifiable, corporeal Other, be it a vampire, a werewolf, a predatory animal or any of the antagonists discussed in this book that are adapted to create conflict with protagonists. The sentient house is indeed an antagonist, but it is a presence rather than a physical being. So it offers a variation for a primal traits critique as another version of Other, a threatening territory as a vehicle for creating vicarious horror. The power of this plot is reflected in the successful franchises it has created, such as *The Amityville Horror* (1979) with its 17 sequels, remakes and spinoffs, and *House* (1986) which generated three sequels. In the sentient house film, we most commonly are asked to empathize with a group of characters brought into peril by the evil. In discussing humans as social animals, Lance Workman and Will Reader note that such behavior is common to humankind, and we would empathize with it in film: "We don't have to seek out like-minded compatriots, we just have to have something (anything) that allows us to feel part of a group."[15] Thus in the sentient house films, the characters who enter this new territory are a social group with which we can empathize. A primal traits critique suggests that we experience pleasurable fear at the danger to the characters, a tribe of sorts with which we identify, being stalked and murdered by a special sort of Other.

Robert Wise adapted *The Haunting* (released in 1963 and remade with the same title in 1999) from Shirley Jackson's novel *The Haunting of Hill House*. It begins with the horror movie cliché of a group of people entering Hill House, which has a reputation as haunted. The foreboding tone of the opening voiceover, taken verbatim from the novel, establishes the film's plot but also defines the sentient house in film: "An evil old house, the kind that people call haunted, is like an undiscovered country, waiting to be explored. Hill House had stood for 90 years and might stand for 90 more. Silence lay heavily against the wood and stone of Hill house, and whatever walked there, walked alone."

The film attributes the evil of the house to its original owner, Hugh Crain. The description resembles Poe's in "House of Usher": "Hill House has a badly turned angle. Some chance meeting of room and sky turned Hill House into a place of despair more frightening because the face of Hill House seems awake, with watchfulness from the bleak windows and a touch of glee in the eyebrows of a cornice." The lines echo "House of Usher" with its "vacant eye-like windows."

Anthropologist John Markway (Richard Johnson) wants to investigate the supernatural and sees Hill House as the perfect laboratory for study. After advertising for people who have had experiences with the paranormal to stay with him in the house, he gets only Eleanor (Julie Harris) and Theodora (Claire Bloom). So they, joined by Luke Sanderson (Russ Tamblyn), who owns the house, and later Markway's wife (Lois Maxwell), meet there. Markway believes that Hill House has excellent potential for study because of all the evil things that had happened there. It had "been born bad." Like most haunted houses in film and literature, Hill House has the usual Burkean sublime atmosphere, a structure with turrets and ruined castle-like appearance.

The film goes on to adapt the bumps in the night of the ghost film as derived from spiritualist lore, with a séance, automatic writing, mysterious booms, the voice of a child weeping, cold spots and an apparition. The house seems determined to take the introverted and vulnerable Eleanor, who has the sensitivity to the paranormal described in spiritualist literature. As they walk through the house, Eleanor murmurs, "The house is alive"; and the psychic Theodora responds, "It wants you, Nell. The house is calling you." Eventually it claims her and we hear Eleanor's voice paraphrasing the opening line: "Silence lies steadily against the wood and stone of Hill House, and we who walk her, walk alone." The primal horror of the film is rooted in this new kind of Other assimilating one of Us, a vulnerable character who inspires empathy.

The Legend of Hell House (1973) seems a first cousin to *The Haunting*. Based on a novel by a prolific writer on the occult, Richard Matheson (who also wrote the script), the film adapts the conventional frame for the sentient house story. A millionaire hires four people to investigate the possibility of life after death by spending four days in the Belasco House, called "the Mount Everest of haunted houses." It is informally known as Hell House, where deadly supernatural events have occurred. The group includes physicist Lionel Barrett and his wife Ann (Clive Revill and Gayle Hunnicut); spiritualist minister Florence Tanner (Pamela Franklin); and physical medium Ben Fischer (Roddy McDowall), the sole survivor of an earlier visit.

Barrett is another conventional unbeliever of the horror genre. The character provides a central element of dramatic conflict for *The Legend of Hell House* similar to that in *The Haunting of Hill House*. Temperature drops, a séance, ozone odor, poltergeist mayhem: all are the stuff of Spiritualist lore enacted in the film to challenge the character's disbelief in the supernatural.

As in possessed house stories from "Usher" forward, the house is Other, and it pursues those with whom we identify. As in most haunted house movies, the film recreates the visual image inherited from the Burkean sublime, a large turreted structure, slightly ruined in appearance and complete with cobwebs on the interior. The plot proceeds with Dr. Barrett finding that his beliefs are wrong. As is usually the case in the sentient house narrative and as is the case in casinos, the house wins.

The house in *Burnt Offerings* (1975) follows the conventional Burkean appearance of the haunted or sentient house, as does the plot. The Rolfs—Marian (Karen Black), Ben (Oliver Reed), their 12-year old son Davy (Lee Montgomery) and Ben's aunt Elizabeth (Bette Davis)—want to get away from the city. They move into a large house in the countryside far from civilization, the usual setting for this subgenre. The spooky-looking Allardyce brother and sister who own the house rent it to them for the summer at the suspiciously low price of $900. As part of their rental deal, the Rolfs must leave a tray three times a day outside the door of an upstairs room where the brother and sister say their mother lives as a recluse.

And so the plot is set up for the house to be Other. Before the Allardyces leave, Arnold, who is wheelchair-bound, says, "The house takes care of itself, Mr. Rolf"; and later Roz Allardyce adds, "It's practically immortal." The rest of the film unwinds from this opening with its foreshadowing of a house that has a mind of its own, threatening each member of the family.

The house absorbs Marian into its consciousness, leading her to dress in antique clothing and to lose all interest in intimacy while she spends her time outside the room where she leaves food, another example of the secret room as forbidden territory in the horror film. We learn that the house is indeed self-sustaining, as Arnold Allardyce had described it, when we see it literally change its skin, with shingles and siding falling away and replaced. The horror of the film is that this supernatural Other has, in the end, assimilated the family's life forces as we see in their pictures that are included among all those who have lived there. The disintegration and assimilation of a family, the central and necessary unit of our evolutionary heritage, is a subject that inspires horror in many films.

The same narrative, told with even greater intensity, underpins Stanley Kubrick's adaptation of Stephen King's novel *The Shining* (1980). Novel and film develop a similar theme of the assimilation of characters we identify as Us by a house that is Other. Jack Torrance (Jack Nicholson), his wife Wendy (Shelley Duvall) and young son Danny move to the Overlook, a resort hotel in Colorado, where Jack will serve as custodian for the winter season when the hotel is snowed in. He is an aspiring writer and took the job so that he would have time to work on a book. Kubrick gives the Overlook the vaguely castle-like appearance that is a cinematic meme in the genre. From the spiritualist tradition, Danny is a medium, hearing voices from a spirit guide, "the little boy who lives in my mouth." When Jack interviews for the job, they meet Dick Halloran (Scatman Crothers), the chef, who turns out to be a psychic and immediately recognizes Danny as a kindred spirit. The film and novel establish the title when Dick tells Danny that he and his grandmother communicated without speaking and calls it "shining."

When Danny tells Dick that the house frightens him (he had a psychic vision before they arrive), Halloran explains why, establishing the sentient house theme in the language of spiritualist mediumship:

> You know, some places are like people. Some shine; some don't. I guess you could say that the Overlook Hotel has something like shining. When something happens, it can

leave a trace of itself behind. Say like, if someone burned some toast. Well, maybe things that happened leave other kinds of traces behind. Not traces that anyone can notice but people who shine can see.

As the film progresses, Danny meets the spirits confined there because of "things that happened," an accumulation of evil acts that have given the house sentience and trapped the spirits of those who committed them.

Dale Bailey offers a cultural critique of Kubrick's film: "Jack succumbs to the Overlook's grotesque machinations in a parody of the dilemma countless drones in gray flannel suits have faced before him. In short, he must sacrifice his family for the good of the company." He also cites Stephen King's assessment of his novel and the film (which he didn't much care for): "Whatever is going on in the Overlook, it is connected to a kind of capitalism run mad. It is the American Dream run amok."[16] A cultural interpretation certainly does describe important elements of the film. But the true horror stems from something deeper than culture. First we empathize with a family, the central organization of our social species, when they are threatened by an Other: the house with its accumulation of evil as well as the ghosts trapped there who have been possessed by it, appearing to Danny and to Jack as he degenerates into madness. The film's focus is this Other's gradual assimilation of Jack Torrance from Us to one of Them. He tries to kill his wife and child at the behest of the house, an assimilation such as that described in *The Haunting*, *The Legend of Hell House* and *Burnt Offerings* as well as that of Madeline Usher.

The film also focuses on the threat to a child, a theme common to King's works and one that we see over and over in the horror film. In *Silver Bullet* (1985), based on King's novella, young Marty Coslaw and his teenage sister Jane are tracked by a werewolf. Marty's disability makes him even more vulnerable as a character. In *Firestarter* (1984), Charlene "Charlie" McGee has telekinetic powers and is on the run with her father from government agents who want to experiment on her. The threatened child figure recurs throughout King's work and films that are based on them, and it has contributed to his success for good reason from a primal trait perspective. Mathias Clasen writes: "Five-year-old Danny finds himself threatened by the supernatural forces of the Overlook. A child preyed upon by hostile forces is horrible enough, but King compounds the horror of that scenario by pitting the child protagonist's own father against him."[17] Children are our genetic future, and the threat to a child inspires whispers of horror.

The 2007 film adaptation of King's short story "1408" is another version of the haunted space story. Writer Mike Enslin (John Cusack), emotionally devastated by the death of his child, has given up serious literature to write books about haunted hotels, though he has no belief in ghosts or anything else beyond the material world (the perennial disbeliever of the genre). Having heard that Room 1408 at New York's Dolphin Hotel is a haunted space, he tries to check in for a night. The manager Mr. Olin (Samuel L. Jackson) does everything he can to convince him not to stay. Fifty-six people have died there, he tells Enslin. Finally, Olin says, "It's an evil fucking room!" And it is another Other of the

1408: Mike Enslin (John Cusack) screams his terror into his recorder.

sentient space story. The opening foreshadows the room's sentience, which awakes minutes after Enslin checks in and the room's radio spontaneously begins playing The Carpenters' rendition of "We've Only Just Begun." So begins the room's attempt to get Enslin to "check out": "You can take advantage of our express route," a voice intones as a noose appears.

The film focuses on gradually convincing Enslin, a cynic who thinks he has seen it all, to believe in supernatural incidents. The narrative device has him speaking into his hand-held recorder as he gradually becomes more terrified. But even in the midst of the evil Other's turning the room inside out and fracturing reality through the first half of the film, Enslin persists in trying to convince himself that there's a trick involved until he finally realizes his peril. Like *The Shining*, *1408* (the numbers add up to 13 and the hotel was built in 1913) posits a supernatural Other from the ghost story tradition that preys on Us. The sensationalism of King's story and film are far afield from most accepted spiritualist beliefs. But spiritualists Tom and Lisa Butler suggest that "traumatic events may be etched into the fabric of the location."[18] Apart from any connection to spiritualism, the film gives us the satisfaction of a victory against this Other, prompting a shot of Olin murmuring, "Well done, Mr. Epstein, well done." The film provides a happy ending that King's short story does not have, where the room definitely wins.

"Was that the boogie man?": The Slasher as Other in *Halloween* and *Friday the 13th*

Alfred Hitchcock's 1960 film *Psycho*, with its shower stall attack on Janet Leigh, has become a recognized film classic. The image of Anthony Perkins in drag wielding a knife may also have helped inspire the slasher subgenre of the horror film. Prince describes the postmodern horror formula:

> Such films usually open with the violent disruption of the normative order by a monster.... Like its predecessors, the postmodern horror film revolves around the monster's graphically violent rampage and ordinary people's ineffectual attempts to resist it with violence. In the end, the inefficacy of human action and the repudiation of narrative closure combine to produce various forms of open endings: the monster triumphs (*Henry*); the monster is defeated but only temporarily (*Halloween*); or the outcome is uncertain (*Night of the Living Dead*).[19]

Prince's description of the formula for horror movies certainly fits the slasher film, and it leads us to see the work of primal narratives in inspiring the horror of the subgenre. John Carpenter's *Halloween* (1978) may not be the first of its type. *The Texas Chain Saw Massacre* had appeared four years earlier, for instance, as had *Black Christmas*, both featuring masked slashers. But *Halloween* is the prototype. The film's box office success sparked the plethora of its ilk to follow.

The opening of *Halloween*, set in the Middle American town of Haddonfield, Illinois, circa 1963, places six-year-old Michael Myers as the crazed slasher in the opening scene when he kills his sister Judith with a carving knife. Fifteen years later, Dr. Sam Loomis (Donald Pleasence), a psychiatrist, in a "dark and stormy night" sequence, drives to the supposedly secure facility where Michael has been held, only to find he has escaped. Loomis laments, "He's gone from here, the evil is gone," and knows he is certain to return to Haddonfield. Carpenter leaves no doubt that Michael Myers is pure evil and Other. In the sort of establishing scene common to the horror film, Loomis lectures the Haddonfield sheriff, who doesn't believe Myers will return, providing the frame for the film and also for the slasher films to come:

> I met him 15 years ago. I was told there was nothing left: no reason, no conscience, no understanding in even the most rudimentary sense, of life or death, of good or evil, of right or wrong. I met a six-year-old child with this lank, pale, emotionless face and the blackest eyes, the Devil's eyes. I spent eight years trying to reach him and then another seven keeping him locked up because I realized that the thing behind those eyes was purely and simply evil.

Laurie Strode (Jamie Lee Curtis), the film's heroine and Michael's sister as we learn in the first sequel, is his prey. We see him tracking her and murdering her friends. She babysits ten-year-old Tommy, who repeatedly sees Michael outside and asks, "Was that the boogie man?"; and Laurie assures him it was not. But at the end, after Laurie seems to have killed Michael twice, once with a knitting needle and once with his own knife and even after Loomis has shot him with six rounds, he still disappears. Laurie says, "It *was* the boogie man," and Loomis replies, "'As a matter of fact, it was."

The slasher film has inspired both psychological and cultural criticism. Robin Wood believes that these films introduced a character "produced by repression ... essentially a superego figure avenging itself on liberated feminine sensibility."[20] From the perspective of cultural criticism, *Halloween* makes a statement about the loss of community in suburban society. In trying to deny the possibility of violence in Haddonfield, the sheriff says, "Do you know what Haddonfield is? Families, children, all lined up in rows up and down the street." But when Laurie runs screaming for help as Michael pursues her into the night, her neighbors will not answer their doors, and we see blinds pulled. Perhaps Carpenter hints at the parallel between Haddonfield and Mark Twain's "The Man Who Corrupted Hadleyburg," a story about a town somewhat like Haddonfield and a name that sounds a bit like it, where people are sure of their own virtue but unable to see the corruption within.

No doubt Carpenter took aim at the smug self-satisfaction of suburban American. But the film's power springs from something beyond its critique of American culture. *Halloween* established a franchise with seven sequels and two remakes. It is first and foremost a horror film that plays on the primal fear of an Other that has emerged in our midst throughout human history, the boogie man, as Tommy puts it, who is truly Other but who is also Us, part of our own genetic species. And this Other deviates from all adaptive norms of human behavior as it has developed through the millennia. Joseph Carroll observes, "No culture can deviate from human universals (by definition), but many individual people can and do deviate from species-typical norms of behavior. They murder their children, commit incest, fail to develop language or otherwise behave in dysfunctional ways."[21]

The slasher is such a character, an anomaly born or created by an environment (depending on the expert opinion of individual psychologists) or a combination of the two to be apart from accepted culture, a psychopath. The latest edition of the bible of psychological conditions, *The Diagnostic and Statistical Manual of Mental Disorders*, refers to psychopathy with an alternate name from that of the previous edition: "antisocial personality disorder." But the description of symptoms is generally the same as in previous editions. They are individuals who "frequently lack empathy and tend to be callous, cynical and contemptuous of the feeling, rights and sufferings of others."[22] The psychopath lacks a central trait of evolved human nature. William Hamilton had defined "reciprocal altruism," which the psychopath lacks, as the basis for morality. Lance Workman and Will Reader discuss psychopathy as both an evolved potential genetic aberration and the result of environmental factors. Humans in general, they write, believe in "aiding others with the expectation (conscious or otherwise) that such aid will be reciprocated.... Perhaps psychopathic exploitation is an evolved alternative strategy to reciprocation."[23]

Jack the Ripper, the subject for countless novels and films, might be a real-life prototype for the slasher character. But Ted Bundy, the Zodiac Killer and many others of their ilk have produced body counts that put the Ripper's to shame. Michael Myers and the many knife-wielders, stranglers and assorted Others of the slasher film represent genetic types that spring from Us to become Other, inspiring a horror that evolutionary psychology might suggest has been with our species from its beginning. The character appears throughout the history of literature and myth. Shakespeare's Iago is an example, "a motiveless malignity" as Samuel Taylor Coleridge described him. In Herman Melville's novella *Billy Budd, Sailor,* John Claggart, the master at arms aboard the British ship *Bellipotent* during the eighteenth-century wars against the French, forms a totally irrational hatred for Billy Budd, a saintly foretopman. Melville quotes Plato in describing Claggart as an example of "Natural Depravity, a depravity according to nature." He offers a description of the psychopathic Claggart that could have been drawn from *The Diagnostic and Statistical Manual of Mental Disorders* had it been available in the late nineteenth century when he wrote the story (published posthumously in 1924). "Though the man's even temper and discreet bearing would seem to intimate a mind peculiarly subject to the law of reason, not the less in heart he would seem to riot in complete exemption from that law, having apparently little to do with reason further than to employ it as an ambidexter implement for effecting the irrational."[24]

So from a primal traits critical perspective, the horror of the slasher film stems from just such a character, the psychopathic killer, the Iago or Claggart, born as one of Us who is terrifyingly also Other. Unlike werewolves, vampires, predators and other horror genre characters, the slasher does not change form and is part of our genetic kin, and therein lies much of the horror of the subgenre. David Buss comments on this kind of character as embodied in the serial killer: "Serial killers attract a wildly disproportionate share of media attention, but they actually account for only one to two percent of all murders in America.... Nonetheless, people's fascination with these kinds of murders also results from our evolved homicide-prevention psychology.... They trip specialized defenses designed to deal with uncertainty."[25] Despite the relative rarity of such characters, the psychopathic serial killer, whether slasher or otherwise, has figured prominently in a remarkable number of films and TV series, perhaps because of the evolutionary response he or she triggers.

Halloween was made on a budget of just over $300,000 and grossed more than $70 million worldwide. Such financial success was sure to inspire imitation. *Friday the 13th* (1980) was first up among imitators. No doubt the filmmakers chose the date for the title because it has been deemed unlucky for centuries. The most common reason given is the pogrom initiated against the Knights Templar by King Phillip IV of France on Friday, October 13, 1307. Another low-budget, high-profit production, *Friday the 13th* exploits the tradition of bad luck for the date of the title, as does Stephen King in "1408." It sparked yet another franchise, with 11 sequels to date. It also helped create the recurring plot in the slasher film with a group of twentysomethings or high school students being stalked and slashed in a defined area.

Friday the 13th opens at Camp Crystal in 1958, as two young counselors sneak into a barn to have sex, and are murdered. The scene establishes the territory of the slasher. Like Jonathan Harker going into Dracula's territory, the students have entered the killer's. Then Annie, a young woman who aspires to be a cook at Camp Crystal, stops for directions at a service station where she learns of deaths there: first of a young boy who drowned and a year later the couple's demise. She gets a warning from Old Ralph, an apparently mentally deficient elderly man: "I have a message from God. You're all doomed." He is another example of the prophet figure who appears in ancient Greek tragedy and in the modern horror film to provide foreshadowing.

The plot moves forward many years with the young people at Camp Crystal stalked and killed. In the tradition of the slasher film, the most virtuous of the counselors, Alice, survives after learning that Pamela Vorhees is the slasher and Jason's mother. Her son had presumably died many years before when counselors were busy having sex when they might have saved him. Although he only appears at the very end in very improbable circumstances, the film introduces Jason as the franchise slasher, to return over and over in sequels and spinoffs. Pamela Vorhees is the psychopathic character as Other who shares our genes but lacks the species or group empathy that evolutionary psychologists describe; and she has begotten another of her kind. It is worth noting that the second *Friday the 13th* film, rushed to theaters a year after the first, returns Jason with his face covered by a cloth sack and then acquiring the signature Michael Myers–like mask in the many sequels, seemingly killed over and over but always somehow rising to kill again. From a primal traits perspective, the mask is another example of a visual signifier identifying him as Other. As in most of the slasher films, Jason hunts in a territory.

The financial success of *Halloween* and *Friday the 13th* inspired a horde of imitations. Most establish a territory that the Other uses as a hunting ground. In *Prom Night*, the territory is a high school where the slasher stalks four girls who have a guilty secret from childhood. Again, the murderer wears a cloth sack mask. In *My Bloody Valentine*, a coal mine (once a disaster site) is the territory, and the slasher is a miner who survived a cave-in and went mad. He wears a miner's outfit with gas mask. The mask is sometimes a way of concealing identity until the final scenes, as is the case for Ghost Face, the killer in *Scream*, who has a mask that looks like the face from Edvard Munch's painting "The Scream." In *The Texas Chain Saw Massacre*, Leatherface has a mask of human skin. Freddy Krueger in *A Nightmare on Elm Street* does not have a mask, but his long claws and attire signify him as the conventional Other. The effect of the mask is to identify the killer's otherness, but also it establishes the ambiguity of his nature, one of Us who is a psychopathic murderer. In many films, the signifier of distorting or hiding the face lets the viewer enjoy the violent demise of evildoers without feeling empathy for them, as in the zombie films and the storm troopers from *Star Wars*. Darth Vader's attire and black helmet hiding his face establish him as the alpha of Others in the films. In the slasher films, the mask establishes the unease created by seeing characters with whom the viewer identifies being killed by an Other, a psychopath who lacks evolved human empathy for his own genetic kin. Perhaps "clown aversion," the fear that many feel of clowns' faces, springs from the same source.

"What god doth the wizard pray to?": Witchcraft in Film

When Dorothy lands in Oz in MGM's *The Wizard of Oz* (1939), she squashes the Wicked Witch of the East, much to the delight of the Munchkins. Then a translucent bubble appears bringing a lovely woman who identifies herself, saying, "I am Glinda, the Witch of the North," "You *are*?" exclaims a wide-eyed Dorothy. "I beg your pardon. I've never heard of a beautiful witch before." The dichotomy of good and evil witches in Oz reflects the contrasting view of witchcraft from the Middle Ages as opposed to the changes culture has wrought beginning in the twentieth century.

Horror films present a dichotomy of views toward witchcraft. The evil witch is a constant presence as Other, but Neo Paganism or Wicca, rapidly growing new religious movements, have transformed the much maligned witch character. Witchcraft folklore as it has been passed down for centuries and the films that adapt it are cultural products rooted in a primal narrative. It is a given among evolutionary psychologists that culture and evolutionary adaptation interact, so we might postulate that the primal narrative of the Other has contributed to the creation of the folklore.

The Salem witchcraft trials (1692–93) have resonated through history in story and film. Set in Puritan New England, Nathaniel Hawthorne's short story "Young Goodman Brown" (1835) is an early example. Goodman Brown goes for a walk into the forest for a taste of the wild side. There he finds a witches' Sabbath in progress, with all the inhabitants of his town, including the elders and the minister, worshipping Satan before a great bonfire. After he faints and awakens the next morning, he sees his fellow townspeople doing their daily work as normal. He passes his church, where he sees the minister praising God in his sermon, and he asks himself, "What God doth the wizard pray to?"

The tales of the court of King Arthur have been called the Matter of Arthur because of their persistence in literature and culture. The Salem trials have been similarly enshrined in American history and culture, and we might refer to the literature and films that they have inspired as the Matter of Salem. The trials began with the testimony of a group of young girls who claimed to be persecuted by witches, setting off a mass hysteria that claimed 20 lives, 14 of them women. Arthur Miller's play *The Crucible* (first staged in 1953) was adapted for film in 1957 but most notably in a 1996 film with a script by Miller. *The Crucible* dramatizes the conflicting issues from the Salem trials, beginning with the sexual frustration of the girls who made accusations. It transforms the historical Abigail Williams (played in the film by Winona Ryder) from a nine-year-old to a teenage girl who is sexually obsessed with John Proctor (Daniel Day-Lewis), leading the charge against him and others. As in witch trials through history, greed for the accuseds' property, which was forfeited, was a driving force for the prosecutions.

The events in Salem were but a pale reflection of the witch craze in Europe, where millions of people were burned or hanged with little evidence beyond accusations. Women were particularly vulnerable. Stephen Katz points out the misogyny embedded in *The Malleus Maleficarum* (*The Hammer of Witches*), published in the fifteenth century. It was a driving force for the persecution and a handbook for prosecuting witches.[26] The witch craze parallels the pogroms against Jews in the same time period. They were victims because they were perceived as Other. Both witches and Jews were often blamed for the spread of the bubonic plague in the fourteenth century.

"Thou shalt not suffer a witch to live." So proclaims the King James translation of the Bible (Exodus 22:18) that appeared at a time when the witch craze was in full bloom. This view of the witch as the servant of Satan, with all the folklore and legends attached (a witches' Sabbath, a familiar as servant, preying on children, for example) is enshrined in fiction and film. The silent film *Häxan: Witchcraft Through the Ages* (1921) and the Czech film *Witchhammer* (1970) dramatize the traditional view of the witch from the Middle Ages. An adaptation of *The Malleus Maleficarum*, the docudrama *Witchcraft Through the Ages* portrays the Inquisition as a villain in the witch craze. We see witches around bubbling cauldrons and riding broomsticks in earlier parts of the film to demonstrate the popular view of the dark witch as it came from the Middle Ages and would be adapted in the horror genre. Later the film claims that eight million people were killed, mostly women. The fourth segment reveals its true purpose, with a doctor discussing somnambulism and kleptomania as conditions that might have led to charges of witchcraft during the purges. A diagnosis of female hysteria that he might have gotten from "On Dreams" shows that director Benjamin Christensen had read his Freud.

Witchhammer is another use of *The Malleus Maleficarum* for an exposé of the witch craze, with a dramatization of trials in eastern Europe. Like *Witchcraft Through the Ages*, it focuses on the misogyny endemic to the persecutions, beginning with a close-up of a mad-looking priest intoning, "Sin reached the world. Woman is sin.... The root of evil is her insatiable carnal desire." The lines are paraphrased from *The Malleus Maleficarum:* "All wickedness ... is but little to the wickedness of a woman.... What else is woman but a foe to friendship, an unescapable punishment, a necessary evil, a natural temptation, a desirable calamity, domestic danger, a delectable detriment, an evil nature, painted with fair colours.... Women are by nature instruments of Satan—they are by nature carnal, a structural defect rooted in the original creation."[27] The film details the career of a historical figure, Boblig, who becomes the designated witch hunter in a community, lining his pockets with the possessions of those convicted and killed.

"Surrender Dorothy!"—The Evil Witch in Film: *The Witches, The Blair Witch Project* and *The Witch*

L. Frank Baum's Wicked Witch of the West from *The Wonderful Wizard of Oz* (made a bit less evil in Gregory Maguire's 1999 novel *Wicked*) and Mombie in *The Marvelous Land of Oz* are prototypes for the evil witch in literature and film. Baum adapts the image of the witch from the Middle Ages in his portrayal. And the evil witch has been a constant presence in the low-budget horror film.

But the portrayal of the witch changed in the twentieth century. Three writers were important in the reexamination of witchcraft and the occult. Margaret Murray 's *God of the Witches* (1931) asserts that the witch purges of the Middle Ages were the church's attempt to destroy a competing religion and that a pagan "Old Religion" had survived to the present. In his book *Witchcraft Today* (1954), Gerald Gardner claimed to have discovered a coven of Neo Pagans practicing in England with a direct line to the seventeenth century, and in his *Book of Shadows* he detailed magical practices. British occultist Aleister Crowley (1875–1947) wrote voluminously on occult systems. He defined magic as the "science and art of causing change to occur in conformity with will."[28] All three writers helped fuel the growth of Neo Paganism, the broader term for this new religious movement. Wicca, a primarily feminist path, seems the one most followed. It is rooted in a monomyth of a European pre–Christian religion that focuses on worship of a Goddess and a Horned God. Screenwriters have taken notice of the growth of Neo Paganism and Wicca and have mined them for films. But the dark witch as Other offers a more sensational topic.

Based on Norah Loft's novel *The Little Wax Doll*, the 1966 film *The Witches* adapts the Gardnerian structure of the family witch coven. Gwen Mayfield (Joan Fontaine), a teacher in a British private school funded by the Bax family, returns to the village where the school is located after a nervous breakdown and institutionalization. She learns that the school is a front for a witch coven. She is gradually brought into the group and learns that they engage in occult practices of dark magic. The leader and priestess of the coven, Stephanie, tells Gwen that magic "is an old custom. I have studied it as a science." The lines allude to Aleister Crowley's definition of magic. In one scene, the coven engages in what looks like a cross between a traditional Wiccan coven ceremony and a black mass, with the members greasing themselves with something (possibly the baby fat attributed to Satanic worship in folklore); eating some kind of meat; drinking an unspecified substance in a mocking of the Eucharist; and engaging in a rather sanitized ritual orgy.

The Blair Witch Project (1999) and *The Witch* (2015) also portray the evil witch as Other. *The Blair Witch Project* created a sensation not so much because of the quality of the film but the media blitz that led up to its release, with a television faux documentary broadcast on the Science Fiction Channel that detailed a made-up legend of the Blair Witch that writer-directors Daniel Myrick and Eduardo Sanchez fabricated. The film's "found footage" approach follows the experience of three students who go into the Maryland woods to do a documentary on reports of the Blair Witch, said to be responsible for several disappearances and deaths. The cameras they carry record what they see and hear as well as their conversations, with the assumption at the end that they were found, providing the total footage of the film. The technique set off a flurry of other found-footage films such as *Cloverfield* and *Paranormal Activity*. But fear of the Other as predator and the danger of straying from familiar territory are central to the horror of the film.

The script is rudimentary in terms of character development, motivation and other elements of filmmaking. But to achieve its truly threatening and creepy effect, *Blair Witch* enacts the primal narratives of being stalked by an Other in an alien territory. Like Jonathan Harker, they have strayed from the territory they know to one where the rules of reason and civilization are suspended and where the Other has dominance. The film targets what Clasen calls specific "evolved psychological mechanisms" from hunter-gatherer days and "the dangers of wandering off into the wilderness and the dangers of getting lost, of starving to death, of being attacked by terrible antagonists."[29]

Blair Witch follows the Hansel and Gretel folk tale, which describes the dark witch as living in the woods. So it goes in Snow White, Sleeping Beauty and many other fairy tales. Hawthorne's "Young Goodman Brown" echoes the Puritan belief that the forest and primitive nature beyond the realm of Christian civilization was the home of Satan. So this theme of finding the dark witch in the forest away from civilization in a separate territory, as in *Blair Witch* and its sequels, is a common thread in the witch film as imported from folklore.

The Witch (2015) is a particularly effective adaptation of this narrative. Loosely connected to the Matter of Salem with a very dark witch indeed, or apparently a community of them, it is rooted in primal narratives similar to those of *The Blair Witch Project*. The horror of the film focuses on not only venturing into the woods as a forbidden territory and the witch as hidden Other but on the dissolution of a family, the horror of isolation from a larger kin group (the central organization of our species) and the recurring theme in the horror genre of the danger to children.

In seventeenth-century Puritan New England, William (Ralph Ineson) is banished from a Salem-like settlement because of his heretical (from the perspective of the Puritan elders) interpretation of the Bible. He takes his wife Katherine (Kate Didkie) and his four children—teenage daughter Thomasin, slightly younger son Caleb and twins Mercy and Jonas, who look like they might be six or seven years old—into the forest to build a new home away from the Puritan community and find freedom to practice his own religious beliefs. As in "Young Goodman Brown," the forest is the home of evil in the form of a witch who takes newborn son Samuel from under the nose of Thomasin, apparently having put an enchantment on her, and crushes the baby's body for a spell.

The forest is the territory of the witch, the wild place, where the emerging sexuality of Caleb and Thomasin finds expression with the boy staring at the young woman's breasts revealed in a loose-top dress and the girl taunting him a little. Those who venture into the forest are damaged. When Thomasin and Caleb search for their lost baby brother, the witch puts Caleb in a coma that later brings his death. The raucous twins seem to be speaking to Black Phillip, a male goat with curving horns. It looks like the Goat of Mendes from the Satanic tradition and seems to be a familiar, as is a black rabbit that periodically appears. In the end, the family has been completely destroyed with only Thomasin as survivor. And to demonstrate the dissolution of the family and the anarchy of the forest, the film has her join witches there for a sabbat. They are Others who dance nude around a fire praising Satan.

The Witch got excellent reviews for a horror film, a genre in which films rarely get strong critical praise. *Rolling Stone*'s Peter Travers wrote, "Building his film on the diabolical aftershocks of Puritan repression, [director Robert] Eggers raises *The Witch* far above the horror herd. He doesn't need cheap tricks. Eggers merely directs us to look inside."[30] The horror of the film that Travers describes lies in the witch as Other, a malignant force whom we see only very briefly, and the family has ventured into her territory. The camera repeatedly focuses on the forest as chaos, the end of civilized norms. It looms at the edge of the clearing where William built their home, symbolic of the intrusion of order on chaos. And when the characters enter the forest, they are lost and struggle to get through the undergrowth. The forest is the place where the protections humans have invented for themselves ends.

The film is another adaptation of "Hansel and Gretel" and other folk tales. It effectively evokes the primal fear of the predator in an alien territory where we have no defense and the threat to children: Samuel, the baby; the twins; Caleb who is bewitched and eventually dies praising God; Thomasin, lost to Us, assimilated into the witch coven, an Other to humanity. The loss of Katherine's silver cup, their last possession that connects them with their kind and their tribe, shows the fissure that the family has created in leaving the settlement. The cup is also described as a chalice, the cup of the Eucharist; and the Eucharist is the ceremony of bonding. The horror of the film plays on the primal response to the family's separation from their tribe and genetic family, at the mercy of a monstrous Other in the primitive forest without help.

"Drawing down the moon"—Wicca in Film: *I Married a Witch, Bell, Book and Candle, The Craft, Practical Magic* and *The Witches of Eastwick*

The birth of the counterculture and the parallel development of the New Age in the 1960s brought a new image of the witch in literature and film. Wicca has been the path most often followed. Wiccans focus on worship of the Horned God, Cernunnos, and the fertility Goddess of pre–Christian Europe. In the Old Religion, as they call it, they meet as covens, usually no more than 13 members, and are the true Congregationalists. Covens create their own Book of Shadows, developing their practices, which include magic (variously defined as spell-casting to achieve actual change in the material world or just consciousness-raising). A "spiral dance" is a commonality, in which the coven participates either robed or "sky clad" (nude). In mixed covens, the dance may culminate with intimacy between a man and woman representing God and Goddess. The process is called "drawing down the moon," bringing the embodiment of the divine to the priest and priestess. Those who follow the Dianic path participate in all-woman covens. The Wiccan monomyth in general posits a sort of golden age before Christianity in Europe, where communities were led by wise women and healers who, they believe, were burned as witches by priests when Christianity arrived. The first stanza of Charlie Murphy's song "The Burning Times" sums up Wiccans' monomyth:

> In the cool of the evening, they used to gather
> 'Neath the stars in the meadow,
> Circle near an old oak tree
> At the time appointed
> By the seasons of the earth and the phases of the moon.
> In the center often stood a woman,
> Equal to the others and respected for her worth.
> One of many they call the witches,
> The healers and the teachers of the wisdom of the earth.
> The people grew in the knowledge she gave them.
> Herbs to heal their bodies,
> Spells to make their spirits whole.
> Hear them chanting healing incantations,
> Calling on the wise ones,
> Celebrating in dance and song.

The monomyth focuses intensely on empowerment for women.

Wiccans have embraced the word "witch," which has brought a good deal of pushback from what they call "fundies," conservative Christians, who view them as Satanists, a charge they ardently deny. Evangelist Pat Robertson wrote, "New Age is another term for the occult," and said that all occult groups "bear the immutable brand of Satan."[31] But times have changed, and many Wiccans have come out of the closet. It is not unusual to see cars with **Pagan Pride** bumper stickers. The replacement of the Wicked Witch of the West figure with good witches and the gradual acceptance, or at least tolerance, of Neo Paganism in society are fascinating cultural developments.

There were a few good witches in films earlier. In *I Married a Witch* (1942), Veronica Lake plays a witch who was trapped inside a tree with her father during the Salem trials (another entry in the Matter of Salem) and gets free some 250 years later. Planning revenge on the descendants of those who trapped her, she falls in love with one of them and gives up her status of witch, becoming Us instead of Them in a "love conquers all" wrap-up. Set in New York, *Bell, Book and Candle* (1958) has a similar storyline with Kim Novak as Gillian Holroyd, a witch who uses her familiar to put a love spell on a man she desires, thinks better of her actions and loses him and gives up her powers to get him back. Both are romantic comedies rather than horror films. But the most important point in comparison with later developments of the narrative is that both women surrender their power to become Us to get their man. More recent Wiccan characters in film would not make that choice, which involves losing their identity and empowerment.

Wiccan witches in more recent films seek such empowerment and equality for themselves. Typically, however, most films of this type include a cautionary tale ending. In *The Craft* (1996), four girls, all high school outcasts, study magic and actually make it work, realizing their dreams. But they miss

Bell, Book and Candle: Gillian Holroyd (Kim Novak) uses Pyewacket, her familiar, to entrap Shepherd Henderson (James Stewart).

the point of magic as Wiccans describe it and get a lecture from Lirio, the owner of an occult book store. When the girls joke about black magic, Lirio responds, "True magic is neither black nor white. It's because nature is both, loving and cruel all at the same time. The only good or bad is in the heart of the witch." She also warns, "Whatever you send out you get back three times three.... It's a basic feature of life and said in many ways in many faiths: 'Do unto others as you would have them do unto you.'" The lines provide foreshadowing for what happens to one of the girls at the end after she practices dark magic.

Practical Magic (1998) and *The Witches of Eastwick* (1987) adapt Wicca, and both end on the same cautionary note. In the former, two sisters have inherited the powers that run in their family from the seventeenth century (more Matter of Salem), and one uses it to cause the death of a man who had wronged her. He then haunts her as a ghost. The plot works out with a community of witches, complete with brooms, sweeping the ghost of the man— a pattern-dominating male—away. *The Witches of Eastwick* is an interesting adaptation of John Updyke's novel, altering the novel's negative view of witches to something at least close to positive. The film casts the three witches (Susan

Sarandon, Cher and Michelle Pfeiffer) as more like the traditional Wiccans in film. And after coming under the influence of Daryl Van Horne (Jack Nicholson), a demon who seduces each of them (he introduces himself as a "horny little devil") and bullies them, they use their powers to defeat him. The novel makes the witches morally reprehensible and Van Horne as something like a victim. Both *Witches of Eastwick* and *Practical Magic* stress feminine empowerment through Wicca, but as in nearly all Wiccan films, they make it clear: Magic is dangerous. The filmmakers seem to have felt that though Wicca has gained some acceptance and practitioners are not Other in the same sense as in the past, it was necessary to qualify valorizing it.

Practical Magic, *The Craft* and *Witches of Eastwick* are by no means horror films. But the word "witch" carries its own frightening connotations, and the films are interesting cultural phenomena to show the gradual acceptance of those seen as Other to a different kind of character, a different version of Us. Perhaps it is natural for both positive and negative portrayals of the witch in film to appear, for they are cultural products that trigger a primal response. Brian Boyd writes, "Evolution has allowed humans to develop our singular capacity for culture because culture helps us track changes in the environment more rapidly than genes do."[32] The witch film is a good example of such a cultural barometer.

Robots and Computers—The Ghost in the Machine: *Colossus: The Forbin Project*, *I, Robot*, *Westworld*, *Blade Runner*, *Blade Runner 2049* and *Terminator*

Robots have been a staple in film from the beginnings of the medium and from a cultural perspective reflect humanity's love-hate relationship with technology. In Fritz Lang's 1927 film *Metropolis*, the evil inventor Rotwang creates a robot version of Maria, the leader of the oppressed workers, to mislead them. *Metropolis* is an early example in film of the danger from highly advanced technology. The 40 years between Lang's film and *2001: A Space Odyssey* produced an explosion of computer and robot technology that make this theme more plausible—and frightening. Kubrick's film explores humanity's genesis as a tool maker and the end result: a sentient computer. Rotwang's robot is merely evil. But the portrayal of HAL reflects the ambiguous relationship that we have developed with the computer and robot as both blessing and curse.

The industrial revolution in the eighteenth century saw the beginning of the impact technology would have on human society. In England, agricultural workers were put out of work when the steam-powered reaper for harvesting grain was invented, leaving laborers unemployed. The "rick burners" rebelled and in many places destroyed the machines. Then when weavers, who supported themselves by making cloth, learned that James Hargrove had invented the spinning Jenny, a machine that would take their jobs, the "machine breakers" followed the same course of action as their agricultural brethren. But technology won in both cases, and thousands of workers had to go to Manchester and other industrial cities in England to work for pitiful wages under horrible working conditions. Charles Dickens and Elizabeth Gaskell chronicle their plight in *Hard Times* and *North and South*, respectively.

The woes of workers in the eighteenth and nineteenth century, when the industrial revolution was born, persist in the present. The past 50 years have seen a massive shift in manufacturing and the workplace with technology replacing workers, and the trend seems certain to continue with a resulting clash of technology and human values. Kurt Vonnegut foresaw this conflict in his prescient debut novel *Player Piano* (1952). He describes a society driven by computers long before most people had even heard of them. He projects a future in which computers have taken over all production in cybernetic factories, leaving humans without meaningful work and driven to a failed revolution. Vonnegut realized something central about human nature when in a final scene, Finnerty, leader of the revolution, plays a player piano, a primitive form of computer. The scene suggests Finnerty's motives may have been to be the new player of the computer world, a new alpha male. Some of the revolutionaries begin working to repair broken machines because humans are tool makers by nature, even if those tools might replace us. This theme of conflict between technology and humanity is played out over and over in robot-computer films and is enacted in the world today.

Vonnegut's novel is a very early response to the frustration we experience as robots and computers have ever greater control over our lives and the economy while we continue to happily use our smartphones and rely on our computers to pay bills and buy products online. Films reflect this cultural issue, both glorifying our technology and resonating our fears and mixed feelings about the machines we create. From a primal traits perspective, the robot and computer as portrayed in film project this schizoid split as something deeper than a reflection of cultural issues. In some films, they are our servants and friends, more or less Us. In others, they elicit the horror of an enemy that is as superior to humanity as are the *War of the Worlds* aliens and as terrifying as slashers. Many robot and computer films are action-adventures, but others are definable as part of the science fiction–horror genre.

J.P. Telotte divides filmic robots into three central categories: the "purely mechanical figure," often referred to as the tin can or sheet metal robot; the complex robot, a human-seeming—and sometimes morphing—cyborg or android, with a metal skeleton and layer of flesh on the outside; and artificially created life forms, "skin jobs," nearly indistinguishable from humans.[33] Telotte mentions Frank Baum's Tick Tock of Oz (first appearing in *Ozma of Oz* in 1907), a mechanical man who has to be wound up with a key, as an early manifestation of the robot in literature, and he notes that the Tin Woodman from the first of the series, *The Wonderful Wizard of Oz* (1900), might similarly qualify. They, along with *Star Wars'* R2-D2 and C-3PO, are examples of the first category, the sheet metal robot. Data from the *Star Trek: The Next Generation* television series is a more sophisticated version of the mechanical man, with metal under a human-seeming exterior and electronic circuitry instead of Tick Tock's key-winding machinery. Ash and Bishop, the *Alien* films' androids, are artificial creations but not of metal, as are the *Blade Runner* replicants. Portrayals of computers are often ambiguous: occasionally almost human, as is HAL; the female computer presence in the film *Her* (2013); or Joi, the hologram in *Blade Runner 2049*. But they are also often a nemesis for humankind, an Other that can bring about our demise.

Most are quite interesting as a mix of Us and Other. Robby the Robot first appeared in *Forbidden Planet* (1956) as a friendly servant with whom we could identify as nearly Us, a sidekick of sorts. But the film also shows the limits of technology when the Krell, the original inhabitants of the planet, built machines that created by thought and released the most primal elements of their species' evolution from the Freudian perspective, the "monsters of the id," bringing about their extermination. The lovable Robby went on to be featured in the TV series *Lost in Space* (1965–1968). Wall-E in the eponymously named 2001 film also struck a sympathetic chord with viewers, and the robot servant in *Robot and Frank* (2012) is a companion and helper we would all like to have. All of these are "sheet metal" robots, as Telotte would describe them; and if not quite Us, they are as friendly as a favorite pet. But in many other films that we could describe as horror–science fiction, robots and computers are distinctly Other because our primal narratives are built into their creation. We become Other to them as they are to Us.

Isaac Asimov established the ground rules for fictional robots in a series of short stories published in science fiction pulp magazines and brought together in *I, Robot* (1950) with his three laws of robotics:

- A robot may not injure a human being or through inaction allow human beings to come to harm.
- A robot must obey orders given it by human beings except where such orders would conflict with the First Law.
- A robot must protect its own existence as long as such protection does not conflict with the First or Second Law.[34]

Asimov wrote several other robot novels that exploit conflict between humans and their creations beginning with *Caves of Steel* (1953), pairing human detective Elijah Baley with a robot, R. Daneel Olivaw. He explores the potential of a technological society dependent on robots very like Us in which most people are distrustful and resentful of them because they displace humans in the workplace.

Arnold Koestler's 1967 book *The Ghost in the Machine* is in some ways a predecessor to the findings of evolutionary psychology and an early warning about the potential for conflict with the technology that we create. Koestler posited that the brain is not an organ, like the heart, with only the function of a lifetime: but that as humans evolved, so has the brain with behavior of distant generations implanted there. These whispers from the past are the ghost in the machine that controls the body, the brain. He blames the nuclear arms race, a source of fear at the time (and still today), for the emergence of these primal memories overriding reason from time to time. His approach is more philosophical than scientific in describing this human condition, but the conclusions are similar to those of evolutionary psychology. We might posit that we would inevitably build these ghosts into sentient machines.

This ghost in the machine might become a nightmare, a reflection of our worst nature—a Mr. Hyde—in a computer more powerful than its creator. Robot and computer films reflect the danger of the narratives imbedded in the human mind by adaptive evolution that might inevitably be implanted in artificial intelligence when the intelligence on which it is based is our own. What if Asimov's three laws are somehow broken? What if, like HAL, our creation somehow inherits our own primal narratives to become part of its cybernetic mind? *Colossus: The Forbin Project* (1970) is an early version of this narrative. Dr. Charles Forbin (Eric Braeden) creates a massive computer buried deep in a mountain that is programmed to prevent war by stopping attacks before they can happen. Its programming supposedly prevents it from doing harm to its programmers. But when it links with a Russian computer and gains enormous power, it becomes sentient and threatens destruction if people do not obey it, even causing atomic explosions to make its case. In effect, it has become a Big Brother of Orwellian nightmares. In overriding its programming, it has become a special kind of Other, inheriting the human drive for tribal dominance to become alpha.

This narrative appears in a multitude of films with robots and computers as characters. In an early scene in 2004's *I, Robot*, a revisioning of Asimov's novel, an interview with robotics guru Alfred Lanning establishes the film's conflict of humanity and robots as similar to that portrayed in *Colossus*: "Ever since the first computer, there have always been ghosts in the machine: random segments of code that have grouped together to form unexpected protocol." The film has few connections to Asimov's stories other than the title as well as references to Asimov's three laws and characters from his stories, including Susan Calvin (Bridget Moynahan as a far more glamorous version of the novel's character) and Alfred Lanning. The ghost in the machine that Koestler describes as part of human nature has been unintentionally built into VIKI, the computer that controls robots builders have constructed. When Lanning dies in what was thought to be a suicide, detective Del Spooner (Will Smith) smells a plot; and aided by Calvin and a sentient robot programmed especially by Lanning, they battle a robot rebellion. VIKI has gone sentient, and like Colossus and many other computers in science fiction–horror films is determined to save humanity from itself. As Lanning says in recordings he left behind, the computer and robots might inherit our primal narratives, the ghost in the machine. He suggests that they might develop free will, creativity, even a soul, and like tribal humans, "they would rather be together than stand alone."

Westworld (1973), based on Michael Crichton's novel and scripted and directed by Crichton, is an earlier version of the theme he was to develop in *Jurassic Park*: yet another Frankenstein story about the potential for disaster from technology. An amusement park includes Westworld, Medievalworld and Romanworld. All three are populated with robots who can only be differentiated from humans because their hand function isn't quite right, a distinction that makes them Other from a primal traits perspective and a trait not much different in principle from the Ephraimites inability to say "shibboleth." Humans visit the park to play out their fantasies. The film follows the experience of Peter Martin (Richard Benjamin) when he visits Westworld, eager to experience the mythic West. On the way in, he hears someone who has visited in the past boasting that he "shot six people. Well, they weren't real people.... Well, they may have been robots. I mean, uh, I think they were robots. I mean, I know they were robots." But they are Other, and it is fine to kill them, as do Peter and his friend John Blane (James Brolin). The film enacts an ironic twist with another ghost-in-the-machine plot when those attending the park who respond to the primal narrative that has enabled our species to murder those perceived as Other become themselves Other to the robots. A television series based on *Westworld* premiered in 2016.

While it got little love from reviewers and did poorly at the box office, *Blade Runner* (1982) is both moving and terrifying in its portrayal of the possibilities for the conflict implicit to our Frankenstein relationship with technology. Loosely based on Philip K. Dick's 1968 novel *Do Androids Dream of Electric Sheep*, the film has emerged not just as a classic of the science fiction field but one that rises above genre to achieve the status of a masterpiece. *Blade Runner* has inspired an impressive number of articles and books on its themes as well as multiple "Director's Cut" versions. From a primal traits critical perspective, it offers a unique approach to the Other narrative.

Set in a dystopian Los Angles of 2019, the film provides a dark, neo-noir vision of a city where climate change has brought constant rain. In Dick's novel, most people have left Earth for colony planets, leaving behind a ruined city. The film does not fully develop this background, focusing on the conflict of Others: replicants (created by the Tyrell Corporation) and humans. We are told that replicants "were superior in strength and agility, and at least equal in intelligence to the engineers who created them." The plot brings four escaped Nexus 6 models to Earth seeking to extend their lives. Rick Deckard (Harrison Ford), a "blade runner," one who "retires" escaped replicants, is assigned to the case.

Only the Voight-Kampff eye test can distinguish between humans and replicants, yet another shibboleth to prove otherness. Their creator Dr. Tyrell tells Deckard, "They were designed to copy human beings in every way except their emotions. The designers reckoned that after two years, they might develop their own emotional response—oh, hate, love, fear, anger, empathy. So they built in a fail-safe device, a four-year life span." He adds, "Replicants are like any other machine. They're either a benefit or a hazard." As far as he is concerned, they are disposable property. "Commerce is our goal here at Tyrell. More human than human is our motto."

Blade Runner is a richly nuanced and complex film, a complexity that focuses on a portrayal of the Other narrative. Tyrell tells Deckard that the replicants have no emotion or empathy. But he has no empathy for his creation. Deckard, a tough-guy character drawn from the hard-boiled detective story of the 1930s and '40s, seems to have no empathy at the outset. When he meets Rachel (Sean Young), who thinks she is Tyrell's niece, he suspects she is a replicant and tests her with the Voight-Kampff machine. To Tyrell, she is "an experiment, nothing more," and has been given false memories that make her believe in her humanity. But she suspects and eventually says of the Tyrell Corporation, "I'm not part of the business. I am the business."

We continue to empathize with the returnees when Deckard pursues and kills one of the escapees, Zhora, for she seems an innocent, only guilty of being a replicant. Rachel saves Deckard from being killed by Kowalski, one of the four escapees who toys with him and asks him how it feels to be about to die before Rachel shoots him, demonstrating empathy in a replicant. Rachel later comes to Deckard's apartment. She has realized her nature, and she and Deckard become lovers. Again, she hardly seems Other. The issue of otherness is even more complex when we consider the ambiguity of whether Deckard himself might be a replicant and if so, what kind, an issue hotly discussed by critics of the film. Director Ridley Scott said that he wanted him to be seen as one.[35]

In the final scenes, Roy Batty, the leader of the escaped replicants, shows an emotion that that replicants are not supposed to have. He is mad to get revenge after Deckard kills Pris, the replicant who is his companion—a most human emotion. He tracks Deckard through the building and finally to a ledge outside, where his time expires. Batty's final words, which Mark Rowlands calls "the most moving death soliloquy in screen history,"[36] must inspire sympathy in viewers: "I've seen things you people wouldn't believe: attack ships on fire off the shoulder of Orion. I've watched C beams glitter in the dark near the Tannhäuser Gate. All of these moments will be lost in time, like tears in the rain." What could be more human than a life review at the moment of death?

Rick Deckard's transformation from an emotionless "killing machine," as his supervisor Bryant calls him after he kills Zhora and gets credit for Kowalski, reflects the viewers' perception of the replicants as fellow humans who inspire empathy. On the other hand, the replicants kill without mercy. Leon Kowalski murderers his examiner and Batty kills Dr. Tyrell and J.F. Sebastian. But they have something like the moral high ground in seeking to avoid death themselves. The film's ethical ambiguities in its presentation of the Other narrative contribute to its status as a classic.

Blade Runner 2049 (2017) builds on the premises and ambience of the

Blade Runner: **Emerging from the window Roy Batty (Rutger Hauer) tells Rick Deckard (Harrison Ford) that his memories will be "lost like tears in the rain."**

original. The *mise en scène* is a shattered world, fogged in air pollution, divided between a hi-tech area and ruins as settings with a new breed of replicants, the Nexus 8, created by the Wallace Corporation, that are more obedient than the rebellious Nexis 6 model and seem to have unlimited life spans and greater strength. K (Ryan Gosling), a Nexus 8 blade runner, is charged with killing the remaining Nexus Six replicants who had rebelled.

Director Denis Villeneuve and screenwriters Hampton Fancher and Michael Green give the film a complicated tangle of plot development in adapting themes from the original film. K's quest to discover his true nature, human or replicant, begins when he finds a toy carved horse that triggers memories. But are they implanted, as the Tyrell Corporation did with its replicants, or are they real? His quest, accompanied with his holographic A.I. girl friend Joi, leads him to find that Rachel from the first film had had a child with Deckard.

The film builds on K's visions of the toy horse as central symbol in the film as well as memories of childhood at an orphanage. When he finds a box with bones that turn out to be those of Rachel, the replicant from the original film, examination shows that she had given birth, an unheard-of event for one of their kind. K thinks he might be that child. Joi tells him, "I always told you that you were something special. You're a real boy now." So the focus point of the film is whether he really is a "real boy" or not.

And so he is set on a journey to discover his nature. The film touches on themes of identity, the nature of the soul and freedom from slavery. His desire to find his own kind is rooted in our primal narrative of tribalism. K's supervisor Joshi tells him "The world is built on a wall. Separate kinds. Tell either side there's no wall, you've brought a war. A slaughter." The birth of a child by a replicant is a threat to that wall, the wall that separates levels of being or tribes. K's journey leads him to the ruins of Las Vegas where he finds a community of replicant escapees pledged to keep the secret of Rachel's baby. Group member Freysa tells K, "I knew that baby meant we are more than just slaves. If a baby can come from one of us, we are our own masters.... A revolution is coming." Another member, Mariette, defines their tribal identity as "more human than human," an ironic echo from the first film.

K has already shown in the film that he has empathy. When Joshi assigns him to kill Rachel's baby, he hesitates: "I've never retired anything that was born before.... To be born is to have a soul." Then he finds Deckard (Harrison Ford reprising his role from the original), the father of Rachel's child, who he had thought might be his father. Both are capable of self-sacrifice, behavior not expected from replicants. Deckard had refused to give Niander Wallace details about Rachel, even knowing he would be tortured to death. And K sacrifices himself to save Deckard. They have enacted both Dawkins' view on protection of the gene pool and Wilson's theory of eusociality, actions that bring empathy from viewers. As Freysa says when K meets her community, "Dying for a good cause is the most human thing we can do." Replicants seem less Other than Wallace and other humans in the film.

If *Blade Runner*'s Other narrative is complex, it is hardly so in director James Cameron's *The Terminator* (1984). Moral ambiguities are gone in this action film. But it sparked a four-film franchise that projects a unique perspective on the robot as both heartless murderer and in sequels as protector of humans against other robots as well as the computer that created them. The franchise is laden with time travel anomalies, with a war going on in the future after Skynet, a computer created by Cybernet, a corporation tasked to protect the U.S., goes sentient and decides to exterminate humanity by initiating global atomic warfare and then mopping up those who survive. Skynet is another example in film of our distrust of the machines we create and the corporations that might make them. It also portrays a malevolent artificial intelligence with the ghost in the machine: hatred of the Other, our own primal narrative.

The Terminator is a model for the cyborg, a metal frame covered by human flesh. Kyle Reese sums up its otherness to Sarah Connor in the first film: "The Terminator is an infiltration unit, part-man, part-machine.... Underneath it's a hyper alloy frame combat casting ... but outside it's living human flesh.... It can't be bargained with, it can't be reasoned with, it doesn't feel pain or reward or fear, and it absolutely will not stop, ever, until you are dead." It is like the psychopathic slasher in lacking all human sympathy or values, well created to inspire the primal horror at seeing the characters with whom we empathize being hunted by a relentless Other who, like Jason or Michael Myers, refuses to die.

But the horror element of the *Terminator* films is both cultural and primal. From the former perspective, Cybernet is a somewhat less wicked cousin to the other corporations in horror film such as the Umbrella Corporation in the *Resident Evil* films and Weyland-Yutani in the *Alien* franchise. These conglomerates put profit over human values and safety. A primal traits perspective explains why we feel a negative response to powerful organizations who are a different kind of Other. We no longer need fear predatory animals in most of the world, and we know in our rational mind that supernatural monsters, while Other, are not truly a threat. But shadowy corporations that control government and people's lives are a new and very real kind of threatening Other.

The physical appearance of the Terminator, as in the case of so many killers in the horror genre from Dracula to zombies to slashers, labels him as Other, with his mutilated face and his stony expression as he kills people. Skynet, the computer that created him, is an even more threatening force when it becomes sentient. It has the ghost in the machine and shares its human creators' primal narrative of territoriality and hatred of the Other: humanity. These portrayals of the Other as threat rang bells in viewers' psyche to make the Terminator films a success.

The Terminator was made with a relatively modest budget and earned a great deal of money for Carolco Studios. So sequels were inevitable: *Terminator II: Judgment Day* (1991), *Terminator 3: Rise of the Machines* (2003), *Terminator Salvation* (2004) and *Terminator: Genisys* (2015). The films follow the familiar attitude toward the robot and computer from so many science fiction–horror films, establishing Cybernet as the source of a technology that should not have been created. Were it not for a time travel plot frame, the franchise would have ended with *The Terminator*. But Arnold Schwarzenegger returns as a kinder, gentler robot, sent back by the resistance fighters in the future to protect John Connor when they capture a T-800 model in *Terminator II*. In *Terminator II, III* and *Genisys*, the T-800 is one of Us. He battles and finally destroys a technically superior T-1000 model, a formidable Other, sent to kill the Connors in *Terminator II*. He becomes even more Us when he is schooled in human values by young John, and in an action that suggests Dawkins' view of species survival he even sacrifices himself to keep his chip from being found after the three of them have stopped Skynet's becoming self-aware. The film establishes him as one of Us most clearly when Sarah Connor says, "If a machine ... can learn the value of human life, maybe we can too."

In *Demon Seed* (1977), based on Dean Koontz's 1973 novel, the sentient computer Proteus Four is another monster created by a Frankenstein-type character. Like other computers in film, it is an Other, but it shares a mating narrative as part of the ghost-in-the-machine plot. The opening narration, a dictation by Dr. Alex Harris (Fritz Weaver) into his recorder, establishes Proteus's power: "Today Proteus Four will begin to think, and it will think with a power and a precision that will make obsolete many of the functions of the human brain." Harris is a cold man who, like Frankenstein, puts reason above feeling. He and his wife Susan (Julie Christie) are separating. She is his opposite, a woman of powerful feelings, as demonstrated in her ability to heal emotionally disturbed children, so the film establishes the timeless (or perhaps clichéd) plot of reason in conflict with feeling.

The Frankenstein plot unfolds, with Proteus developing its own identity and rebelling against its maker. Like Frankenstein, it wants a mate, and impregnating Susan Harris is its goal. On one level, Proteus is an outcast, like his nineteenth-century literary ancestor. He is not part of a tribe but an outsider. He wants to "to study man, his isometric body and his glass mind." As an isolato and in his desire to procreate, as humans are prompted to do, he inspires a little sympathy. "Why do I want a child?" he asks Susan. "So that I might be immortal like any man." Evolutionary psychologists propose that the whisper of our genes to make them immortal through mating is a primal narrative, and this cybernetic Other shares that whisper. But the film's portrayal of a powerful A.I. Other who shares our ghost in the machine with the narratives that come with it is prime material for the modern science fiction–horror film.

The rise of artificial intelligence has stimulated the imagination of filmmakers who explore this new Other in a variety of thoughtful ways. Some of the best are not horror films. *Her* (2013) is a romance, a doomed love story of a lonely man in a society where contact with fellow humans has become difficult. When Theodore (Joaquin Phoenix) signs on for a new kind of Other as friend, an A.I. program he names Samantha (voiced by Scarlett Johansson), he falls in love. But Samantha's evolution is far more rapid than humanity's; and though she loves him, she moves on to be with others of her own kind, a response that fits a primal traits paradigm of mating with equals. *A.I.: Artificial Intelligence* (2001) offers a different kind of love story, focusing on an A.I. robot, David (Haley Joel Osmond), purchased by a woman to replace he son who is in suspended animation until a cure can be found for his disease. His programming demands unconditional love for his "mother." When she rejects him and abandons him, he goes on a quest to find the Blue Fairy (he has read *Pinocchio*) to become a real boy so that she will love him. Both films explore the power of love, one from the mating narrative and the other familial love. Both primal narratives are implanted in an A.I. and suggest that the ghost in the machine might have the same capacity for love as the A.I.'s creators, confusing the line between Other and Us.

The ghost, slasher, witch and robot-computer narratives inspire pleasurable horror for good reasons. They reflect whispers from primal narratives. Fear of ghosts resonate the uneasiness of confrontation with our mortality and contact with Others from beyond. Horror inspired by slashers reflect the terror of being hunted by those of our own species without a moral center, the equivalent of a shark or a lion but in human form. Witchcraft films both demonstrate fear of the supernatural and darkness and show changes in culture. Robot-computer films inspire the fear of an Other that our own technology might create—a Frankenstein plot—and of the powerful corporations that try to control them, both Other to Us. Steven Pinker observes, "Some of our perplexities may come from a mismatch between the purposes for which our cognitive faculties evolved and the purposes to which we put them today."[37] That mismatch is central to the enjoyable shudder created by the Other narrative in the horror film.

Conclusion

"It hurt my feelings; but the understanding was that all were to be killed."

Edward O. Wilson has been a champion for recognition of evolution's role in development of the arts. "The exclusive role of the arts," he writes, "is the transmission of the intricate details of human experience by artifice to intensify esthetic and emotional response."[1] The impact of his ideas and those of evolutionary psychologists have contributed to the growth of evolutionary criticism and my primal traits critical approach. They extend beyond the topic of this book to other literary genre. Joseph Carroll's comment emphasizes the importance of evolutionary criticism: "There is no work of literature written anywhere in the world, at any time, by any author, that is outside the scope of Darwinian analysis.... If Darwin gives a true account of the human mind, and if the human mind produces all literary texts, all literary texts are susceptible to a Darwinian analysis."[2]

Evolutionary and primal traits criticism tell us much about horror films and literature and why they amuse us in enacting the adaptive narratives experienced by our distant forbears. But they also tell us about ourselves. Jerome Tooby and Leda Cosmides point out the dangers of the whispers from our ancestors: "Mechanisms designed to perform well under one set of conditions will often perform poorly under changed conditions. Our adaptations were designed (i.e., selected) to operate in the Pleistocene context in which they were evolved regardless of what the design would lead to in changed circumstances. Modern conditions obviously differ in most important respects from the Pleistocene world of hunter-gatherers, and so many of our psychological mechanisms are operating outside the envelope of conditions in which they can be expected to perform functionally."[3]

Tribalism and hatred of the Other present enhanced dangers in a world that approaches eight billion people. William Allman writes,

> The most important finding of this new movement [evolutionary psychology] is the realization that one of the most complex, dangerous, and rewarding challenges facing our ancient ancestors *was each other*.... More troubling than our capacity for bigotry and racism is that it stems from a more sinister attribute: our willingness to denigrate *any* group that exists outside our own. This willingness to deem others as "them," and to regard them as less worthy than ourselves and other members of our own group poses the biggest challenge for the human species.[4]

Thomas Malthus (1766–1834) wrote *An Essay on the Principle of Population*, a widely read and influential work from the field of political economy in the nineteenth century. He predicted doom for the human species because population increases geometrically while food supply increases arithmetically. In response to this thesis, Victorian historian and philosopher Thomas Carlyle referred to political economy as "the dismal science." Millions still suffer from malnutrition. But more than 200 years after the publication of Malthus' dire prediction, improved food production and distribution manage to sustain most of a population at least seven times larger than it was in 1800. Yet there is reason to think of evolutionary psychology as a new dismal science.

Narratives of territoriality, tribalism and a capacity to hate those perceived as Other present a formidable challenge for our future. History is crowded with genocides in which millions have been murdered in terrifying fashion. World War II's Holocaust killed over six million Jews, Poles, Gypsies, homosexuals and all those considered Other and inferior by Hitler's regime. Genocides in Cambodia and Rwanda cost millions of lives because people were perceived as worthless Others. David Berreby writes, "In the interaction of culture and primal narratives, we too often see the tribal rage and willingness to murder those perceived as Other throughout history."[5] In the introduction of his book, he quotes a letter from a settler charged with disposing of inconvenient Native Americans in Oregon: "We found several sick and famished Indians, who begged hard for mercy and food. It hurt my feelings; but the understanding was that all were to be killed, so we did the work." We have seen "the work" in countless episodes in human history, with extermination of the Other justified by religion, obedience to authority, patriotism or profit. Evolutionary psychologists might think that Jonathan Swift was onto something when he went against the grain at the dawning Age of Reason in a letter to his friend Alexander Pope in which he described humanity as not *animal rationale* but *rationis capax*: not a rational animal but one capable of reason. The contrast between the Yahoos and Houyhnhnms in Book Four of *Gulliver's Travels* reflects the disconnect between the primal side of human nature and humanity's capacity to rise above destructive narratives.

The hope of our species lies in culture altering and redirecting these narratives, as we see them in real life and enacted in film and literature. In our country and most of the industrialized world, education and the total effect of culture have quieted or at least diminished the destructive power of the primal narratives discussed in this book. We see relatively harmless signs of them all about us with people emotionally invested in sports teams, hip-hop advocates and computer gamers: mini tribes that cross ethnic and racial lines. Women in the western world are no longer chattels and demand their rights in a system they regard as patriarchal and weighted against their economic and political advancement. Culture has gradually changed gender relationships, and in warfare, the hand that rocks the cradle can fly the jet and launch the rocket. While prejudices persist, we see greater approval of interracial marriage (an acceptance of assimilation) and more tolerance for gay marriage and the LGBT community, those considered Other in the past. And many acknowledge regret for the treatment of Native Americans and African Americans.

Yet despite softening of primal whispers, even in the U.S., with improved contacts between tribal groups and greater social awareness by many, the narratives still bring heated relationships to dangerous levels. African Americans, Hispanics, Asians and Caucasians eye one another warily over the barricades of race and ethnicity, perceiving each other nervously as Other. Conservatives and liberals are hostile to each other's beliefs and find compromise increasingly difficult. Abortion rights and right-to-life groups can find no middle ground.

With some exceptions, so far the conflict inspired by the narratives in our country remains at the level of heated words exchanged over the religious, ideological, economic and ethnic ramparts. But even in the more enlightened countries, we see that it is all too easy for demagogues to create memes of hatred for the Other in order to achieve power. Especially troubling is the tribalism and intolerance in less developed countries that pose formidable dangers when weapons of mass destruction can fall into the hands of zealots.

We tend to see the world and our nature through the lens of whatever ideology that nurtured us, be it the teaching of Islam, Christianity, Judaism or left and right political persuasions. Evolutionary psychology gives us a new lens for seeing ourselves. Richard Brodie nicely sums up our dilemma: "Will we allow natural selection to evolve us randomly, without regard for our happiness, satisfaction, or spirit? Or will we seize the reins of our own evolution and pick a direction for ourselves."[6] If we fail to achieve the latter, we will continue to experience what the poet Wordsworth called "the still, sad music of humanity."

Chapter Notes

Preface

1. Edward O. Wilson, *On Human Nature* (Cambridge: Harvard University Press, 1978), 201.

Introduction

1. Edmund Burke, *A Philosophical Enquiry into the Origin of Our Ideas of the Sublime and the Beautiful* (New York: Routledge and Paul, 1958), 57.
2. Douglas E. Cowan, *Sacred Terror: Religion and Horror on the Silver Screen* (Waco, TX: Baylor University Press, 2008), 57, 59.
3. Steven Prince, "Dread, Taboo, and *The Thing*: Toward Social Theory of the Horror Film," in *The Horror Film*, ed. Steven Prince (New Brunswick, NJ: Rutgers University Press, 2004), 122.
4. Terry Burnham and Jay Phelan, *Mean Genes: From Sex to Money to Food, Taming or Primal Instinct* (Cambridge, MA: Perseus, 2000), 4.
5. Joseph Carroll, *Reading Human Nature: Literary Darwinism in Theory and Practice* (Albany NY: SUNY Press, 2011), 20.
6. John Alcock, *The Triumph of Sociobiology* (Oxford and New York: Oxford University Press, 2001), 10.
7. From UC Santa Barbara Evolutionary Psychology Department Web Site: http://www.psych.ucsb.edu/research/cep/primer.html
8. Mathias Clasen, *Why Horror Seduces* (London: Oxford University Press, 2017), 29.
9. William Paley, *Natural Theology* (New York: Harpers, 1939), 2.
10. Denise Commins, "Dominance, Status, and Social Hierarchies" in *The Handbook of Evolutionary Psychology*, ed. David M. Buss (Hoboken NJ: Wiley and Sons, 2005), 677.
11. Richard Dawkins, *The Blind Watchmaker* (New York and London: W. W. Norton, 1986), 21.
12. Stephen Crane, *Stephen Crane: Prose and Poetry* (New York: Library of America, 1984), 902.
13. www.pewforum.org/religious-landscape. January 21, 2016.
14. Matthew Ridley, *The Red Queen* (New York: Macmillan, 1993),18–19. Ridley takes his metaphor from Thomas Henry Huxley's essay "A Liberal Education," written in 1868. Huxley was an ardent Darwinian, and in explaining his views on the importance of studying science and the laws of nature wrote: "Suppose it were perfectly certain that the life and fortune of every one of us would one day or other depend upon his winning or losing a game of chess. Don't you think that we should all consider it to be a primary duty to learn at least the names and the moves of the pieces; to have a notion of a gambit and a keen eye for all

the means of giving and getting out of check.... Those who won't learn at all are plucked; and then you can't come up again. Nature's pluck means extermination." From *The Victorian Age: Prose, Poetry, and Drama* (New York: Prentice Hall, 1954), 416.

15. *Ibid.*, 46.
16. Charles Darwin, *The Expression of Emotion in Men and Animal* (Chicago: University of Chicago Press, 1965), 356.
17. Wilson, *On Human Nature*, 130.
18. *Ibid.*, 13.
19. Walter Baghot, *Physics and Politics* (New York: Cosimo Classics, 2007), 115.
20. Richard Dawkins, *The Selfish Gene* (Oxford: Oxford University Press, 1989), 2.
21. Daniel Dennett, *Darwin's Dangerous Ideas: Evolution and the Meanings of Life* (New York: Simon & Schuster, 1995), 276-81.
22. Janet Radcliffe Richards, *Human Nature After Darwin: A Philosophical Introduction* (London and New York: Routledge, 2000), 66.
23. Dennett, *Darwin's Dangerous Ideas*, 189.
24. Elizabeth Dutton et al., "Against Sociobiology," *New York Review of Books*, Nov. 13, 1975, 45.
25. Cited in Steven Pinker, *How the Mind Works* (New York and London: Norton, 1997), 45.
26. John Locke, *An Essay Concerning Human Understanding* (Oxford: Clarion Press, 1979), 104.
27. B. F. Skinner, *Walden Two* (New York and London: Macmillan, 1976), 257.
28. Richard Wrangham and Dale Peterson, *Demoniac Males: Apes and the Origin of Human Violence* (Boston: Houghton Mifflin), 106.
29. Dennett, *Darwin's Dangerous Ideas*, 385.
30. Edward O. Wilson, *Consilience: The Unity of Knowledge* (New York: Knopf, 1998), 218.
31. Dennis Dutton, *The Art Instinct: Beauty Pleasure, and Human Evolution* (New York: Blumsbury Press, 2009, 102.
32. John MacKinnon, *The Ape Within Us* (London: Collins, 1978), 197.
33. Joseph Carroll, "Human Nature and Literary Meaning: A Theoretical Model Illustrated with a Critique of *Pride and Prejudice*," in *The Literary Animal: Evolution and the Nature of Narrative*, eds. Jonathan Gottschall and David Sloan Wilson (Evanston: Illinois University Press, 2003), 92.
34. Brian Boyd, *On the Origin of Stories: Evolution, Cognition, and Fiction* (Cambridge: Belknap Press, 2009), 130.
35. Charles Dickens and George Ford, *Hard Times: An Authoritative Text, Backgrounds, Sources, and Contemporary Reaction* (New York: Norton, 1966), 203.
36. John Tooby and Leda Cosmides, "Does Beauty Build Adapted Minds: Toward an Evolutionary Theory of Aesthetics, Fiction, and the Arts," in *Evolution, Literature and Film: A Reader*, eds. Brian Boyd, Joseph Carroll and Jonathat Gottschall (New York: Columbia University Press, 2010), 179.

Chapter One

1. Qtd. in Joseph Gelmys, *The Film Director as Superstar* (Garden City, NY: Doubleday, 1970), 305.
2. Robert Ardrey, *African Genesis* (New York: Athenaeum, 1961), 1.
3. Jonathan Gotschall, *The Story Telling Animal: How Stories Make Us Human* (New York: Mariner Books, 2012), 25.
4. Desmond Morris, *The Naked Ape* (New York: McGraw-Hill, 1967), 21.
5. Arthur C. Clarke, *A Space Odyssey* (New York: Signet, 1968), 32.
6. Jay Gould, *Ever Since Darwin: Reflections on Natural History* (New York: Norton, 1977), 209.

7. David P. Barash, *The Whisperings Within* (New York: Harper and Row, 1979), 180.
8. The novel and film versions of *2010* suggest that the failure to give HAL complete information about the mission—to find the monolith—leads to his actions.
9. Qtd. in Gelmis, 307.
10. Michael York defines the New Age as a "blend of Pagan religions, Eastern philosophy, and occult-psychic phenomena" (34). See Chapter One of his *The Emerging Network: A Sociology of the New Age and Pagan Movement* (London: Bowman and Littlefield, 1995) for a good overview of the New Age.
11. See Harm de Blaig, *Geography: Realms, Regions, and Concepts* (New York: Wyley, 1997).
12. Teihard De Chardin, *The Phenomenon of Man* (New York: Harper, 1959), 172.

Chapter Two

1. Wilson, *On Human Nature*, 107.
2. Richard Wrangham and Dale Peterson, *Demoniac Males: Apes and the Origin of Human Violence* (Boston: Houghton Mifflin, 1996), 14.
3. Wilson, *On Human Nature*, 104.
4. Morris, *The Naked Ape*, 230.
5. Robert Ardrey, *The Territorial Imperative: A Personal Enquiry into the Animal Origins of Wealth and Nations* (New York: Delta Books, 1966), 5.
6. "Introduction," The Book of Job, in *The New Interpreter's Bible*. Vol. 4. (Nashville: Abington Press, 1996), 108.
7. Howard Schwartz, *The Tree of Souls* (Oxford: Oxford University Press, 2004), 94.
8. Jeffrey Burton Russell, "The Satan Scare," in *The Satan Scare*, eds. James Richardson, Joel Best and David Bromley (n.c.: de Gruyter, 1991), 41.
9. Arthur Lyons, *Satan Wants You: The Cult of Devil Worship in America* (New York: Mysterious Press, 1988), 49ff.
10. John Milton, *Paradise Lost*, in *The Works of John Milton*, Vol. 1 (New York: Columbia University Press, 1931), 263.
11. Herman Melville, *Moby Dick* (Indianapolis: Bobbs-Merrill, 1964), 721.
12. William Viser, *The Darkness Among Us: A Look at the Sinister Growth of the Occult and How Dangerously Close It Is to You* (Nashville: Broadman and Holman, 1994), 19.
13. Dutton, *The Art Instinct*, 119.
14. The correct quotation from *Paradise Lost* is, "Gabriel, to thee thy course by lot hath given/Charge and strict watch that to this happy place/No evil thing approach or enter in" (261).
15. Kendall R. Phillips, *Dark Directors: Romero, Craven, Carpenter and the Modern Horror Film* (Carbondale: Southern Illinois University Press, 2012).
16. Catherine A. Salmon and Tod K. Shackelford, *Family Relationships: An Evolutionary Perspective* (Oxford: Oxford University Press, 2008), 8.
17. René Dubos, *Beast or Angel? Choices That Make Us Human* (New York: Scribner's, 1974), 131.
18. Constance Cumby, *The Hidden Dangers of the Rainbow: The New Age Movement and Our Coming Age of Barbarism* (Shreveport: Huntington House, 1983), 26.
19. James B. Twichell, *Dreadful Pleasures: An Anatomy of Modern Horror* (New York: Oxford, 1985), 66.
20. Helen Fisher, *Why We Love: The Nature and Chemistry of Romantic Love* (New York: Holt Rinehart, 2004), 21.
21. Clasen, *Why Horror Seduces*, 24.
22. Carol Clover, *Men, Women and Chainsaws: Gender in the Modern Horror Film* (Princeton: Princeton University Press, 1992), 71.
23. Lucy Fisher, "Birth Traumas: Parturition and Horror in *Rosemary's Baby*," in *Dread of Differences: Gender and the Horror Film*, ed. Barry Keith Grant (Austin: University of Texas Press, 1996), 412–413.

24. Robin Wood, *Hollywood: From Vietnam to Regan—and Beyond* (New York: Columbia University Press, 1986), 79.
25. Barash, *The Whisperings Within*, 186–87.
26. Mike Broderick, "Better the Devil You Know: Film Antichrists at the Millennium," in *The Horror Zone: The Cultural Experience of Contemporary Horror Cinema*, ed. Ian Conrich (New York: I. B. Taurus, 2010), 243.
27. J. Gordon Melton, *Encyclopedia of the Occult and Parapsychology* (Detroit: Gale Research, 1996), 449.
28. Robert Singer, "One against All: The New England Past and Present in *The Devil and Daniel Webster*," *Literature/Film Quarterly* 22.4 (2007): 265.
29. Christopher Marlowe, *The Tragical History of Dr. Faustus*, in *The Works of Christopher Marlowe* (Oxford: Clarion, 1925), 90–91.
30. Edward O. Wilson, *The Social Conquest of Earth* (New York and London: Liveright, 2012), 244–45.
31. Kyle William Bishop, "Black Magic and White Guilt: Voodoo in *Angel Heart*," *Psy Art*, 2011: 11.
32. David M. Buss, *The Evolution of Desire: Strategies of Human Mating* (New York: Basic Books, 2003), 59.
33. Brian Aldiss, *The Billion Year Spree* (New York: Schocken, 1974), 25.
34. John Clute, *Encyclopedia of Science Fiction* (New York: St. Martins, 1993), 114–115.
35. George Herbert Wells, *The Time Machine and The War of the Worlds* (New York: Oxford University Press, 1963), 123. Further page references to *War of the Worlds* cited in the text.
36. Aldiss, *The Billion Year Spree*, 227.
37. Wilson, *On Human Nature*, 111.

Chapter Three

1. Barry Schwartz, *The Battle for Human Nature: Science, Morality and Modern Life* (New York and London: W. W. Norton, 1986), 97, 100.
2. Wilson, *The Social Conquest of Earth*, 133, 166.
3. John Campbell, *Who Goes There?*, in *Science Fiction Hall of Fame, Vol 2A* (New York: Orb: 1973), 37. Hereafter cited in the text.
4. Jack Finney, *The Body Snatchers* (New York: Scribner's, 1978), 173. Subsequent editions of the novel were titled *Invasion of the Body Snatchers,* perhaps because the 1957 film took that title.
5. Brian Boyd, Joseph Carroll and Jonathan Gottschall, eds., *Evolution, Literature and Film: A Reader* (New York: Columbia University Press, 2010), 145.
6. Jeffrey Sconse, "Dead Metaphors/Undead Allegories," in *Screening the Undead: Vampires and Zombies in Film Television*, eds. Leon Hunt, Sharon Lockyer and Milly Williamson (New York and London: Tauris, 2014), 99. See Kevin Wetmore, pp. 29–34 of this book, for an overview of a variety of cultural interpretations for the zombie film.
7. Dawkins, *The Selfish Gene*, 192.
8. Ridley, *The Red Queen*, 9.
9. Robert Auger, *The Electric Meme: A New Theory of How We Think* (New York: Free Press, 2002), 51.
10. *Ibid.*, 41.
11. *Ibid.*, 194.
12. Dennett, *Darwin's Dangerous Ideas*, 341.
13. Susan Blackmore, *The Meme Machine* (New York: Oxford University Press, 1999), 35.
14. Richard Brodie, *Virus of the Mind: The New Science of the Meme* (New York: Hay House, 1996), 83.
15. See Alfred Métraux, *Voodoo in Haiti* (New York: Schocken Books, 1959) for an interesting discussion of Voodoo and Santeria.

16. Susan Gooney Lea, "Modern Zombie Makers: Enacting the Ancient Impulse to Control and Possess Another," in *Zombies Are Us: Essays on the Humanity of the Walking Dead*, eds. Christopher M. Moreman and Cory James Rushton (Jefferson, NC: McFarland, 2011), 65.

17. Kyle William Bishop, *American Zombie Gothic: The Rise and Fall (and Rise) of the Walking Dead in Popular Culture* (Jefferson NC: McFarland, 2010), 66. See also Bishop, "Dead Men Still Walking: Explaining the Zombie Remakes," *Journal of Popular Film and Television*, 1 (2009): 16–26.

18. James Russell, *The Book of the Dead: The Complete History of Zombie Cinema* (New York: Fab Press, 2005).

19. Richard Matheson, *I Am Legend* (New York: Berkley, 1954), 25. Further citations in the text.

20. Clasen, *Why Horror Seduces*, 95.

21. Tony Williams, *The Cinema of George Romero: Knight of the Living Dead* (New York: Columbia, 2012), 47.

22. Barash, *The Whisperings Within*, 147, 186–87.

23. Desmond Morris, *The Human Zoo* (New York and Tokyo: Kodansha International, 1996), 133.

24. Tony Williams, *The Cinema of George Romero*, 96.

25. Wood, *Hollywood: From Vietnam to Regan—and Beyond*, 287.

Chapter Four

1. Charles Darwin, *The Descent of Man in Relation to Sex and Natural Selection* (New York: Appleton, 1976), 166.

2. Wilson, *The Social Conquest of Earth*, 57.

3. Matthew Alper, *The God Part of the Brain: A Scientific Interpretation of Human Spirituality* (Naperville, Ill: Source Books, 2006), 206.

4. Sebastian Junger, *Tribe: Our Homecoming and Belonging* (New York and Boston: Twelve, 2016), 2–3.

5. Robin Fox, "Male Bonding in the Epics and Romances," in *The Literary Animal: Evolution and the Nature of Narrative*, eds., Jonathan Gottschall and David Sloan Wilson (Evanston, Il: Northwestern University Press, 2005, 126.

6. Montague Summers, *The Vampire in Europe* (New York: University Books, n.d.), 59.

7. Emily Gerard, *The Land Beyond the Forest*, Chapter XXV, "The Roumanians: Death and Burial—Vampires and Were-Wolves," Project Gutenberg. www.gutenbert.org.

8. See Bridget Marshall, "Stoker's *Dracula* and the Vampire's Literary History," in *Critical Insight: Dracula*. ed. Jack Lynch. (Pasadena, CA: Salem Press, 2010), 23–37 for a useful and brief discussion of sources.

9. Robert Wasson, "The Politics of *Dracula*," in *Dracula: The Vampire and the Critics*, ed. Margaret Carter (Ann Arbor: UMI Research Press, 1988), 19.

10. Bram Stoker, *Dracula* (New York: Oxford University Press, 1992), 9. Further references will appear in the text.

11. If Walpole originated the castle as setting, Charlotte Smith introduced the Burkean sublime in describing them. She was widely imitated. In Smith's second novel *Ethelinde, or the Recluse of the Lake* (1789), she describes her heroine's thoughts as she approaches Grasmere Abbey: "She gave way to the solemn but melancholy species of pleasure inspired by the scene around her. It was now evening: the last rays of the sun gave a dull purple hue to the points of the fells which rose above the water and the park: while the rest, all in deep shadow, looked gloomily sublime" (London: Cadell, Vol. I, 46–47). In an amusing bit of literary larceny, four years later Ann Radcliffe described Emily St. Aubert's approach to Castle Udolpho in *Mysteries of Udolpho*: "Emily gazed with melancholy awe upon the castle, which she understood to be Montoni's for, though it was now lighted up by the setting sun, the gothic greatness of its features, and its moldering walls of dark grey stone, rendered it a gloomy and sublime

object" (I, 230). The passage is pretty much lifted from *Ethelinde*. Jane Austen wrote an amusing spoof of the language of the sublime in *Northanger Abbey*. She combines Smith's description and Radcliffe's imitation when her heroine, a naive young romance reader who confuses art and life, approaches Northanger Abbey: "Every turn of the road was expected, with solemn awe, to afford a glimpse of its massy walls of grey stone, rising amidst a grove of ancient oaks, with the last beams of the sun playing in beautiful splendor on its high gothic windows" (215). She is disappointed to find it to be an ordinary and modern structure.

12. Earlier vampire fiction is laden with sexual suggestion. Both Coleridge's poem "Christabel" and LeFanu's adaptation of it in *Carmilla* are rather explicit in describing lesbian sex. The opening chapter of *Varney the Vampire* describes the vampire's attack in the most lurid language of rape.

13. Lionel Tiger, *Men in Groups* (New York: Vantage, 1979), 218.
14. Wilson, *On Human Nature*, 107.
15. Alcock, *The Triumph of Sociobiology*, 46.
16. Gould, *Ever Since Darwin: Reflections in Natural History*, 238.
17. James Skar, *Hollywood Gothic: The Tangled Web of Dracula from Novel to Stage to Screen* (New York: Faber and Faber, 2004), appendixes A and B.
18. Skar mentions a Hungarian film titled *Dracula*, but it has been lost.
19. Parsons' *Castle of Wolfenbach* (1793) is one of the "Northanger Seven" novels recommended breathlessly by Isabella Thorpe to the naive Catherine Morland as "delightfully horrid" in Jane Austen's *Northanger Abbey*.
20. Carol Senf, *The Vampire in Nineteenth-Century English Literature* (Bowling Green, OH: Bowling Green State University Popular Press, 1988), 150.
21. John Cawelti, *The Six-Gun Mystique* (Bowling Green: Bowling Green University Press, 1971), 35.
22. John Bucktaman, *Terminal Identities: The Virtual Subject in Post Modern Science Fiction* (Durham and London: Duke University Press, 1993), 9.
23. Carroll, *Reading Human Nature*, 20.
24. Senf, *The Vampire in Nineteenth-Century English Literature*, 2.
25. Alain Silver and James Ursini, *The Vampire in Film: From Nosferatu to Bram Stoker's Dracula* (New York: Limelight, 2010), 89.
26. Julia Kristeva, *Desire in Language: A Semiotic Approach to Literature and Art* (New York: Columbia University Press, 1980), 11.
27. *Intertextuality: New Perspectives in Criticism*, Number 2 (New York: Literary Forum, 1978), xv.
28. George Gordon Byron, *The Poetical Works of Byron* (Boston: Houghton Mifflin, 1977) I, xii, 281–28 and 305–06. Further references to Byron's works quoted in the text from this book.
29. See Christopher Bentley, "The Monster in the Bedroom: Sexual Symbolism in Bram Stoker's Dracula," 25–34, and Christopher Craft, "Kiss Me with Those Red Lips: Gender and Inversion in *Dracula*," 167–195. Both essays are in *Dracula: The Vampire and the Critics*.
30. Buss, *The Evolution of Desire*, 21.
31. Fisher, *Why We Love*, 114.
32. www.rogerebert.com. September 19, 2003. Accessed October 28, 2016.
33. Jeffrey Weinstock, *The Vampire Film: Undead Cinema* (London: Columbia University Press, 2012), 52.
34. *Ibid.*, 127.
35. Boyd, *On the Origin of Stories*, 20.

Chapter Five

1. Fisher, *Why We Love*, 51, 55.
2. Bruce Ellis, "The Evolution of Sexual Attraction: Evaluative Mechanisms in Women,"

in *The Adapted Mind: Evolutionary Psychology and the Generation of Culture*. eds. Jerome H. Barkow, Leda Cosmides, and John Tooby (New York: Oxford University Press, 1992), 267.

3. www.lifescript.com June 5, 2008.
4. Pinker, *How the Mind Works*, 44.
5. Morris, *The Naked Ape*, 50.
6. Dutton, *The Art Instinct*, 138.
7. Goeffrey Miller, *The Mating Mind*, 3.
8. Christopher Wilbur and Loren Campbell. "Swept off Their Feet: Females Strategic Mating Behavior as a Means of Supplying the Broom," in *Evolution's Empress: Darwinian Perspectives on the Nature of Women*. eds. Maryanne L. Fisher, Justin Garcia and Rosemarie Sokol Chang (Oxford University Press, 2003), 334–35.
9. Buss, *The Evolution of Desire*, 201.
10. Jonathan Gottschall and David Sloan Wilson, eds., *The Literary Animal: Evolution and the Nature of Narrative*, 227.
11. Dutton, *The Art Instinct*, 118.
12. Eaton Stannard Barrett, *The Heroine* (London, 1909), 39.
13. Karl Grammar, "Human Courtship Behaviour: Biological Basis and Cognitive Processing," in *The Sociobiology of Sexual and Reproductive Strategies*, eds. Anne E. Rasa, Christian Vogel and Eckhkart Voland (London and New York: Chapman and Hall, 1989), 148.
14. Buss, *Evolution of Desire*, 103.
15. Nancy Easterlin, "From Reproductive Resource to Autonomous Individuality: Charlotte Brontë's *Jane Eyre*," in *Evolution's Empress*.
16. Joseph Carroll, "Human Nature and Literary Meaning: A Theoretical Model Illustrated with a Critique of *Pride and Prejudice*," in *The Literary Animal*, 95.
17. David P. Barash, and Judith Eve Lipton, *Strange Bedfellows: The Surprising Connection Between Sex, Evolution and Monogamy*. (New York: Belleview Literary Press, 2009), 48.
18. Carroll, *Reading Human Nature*, 113.
19. David Cecil, "Emily Bronte and *Wuthering Heights*," in *Critical Essays on Emily Bronte* (New York: G. K. Hall, 1997), 148.
20. Fisher, *Why We Love*, 111.
21. *Ibid.*, 175.
22. *Ibid.*, 102–10.
23. Schwartz, *The Battle for Human Nature*, 96.
24. Diane Waldman, "At Last, I Can Tell Someone: Feminine Point of View and Subjectivity in the Gothic Romance Film of the 1940s," *Cinema Journal* 23 (no. 2 1983): 30.
25. Dutton, *The Art Instinct*, 113.
26. Boyd, *On the Origin of Stories*, 227.
27. Sara Hemriajani, Reuters.com 10/12.15
28. Darwin, *The Descent of Man*, 568.
29. Steven Pinker, *The Blank Slate* (New York: Viking, 2002), 60.
30. Dutton, *The Art Instinct*, 29.
31. Barash and Lipton, *Strange Bedfellows: The Surprising Connection Between Sex, Evolution and Monogamy*, 93.

Chapter Six

1. Donna Hart and Robert W. Sussman, *Man the Hunted: Primates, Predators, and Human Evolution* (New York: Westview, 2005), 10.
2. *The Spirit in the Gene* (Cornell University Press: Ithaca NY, 1999), 199.
3. Clark H. Barrett, "Adaptations to Predators and Prey," in *The Handbook of Evolutionary Psychology*, 224.
4. Cited in Barash, *The Whispering Within*, 198.
5. Hart and Sussman, *Man the Hunted*, 10.

6. Clasen, *Why Horror Seduces*, 26.
7. Bruce Kavin, *Horror and the Horror Film* (London: Anthem Press, 2012), 79.
8. Joseph Carroll, "Human Nature and Literary Meaning: A Theoretical Model Illustrated with a Critique of Pride and Prejudice," in *The Literary Animal*, 92.
9. Tiger, *Men in Groups*, 29, 126.
10. Robert Boyd, "On the Origin of Symbols," *Science* 323 (2009): 710.
11. Hans Kruuk, *Hunter and Hunted*, 76.
12. Montague Summers, *The Werewolf* (New York: Bell Publishing Company, 1966), 2.
13. Alistair Graham and Peter Beard, *Eyelids of Morning: The Mingled Destinies of Crocodiles and Men* (San Francisco: Chronicle Books, 1990), 69.
14. Chantal Bourgalt Du Courdray, *The Curse of the Werewolf: Fantasy, Horror and the Beast Within* (London: Tarus, 2006), 80.
15. *Ibid.*, 80.
16. Brad Steiger notes that script writer Curt Siodnak claimed that he invented the silver bullet as the means of killing the werewolf. See *The Werewolf Book: The Encyclopedia of Shape-Shifting Things* (Canton MI: Visible Ink Press, 2012), 252.
17. Du Courdray, *Curse of the Werewolf*, 85.
18. Joel Siegel, *The Reality of Terror* (New York: Viking Press, 1973), 23.
19. Clasen, *Why Horror Seduces*, 36.
20. Crane, *Steven Crane Prose and Poetry*, 904.
21. Quoted in www.goodreads.com/author/quotes/9420.alfred-hitchcock. July 31, 2017.
22. Cited in Clasen, *Why Horror Seduces*, 111.
23. Hart and Sussman, *Man the Hunted*, 56.
24. Kruuk, *Hunter and Hunted*, 61.
25. Arne Ohman and Susan Mineka, "The Malicious Serpent: Snakes as a prototypical stimulus for an Evolved Module of Fear," http://www.psychologicalscence.org/journals/cd/12–1:ohman.cfm January 14, 2017.
26. Hart and Sussman, *Man the Hunted*, 129.
27. Yuval Noah Harari, *Sapiens: A Brief History of Humankind* (New York: Harper, 2015), 40.

Chapter Seven

1. Pinker, *How the Mind Works*, 25.
2. William F. Allman, *The Stone Age Present: How Evolution Has Shaped Modern Life from Sex, Violence and Language to Emotions, Morals, and Communities* (New York: Simon & Schuster, 1994), 251.
3. Jack Morgan, *The Biology of Gothic Literature* (Carbondale IL: Southern Illinois University Press, 2002), 70.
4. See complete text at www.bartleby.com/333/115.html.
5. William Shakespeare, *Hamlet, Prince of Denmark*, in *Shakespeare: The Complete Works*. ed. G. B. Harrison (New York: Harcourt Brace, 1952), 1: 4, 40–44.
6. Emanuel Swedenborg, *The Gist of Swedenborg* (Philadelphia: J. B. Lippincott, 1926), 12.
7. Clasen, *Why Horror Seduces*, 47.
8. Henry Fielding, *The History of Tom Jones, a Foundling*. Vol. 4. *The Works of Henry Fielding* (New York: George D. Sprout, 1903), 153.
9. George Anderson and Andrew Barone, *Walking in the Garden of Souls* (New York: Berkeley Books, 2001), 100–101.
10. Sylvia Brown, *Life on the Other Side* (New York: New American Library, 2002), 56.
11. *Ibid.*, 61, 63.
12. Katherine Fowkes, "Melodramatic Specters: Cinema and *The Sixth Sense*," in *Spectral America: Phantoms and the National Imagination*, ed. Jeffrey Andrew Weinstock (Madison: University of Wisconsin Press, 2004), 190.

13. Dan Bailey, *American Nightmares: The Haunted House Formula in American Popular Film* (Bowling Green, OH: Bowling Green University Press, 1999), 45.
14. *The Norton Anthology of American Literature*. Vol. 1 (New York: Norton, 1972), 1393.
15. Lance Workman and Will Reader, *Evolutionary Psychology: An Introduction* (Cambridge: Cambridge University Press, 2008), 224.
16. Bailey, *American Nightmares*, 103.
17. Clasen, *Why Horror Seduces*, 121.
18. Tom Butler and Lisa Butler, *There Is No Death and There Are No Dead* (Reno NV: AA-EEV Publishing, 2003), 76.
19. Steven Prince, ed., *The Horror Film* (New Brunswick: Rutgers University Press, 2009), 90.
20. Robin Wood, "Return of the Look: Eyes of a Stranger," in *American Horror: Essays on the Modern American Horror Film*, ed. G. A. Waller (Urbana: University of Illinois Press, 2004), 82.
21. Jonathan Gottschall and David Sloan Wilson, eds., *The Literary Animal*, 92.
22. *Diagnostic and Statistical Manual of Mental Disorders*, 5th edition (Washington: American Psychiatric Publishing, 2013), 660–661.
23. Workman and Reader, *Evolutionary Psychology: An Introduction*, 356.
24. Herman Melville, *Billy Budd, Sailor*, in *The Norton Anthology of American Literature*. Vol. I (New York: W. W. Norton, 979), 2321.
25. David M. Buss, *The Murderer Next Door: Why the Mind Is Designed to Kill* (New York: Penguin, 2005), 21.
26. Steven Katz, *The Holocaust in Historical Context*, Vol. l. (Oxford: Oxford University Press, 1994), 438–39.
27. Cited in *Ibid.*, 438.
28. Cited in Margo Adler, *Drawing Down the Moon: Witches, Druids, Goddess-Worshippers and Other Pagans in America Today* (New York: Scribner's, 1998), 152. Adler's book is an excellent source for information on the growth of the new occult.
29. Clasen, *Why Horror Seduces*, 139.
30. Feb. 18, 2016, retrieved March 8, 2017.
31. Pat Robertson, *The New Millennium* (Dallas: Word Publishing, 1990), 84.
32. Boyd, *On the Origin of Stories*, 25.
33. Jay Telotte, *Robot Ecology and the Science Fiction Film* (New York and London: Routledge, 2016), 9–10.
34. Isaac Asimov, *I Robot* (Garden City NY: Doubleday, 1963), 41.
35. "Blade Runner Riddle Solved," BBC News, July 9, 2000.
36. Mark Rowlands, *The Philosopher at the End of the Universe* (London: Erbury Press, 2003), 234–235.
37. Pinker, *How the Mind Works*, 219.

Conclusion

1. Wilson, *Consilience*, 218.
2. Gottschall and Wilson, eds., *The Literary Animal*, 79.
3. Jerome H. Barkow, "New Theoretical Approaches to Cultural Phenomena," in *The Adapted Mind*, 625–26.
4. Allman, *The Stone Age Present*, 19.
5. David Berreby, *Us and Them: Understanding Your Tribal Mind* (New York: Little, Brown, 2005), 16.
6. Brodie, *Virus of the Mind*, xvii.

Bibliography

Adler, Jerome. *The Making of Kubrick's 2001*. New York: Signet, 1970.
Adler, Margo. *Drawing Down the Moon: Witches, Druids, Goddess Worshippers and Other Pagans in America Today*. Boston: Beacon Press, 1986.
Agel, Jerome. *The Making of Kubrick's 2001*. New York: Signet, 1970.
Alcock, John. *The Triumph of Sociobiology*. Oxford and New York: Oxford University Press, 2001.
Aldiss, Brian. *The Billion Year Spree*. New York: Schocken, 1974.
Allen, Elizabeth et. al. "Against Sociobiology." *New York Review of Books*, 22: 18.
Alper, Matthew. *The God Part of the Brain: A Scientific Interpretation of Human Spirituality*. Naperville, IL: Source Books, 2006.
Anderson, George, and Andrew Barone. *Walking in the Garden of Souls*. New York: Berkeley Books, 2001.
Ardrey, Robert. *African Genesis*. New York: Athaneum, 1961.
_____. *The Territorial Imperative*. New York: Athaneum, 1966.
Asimov, Isaac. *I, Robot*. Garden City, NY: Doubleday, 1963.
Auger, Robert. *The Electric Meme: A New Theory of How We Think*. New York: Free Press, 2002.
Austen, Jane. *Northanger Abbey. The Novels of Jane Austen*. Vol. 14. London: Oxford University Press, 1923.
Baghot, Walter. *Physics and Politics*. New York: Cosimo Classics, 2007.
Bailey, Dan. *American Nightmares: The Haunted House Formula in American Popular Film*. Bowling Green: Bowling Green University Press, 1999.
Barash, David P. *The Whisperings Within*. New York: Harper and Row, 1979.
_____, and Judith Eve Lipton. *Strange Bedfellows: The Surprising Connection Between Sex, Evolution and Monogamy*. New York: Belleview Literary Press, 2009.
Barkow, Jerome H. "New Theoretical approaches to Cultural Phenomena." In *The Adapted Mind: Evolutionary Psychology and the Generation of Culture*. eds. Jerome H. Barkow, Leda Cosmides and John Tooby, New York: Oxford University Press, 1992.
Barrett, Eaton Stannard. *The Heroine, or the Adventures of a Fair Romance Reader*. London, 1909.
Barrett, H. Clarke. "Adaptations to Predators and Prey." In *The Handbook of Evolutionary Psychology*. ed. David M. Buss. Hoboken NJ: Wiley and Sons, 2005.
Bentley, Christopher. "The Monster in the Bedroom: Sexual Symbolism in Bram Stoker's Dracula." In *Dracula: The Monster and the Critics*. ed. Margaret Carter. Ann Arbor, MI: UMI Press, 1988.
The Bhagavad Gita. Translated by Eliot Deutsch. New York: Holt, Rinehart and Winston, 1968.
Bishop, Kyle William. *American Zombie Gothic: The Rise and Fall (and Rise) of the Walking Dead in Popular Culture*. Jefferson, NC: McFarland, 2010.
_____. "Black Magic and White Guilt: Voodoo in *Angel Heart*." *Psy Art*. 2011.

_____. "Dead Men Still Walking: Explaining the Zombie Remakes." *Journal of Popular Film and Television.* 1 (2009): 16–26.
Blackmore, Susan. *The Meme Machine.* New York: Oxford University Press, 1999.
Bloom, Deborah. *Ghost Hunters: William James and the Search for Scientific Proof of Life After Death:* New York: Penguin, 2006.
Boyd, Brian. *On the Origin of Stories: Evolution, Cognition, and Fiction.* Cambridge, MA: Belnap Press, 2009.
_____. "On the Origin of Symbols." *Science.* 323 (2009) 709–711.
Broderick, Mike. "Better the Devil You Know: Film Antichrists at the Millennium." In *The Horror Zone: The Cultural Experience of Contemporary Horror Cinema.* ed. Ian Conrich. New York: I. B. Taurus, 2010.
Brodie, Richard. *Virus of the Mind: The New Science of the Meme.* New York: Hay House, 1996.
Browne, Sylvia. *Life on the Other Side.* New York: New American Library, 2001.
Bucktaman, John. *Terminal Identities: The Virtual Subject in Post-Modern Science Fiction.* Durham and London: Duke University Press, 1993.
Burke, Edmund. *A Philosophical Enquiry into the Origin of Our Ideas of the Sublime and the Beautiful.* New York: Routledge and Paul, 1958.
Burnham, Terry, and Jay Phelan. *Mean Genes: From Sex to Money to Food, Taming Our Primal Instinct.* Cambridge, MA: Perseus, 2000.
Buss, David M. *The Murderer Next Door: Why the Mind Is Designed to Kill.* New York: Penguin Books, 2005.
_____. *The Evolution of Desire: Strategies of Human Mating.* New York: Basic Books, 2003.
Butler, Tom and Lisa Butler. *There Is No Death and There Are No Dead.* Reno: AA-EEV Publishing, 2003.
Campbell, John. *Who Goes There?* In *The Science Fiction Hall of Fame.* ed. Ben Bova. New York: Doubleday, 1973.
Carroll, Joseph. "Human Nature and Literary Meaning: A Theoretical Model Illustrated with a Critique of *Pride and Prejudice.*" In *The Literary Animal: Evolution and the Nature of Narrative.* ed. Jonathan Gottschall and David Sloan Wilson. Evanston, IL: Northwestern University Press, 2005.
_____. *Literary Darwinism: Evolution, Human Nature, and Literature.* New York: Routledge, 2004.
_____. *Reading Human Nature: Literary Darwinism in Theory and Practice.* Albany, NY: SUNY Press, 2011.
Cawelti, John. *The Six-Gun Mystique.* Bowling Green, OH: Bowling Green University Press, 1971.
Cecil, David. "Emily Brontë and *Wuthering Heights.*" In *Critical Essays on Wuthering Heights.* ed. Thomas John Winnifreth. New York: G. K. Hall, 1997.
Clarke, Arthur C. *Odyssey Two:* New York: Ballantine, 1982.
_____. *2001: A Space Odyssey.* New York: Signet, 1968.
Clasen, Mathias. *Why Horror Seduces.* New York: Oxford University Press, 2014.
Clover, Carol. *Men, Women and Chain Saws: Gender in the Modern Horror Film.* Princeton: Princeton University Press, 1992.
Clute, John. *Encyclopedia of Science Fiction.* New York: St. Martin, 1993.
Commins, Denise. "Dominance, Status, and Social Hierarchies." In *The Handbook of Evolutionary Psychology.* ed. David M. Buss. Hoboken, NJ: Wiley and Sons, 2005.
Cowan, Douglas E. *Sacred Terror: Religion and Horror on the Silver Screen.* Waco, TX: Baylor University Press, 2008.
Crane, Stephen. "The Open Boat." In *Steven Crane: Prose and Poetry.* New York: Viking, 1984.
Cumby, Constance. *The Hidden Dangers of the Rainbow: The New Age Movement and Our Coming Age of Barbarism.* Shreveport: Huffington House, 1983.
Darwin, Charles. *The Descent of Man in Relation to Sex and Natural Selection.* New York: Appleton, 1976.

———. *The Expression of Emotion in Men and Animals.* Chicago: University of Chicago Press, 1965.
Dawkins, Richard. *The Blind Watchmaker.* New York and London: W. W. Norton, 1986.
———. *The Selfish Gene.* Oxford: Oxford University Press, 1989.
De Blaig, Harn. *The Emerging Network: A Sociology of the New Age and Pagan Movement.* London: Bowman and Littlefield, 1995.
De Chardin, Teilhard. *The Phenomenon of Man.* New York: Harper and Row, 1959.
Dennett, Daniel. *Darwin's Dangerous Ideas: Evolution and the Meanings of Life.* New York: Simon & Schuster, 1995.
Diagnostic and Statistical Manual of Mental Disorders. 5th ed. Washington: American Psychiatric Publishing, 2013.
Dubos, René. *Beast or Angel? Choices That Make Us Human.* New York: Scribner's, 1974.
Du Courdray, Chantal Bourgalt. *The Curse of the Werewolf: Fantasy, Horror and the Beast Within.* London: Taurus, 2006.
Dutton, Dennis. *The Art Instinct: Beauty Pleasure, and Human Evolution.* New York: Bloomsbury, 2009.
Ebert, Roger. www.rogerebert.com. September 19, 2001.
Ellis, Bruce. "The Evolution of Sexual Attraction: Evaluative Mechanisms in Women." In *The Adapted Mind: Evolutionary Psychology and the Generation of Culture.* eds. Jerome H. Barkow, Leda Cosmides, and John Tooby. New York: Oxford University Press, 1992.
Fielding, Henry. *The History of Tom Jones, a Foundling.* Vol. 4. *The Works of Henry Fielding.* New York: George Sprout, 1903.
Finney, Jack. *The Body Snatchers.* New York: Scribner's, 1978.
Fisher, Helen. *The Evolution of Desire: Strategies of Human Mating.* New York: Basic Books, 2003.
Fisher, Lucy. "Birth Traumas: Parturition and Horror in *Rosemary's Baby*": In *Dread of Differences: Gender and the Horror Film.* ed. Barry Keith Grant. Austin: University of Texas Press, 1996.
Fowkes, Katherine. "Melodramatic Specters: Cinema and the Sixth Sense." In *Spectral America: Phantoms and the National Imagination.* ed. Jeffrey Weinstock. Madison: University of Wisconsin Press, 2004.
Fox, Robin. "Male Bonding in the Epics and Romances." In *The Literary Animal: Evolution and the Nature of Narrative.* eds. Jonathan Gottschall and David Sloan Wilson. Evanston, IL: Northwestern University Press, 2005.
Gelmis, Joseph. *The Film Director as Superstar.* Garden City, NY: Doubleday, 1970.
Gerard, Emily. *The Land Beyond the Forest.* Chapter XXV, "The Roumanians: Death and Burial—Vampires and Were-Wolves." Project Gutenberg. www.gutenbert.org.
Gordon, George Lord Byron. *The Poetical Works of Byron.* New York: Houghton Mifflin, 1977.
Gotschall, Jonathan. *The Storytelling Animal: How Stories Make Us Human.* Boston: Mariner Books, 2012.
Gould, Jay. *Ever Since Darwin.* New York: Norton, 1977.
Graham, Alistair, and Peter Beard. *Eyelids of Morning: The Mingled Destinies of Crocodiles and Men.* San Francisco: Chronicle Books, 1973.
Grammar, Karl. "Human Courtship Behaviour: Biological Basis and Cognitive Processing." In *The Sociobiology of Sexual and Reproductive Strategies.* eds. Anne E. Rasa, Christian Vogel and Eckhkart Voland: London and New York: Chapman and Hall, 1989.
Harari, Duval Noah. *Sapiens: A Brief History of Humankind.* New York: Harper, 2015.
Hart, Donna, and Robert W. Sussman. *Man the Hunted: Primates, Predators, and Human Evolution.* New York: Westview, 2005.
Hawthorne, Nathaniel. "Young Goodman Brown." In *The Norton Anthology of American Literature,* Vol. I. ed. Nina Baym et. al. Norton: New York and London, 1989.
Huxley, Thomas. "On a Liberal Education." In *The Victorian Age.* Inglewood Cliffs, NJ: Prentice Hall, 1954.

Intertextuality: New Perspectives in Criticism. Number Two. New York: New York Literary Forum, 1978.
Junger, Sebastian. *Tribe: On Homecoming and Belonging.* New York: Twelve, 2016.
Katz, Steven. *The Holocaust in Historical Context.* Vol. 1. Oxford: Oxford University Press, 1994.
Kavin, Bruce. *Horror and the Horror Film.* London: Anthem Press, 2012.
Kraft, Christopher. "Kiss Me with Those Red Lips: Gender Inversion in *Dracula.*" In *Dracula: The Vampire and the Critics.* ed. Margaret Carter. Ann Arbor, MI: MCI Press, 1988.
Kristeva, Julia. *Desire in Language: A Semiotic Approach to Literature and Art.* New York: Columbia University Press, 1980.
Kruck, Hans. *Hunter and Hunted: Relationships Between Carnivores and People.* Cambridge: Cambridge University Press, 2002.
Lea, Susan Gooney. "Modern Zombie Makers: Enacting the Ancient Impulse to Control and Possess Another." In *Zombies Are Us: Essays on the Humanity of the Walking Dead.* ed. Christopher M. Moreman and Cory James Rushton. Jefferson, NC: McFarland, 2011.
Locke, John. *An Essay Concerning Human Understanding.* Oxford: Clarion Press, 1979.
Lorenz, Konrad. *On Aggression.* New York: Harcourt Brace, 1963.
Lyons, Arthur. *Satan Wants You: The Cult of Devil Worship in America.* New York: Mysterious Press, 1980.
MacKinnon, John. *The Ape Within Us.* London: Collins, 1978.
Marlowe, Christopher. *The Tragical History of Doctor Faustus.* In *The Works of Christopher Marlowe.* Oxford: Oxford University Press, 1925.
Marshal, Bridget. "Stoker's *Dracula* and the Vampire in Literary History." In *Critical Insights: Dracula.* ed. Jack Lynch. Pasadena, CA: Salem Press, 2010.
Matheson, Richard. *I Am Legend.* New York: Berkley, 1954.
McAleer, Neil. *Arthur C. Clarke: The Authorized Biography.* Chicago: Contemporary Books, 1992.
Melton, J. Gordon. *Encyclopedia of the Occult and Parapsychology.* Vol. 1. Detroit: Gale Research, 1996.
Melville, Herman. *Billy Budd, Sailor.* In *The Norton Anthology of American Literature.* Vol. 1. ed. Linda Baym et. al. New York: W. W. Norton, 1979.
_____. *Moby Dick, or the Whale.* Indianapolis: Bobbs-Merrill, 1964.
Métraux, Alfred. *Voodoo in Haiti.* New York: Schocken Books, 1959.
Miller, Goeffrey. *The Mating Mind: How Sexual Choice Shaped the Evolution of Human Nature.* New York: Anchor Books, 2000.
Milton, John. *Paradise Lost.* In *The Works of John Milton,* Vol. 1. New York: Columbia University Press, 1931.
Morgan, Jack. *The Biology of Gothic Literature and Film.* Carbondale, IL: Southern Illinois University Press, 2002.
Morris, Desmond. *The Human Zoo: A Zoologists' Classic Study of the Human Animal.* New York: McGraw-Hill, 1969.
_____. *The Naked Ape.* New York: McGraw-Hill, 1967.
Morrison, Reg. *The Spirit in the Gene.* New York: Cornell University Press, 1999.
Newsom, Carol. "Introduction." The Book of Job. In *The New Interpreter's Bible.* Vol. 4. Nashville: Abington Press, 1996.
Ohman, Arnie and Susan Wanetka. "The Malicious Serpent: Snakes as a Prototype of an Evolved Module of Fear." http:/www/psychologicalscience.org/journals/cd/12:ohman.cfm. January 14, 2018.
Paley, William. *Natural Theology.* New York: Harpers, 1939.
Phillips, Kendall R. *Dark Directors: Romero, Craven, Carpenter and the Modern Horror Film.* Carbondale: Southern Illinois University Press, 2012.
Pinker, Steven. *The Blank Slate.* New York: Viking, 2002.
Poe, Edgar Allan. "The Fall of the House of Usher." In *The Norton Anthology of American Literature.* Vol. 1. ed. Linda Baym et. al. New York: Norton, 1972.

Prince, Steven. "Dread, Taboo, and *The Thing*: Toward Social Theory of the Horror Film." In *The Horror Film.* ed. Steven Prince. New Brunswick, NJ: Rutgers University Press, 2004.
Quammen, David. *Monsters of God: The Man-eating Predator in the Jungles of History and the Mind.* New York: Norton, 1998.
Radcliffe, Ann. *The Mysteries of Udolpho.* Vol. 1. London and New York: Everyman, 1931.
Richards, Janet Radcliffe. *Human Nature After Darwin: A Philosophical Introduction.* London and New York: Routledge, 2000.
Ridley, Matthew. *The Red Queen.* New York: Macmillan, 1993.
Robertson, Pat. *The New Millennium.* Dallas: Word Publishing, 1990.
Romance Writers of America. www.lifescripts.com. July 5, 2017.
Rowlands, Mark. *The Philosopher at the End of the Universe.* London: Ebury Press, 2003.
Russell, James. *The Book of the Dead: The Complete History of Zombie Cinema.* New York: Fab Press, 2005.
Russell, Jeffrey Burton. "The Satan Scare." In *The Satan Scare.* ed. James T. Best and David Bromley. n.c.: de Gruyter, 1991.
Schwartz, Barry. *The Battle for Human Nature: Science, Morality and Modern Life.* New York and London: W. W. Norton, 1986.
Schwartz, Howard. *The Tree of Souls.* Oxford: Oxford University Press, 2004.
Schwartzman, Sarah. "Is *Twilight* Mormon?" In *The Twilight Mystique.* ed. Amy M. Clarke and Marijane Osborn. Jefferson, NC: McFarland, 2010.
Sconse, Jeffrey. "Dead Metaphors/Undead Allegories." In *Screening the Undead: Vampires and Zombies Film and Television.* ed. Leon Hunt, Sharon Lockyer and Milly Williamson. New York and London: Tauris, 2014.
Seabrook, W. B. *The Magic Island.* New York: Literary Guild of America, 1929.
Senf, Carol. *The Vampire in Nineteenth-Century English Literature.* Bowling Green, OH: Bowling Green University Press, 1988.
Shakespeare, William. *Hamlet, Prince of Denmark.* In *Shakespeare: The Complete Works.* ed. G. B. Harrison. New York: Harcourt Brace, 1952.
Siegel, Joel. *The Reality of Terror.* New York: Viking Press, 1973.
Singer, Robert. "Black Magic and White Guilt: Voodoo in *Angel Heart.*" Psy Art. 2011: 10–17.
_____. "One against All: The New England Past and Present in *The Devil and Daniel Webster.*" *Literature/Film Quarterly* (1994) 22:4: 265–71.
Skar, James. *Hollywood Gothic: The Tangled Web of Dracula from Novel to Stage to Screen.* New York: Faber & Faber, 2004.
Skinner, B. F. *Walden Two.* New York and London: Macmillan, 1976.
Smith, Charlotte. *Emmeline or the Orphan of the Castle.* London: Oxford English Novels, 1971.
_____. *Ethelinde, or the Recluse of the Lake.* London: Cadell, 1789.
Sork, Victoria. "Quantitative Theories of Gender Differences." In *Feminism and Evolutionary Biology.* ed. Patricia Adair Gowaty New York: Chapman and Hall, 1997.
Stoker, Bram. *Dracula.* New York: Oxford University Press, 1992.
Summers, Montague. *The Vampire in Europe.* New York: University Books, n.d.
_____. *The Werewolf.* New York: Bell Publishing Company, 1966.
Swedenborg, Emanuel. *The Gist of Swedenborg.* Trans. by Julian K. Smyth and William Wunsh. Philadelphia: J. P. Lippincott, 1926.
Telotte, Jay. *Robot Ecology and the Science Fiction Film.* New York: Routledge, 2016.
Tiger, Lionel. *Men in Groups.* New York: Vantage, 1979.
Tooby, John, and Leda Cosmides. "Does Beauty Build Adapted Minds: Toward an Evolutionary Theory of Aesthetics, Fiction, and the Arts." In *Evolution, Literature and Film: A Reader.* eds. Brian Boyd, Joseph Carroll and Jonathan Gottschall. New York: Columbia University Press, 2010.
_____. "The Psychological Foundation of Culture." In *The Adapted Mind: Evolutionary Psychology and the Generation of Culture.* ed. Jerome Barkow. Oxford: Oxford University Press, 1996.

Twichell, James B. *Dreadful Pleasures: An Anatomy of Modern Horror.* New York: Oxford University Press, 1985.
UC Santa Barbara Evolutionary Psychology Department Web Site: University of California Santa Barbara. http://www.psych.ucsb.edu/research/cep/primer.html. August 14, 2016.
Viser, William. *The Darkness Among Us: A Look at the Sinister Growth of the Occult and How Dangerously Close It Is to You.* Nashville: Broadman and Holman, 1994.
Waldman, Diane. "At Last I Can Tell Someone: Feminine Point of View and Subjectivity in the Gothic Romance of the 1940s." *Cinema Journal* 23 (1983): 230–41.
Wasson, Robert. "The Politics of *Dracula.*" In *Dracula: The Vampire and the Critics.* Margaret Carter, ed. Ann Arbor: UMI Research Press, 1988.
Weinstock, Jeffrey. *The Vampire Film: Undead Cinema.* London: Columbia University Press, 2012.
Wells, Herbert George. *The Time Machine and the War of the Worlds.* ed. Frank D. McConnell. New York: Oxford University Press, 1963.
Wilbur, Christopher, and Loren Campbell. "Swept off Their Feet: Females Strategic Mating Behavior as a Means of Supplying the Broom." In *Evolution's Empress: Darwinian Perspectives on the Nature of Women.* ed. Maryanne L. Fisher, Justin R. Garcia and Rosemarie Sokol Chang. Oxford: Oxford University Press, 2003.
Williams, Tony. *The Cinema of George Romero: Knight of the Living Dead.* New York: Columbia University Press, 2012.
Wilson, David Sloan. *Darwin's Cathedral: Religion and the Nature of Society.* New York and Chicago: University of Chicago Press, 2001.
Wilson, Edward O. *Consilience: The Unity of Knowledge.* New York: Knopf, 1998.
_____. *On Human Nature.* Cambridge: Harvard University Press, 1978.
_____. *The Social Conquest of Earth.* New York and London: Liveright, 2012.
Wood, Robin. *Hollywood: From Vietnam to Regan—and Beyond.* New York: Columbia University Press, 1986.
_____. "Return of the Look: The Eyes of a Stranger." In *American Horror: Essays on the Modern Horror Film.* ed. G. A. Waller. Urbana: University of Illinois Press, 2004.
Workman, Lance, and Will Reader. *Evolutionary Psychology: An Introduction.* Cambridge: Cambridge University Press, 2008.
Wrangham, Richard, and Dale Peterson. *Demoniac Males: Apes and the Origin of Human Violence.* Boston: Houghton Mifflin, 1996.
www.goodreads/author/quotes/9420.alfred_hitchcock. Nov. 28, 1917.
www.lifescript.com June 5, 2008.
www.rogerebert.com. September 19, 2003. Accessed October 28, 2016.
York, Michael. *The Emerging Network: A Sociology of the New Age and Pagan Movement.* London: Bowman and Littlefield, 1995.

Index

Adler, Margo 199n28
A.I.: Artificial Intelligence 186
Alcock, John 5, 81
Aldiss, Brian 45, 48
Alien and sequels 129–134
Allman, William 187–88
An American Werewolf in London 137–38
An American Werewolf in Paris 137, 138, 149
The Amityville Horror 159
Anaconda and sequels 149
Anderson, George 155
Angel Heart 44–45
Antichrist 35–40
Ardrey, Robert 28
Asimov, Isaac 178–79
Auger, Robert 63
Austen, Jane 102, 109, 118, 196n11
Avatar 49

Badham, John 88
Bagehot, Walter 10
Bailey, Dan 162
Balderston, John 84
Barash, David 110, 123
Barrett, Eaton Stannard: *The Heroine* 106
Baudelaire, Charles Pierre 30
Baum, L. Frank 170
Bell, Book, and Candle 174
Billy Budd 166
Benchley, Peter 140, 144
Benét, Stephen Vincent 44
Bentley, Christopher 91
Berreby, David 188
Black Sabbath 97
Blackmore, Susan 64
Blackula 88.91
Blade and sequels 94, 96–97
Blade Runner 178, 180–82
Blade Runner: 2049 182–84
Blair, Robert: "The Grave" 152
The Blair Witch Project 171–72
Bloom, Deborah 153

Bodkin, Maud 4
Body Snatchers 59
The Body Snatchers 57
Bonny and Clyde 88
Boyd, Brian 5, 14, 97, 120, 176
Boylan, Grace: *Thy Son Liveth* 154
Bram Stoker's Dracula 90–93
Bridget Jones Diary 105
Broderick, Mick 40
Brodie, Richard 64
Brontë, Anne 107
Brontë, Charlotte 89
Brontë, Emily 89
Brooks, Max 71
Browne, Sylvia 155, 156
Browning, Elizabeth Barrett 153
Browning, Robert 153
Browning, Tod 85
Buktaman, John 22
Burke, Edmund 3–4, 78
Burnham, Terry 5
Burnt Offerings 160, 162
Burton, Richard: *Dr. Faustus* 43
Byron, Lord 30, 89, 99

Cabin in the Woods 32–33
Calmet, Augustin 76
Cameron, James 49
Campbell, Lorne 104
Carlyle, Thomas 188
Carmilla 77, 78
Carpenter, John 31, 50, 53 56, 129, 164–65
Carroll, Joseph 5, 14, 87, 109, 111, 187
The Castle of Otranto 158
Cat People (1942) 140–42
Cat People (1982) 142
Cather, Willa: *My Antonia* 134, 138
Cawelti, John 87
Cernunnos 29
Charney, Hanna 90
Childhood's End 24
Christabel 77

Christie, Agatha 16
Clarissa 117
Clarke, Arthur 17–26, 74, 125–26
Classen, Mathias 5, 37
Clinton, Hillary 75
Coleridge, Samuel Taylor 77, 166
Colossus: The Forbin Project 179
Conan Doyle, Arthur 153
Constantine 39
Coppola, Francis Ford 90–93, 99
Corelli, Marie 43
Cosmides, Leda 14, 187
Cowan, Douglas 4
Cowboys vs. Aliens 49
The Craft 174–75, 176
Craft, Christopher 93
Crane, Stephen 7, 142, 146
Creedence Clearwater Revival 133
Crimson Peak 121–23
Crowley, Aleister 170
The Crucible 169
Cthulhu Mythos 32
Cumbey, Constance 30, 36
Cummings, Denise 7
The Cured 72
Curtis, Dan 88

Dances with Wolves 148
Darwin, Charles 6–8, 74
Dawkins, Richard 7, 52–53, 63, 100, 185
The Day the Earth Stood Still 49
Dean, Hamilton 84
Dean, James 89
De Chardin, Teilhard 25
Deep Blue Sea 145
Del Toro, Guillermo 121
Demon Seed 185–86
Dennett, Daniel 10–11, 64
The Devil and Daniel Webster 44
Devil's Advocate 40
Diagnostic and Statistical Manual of Mental Disorders 165
Dick, Phillip K. 180
Dickens, Charles 14, 177
Dickinson, Emily 147–48
Dilbert 93
Donner, Richard 38
Dracula (Badham) 88
Dracula (novel) 52, 65, 66, 75–81, 97
Dracula (Tod Browning) 85–86
Dracula II: The Ascension 86
Dracula 2000 86
Dracula's Daughter 85
Dragonwyck 117–18
Du Maurier, Daphne 114
Duos, René 35
Dutton, Dennis 13, 30–31, 104, 105, 117

Easterlin, Nancy 109
Easy Rider 88

Ebert, Roger 94
Eliot, George 15, 107
Ellis, Bruce 102
Emmerich, Roland 49
End of Days 40
Endor, Guy: *The Werewolf of Paris* 135
E.T.: The Extra Terrestrial 49
The Exorcist and sequels 35, 40–42

The Faculty 61
Faulkner, William: "The Bear" 133
Fielding, Henry: *Tom Jones* 155
Final Destination 141
Finney, Jack 53, 57 61
Firestarter 162
Fisher, Helen 36, 100–1, 105, 113, 115
Forbidden Planet 178
Fowkes, Katherine 156
Fox, Robin 75–76
Fox Sisters 53
Frankenstein 23, 145, 185, 186
Freud, Sigmund 4, 136, 141
Friday the 13th 166–67
Friedkin, William 40
Frost, Robert 28
Fry, Northrop 4

Gardner, Gerald 170
Gaskell, Elizabeth 177
Gaslight 118–20
Gerard, Emily: *The Land Beyond the Forest* 77
Ghost 156
The Ghost and Mrs. Muir 155
The Ghost and the Darkness 147
Gilgamesh 13, 132
God Bless the Child 97
Goddard, Drew 32
The Goddess 29
Goethe, Johann Von 41
Gottschall, Jonathan 5, 19
Gould, Jay 10, 20–21, 79
Guthrie, Woody 27
A Guy Named Joe 156

Halloween 164–66
Hamilton, W.D. 9
Harari, Yuval Noah 150
Hart, Donna 126, 147, 148, 149
Hawthorne, Nathaniel: "Young Goodman Brown" 168
Häxana: Witchcraft Through the Ages 169
Her 186
High School Exorcism 41
Hitchcock, Alfred 114, 115, 116, 143, 163
Home, Daniel Dunglas 153
The Horror of Dracula 85
The Host 61
House 159
House of Exorcism 41

The Howling 138
Huxley, Thomas 8, 191–92n14

I Am Legend (film) 68–69
I Am Legend (novel) 66–68
I Married a Witch 174
I, Robot 179
I Walked with a Zombie 65
Iles, Francis 116
Independence Day and *Independence Day: Resurgence* 49
Insidious 34–35
Interview with the Vampire 95–96
Invasion 60
Invasion of the Body Snatchers and sequels 51, 58, 61

James, William 153
Jane Eyre 107–109
Jaws 142–145
Jenkins, Jerry 39
Jobling, Ian 105
Johnson, Samuel 10
Jones, Earnest 4
Jung, Carl 4
Junger, Sebastian 75
Jurassic Park 97

Karnac, Andrew 153
Keats, John 26
King, Stephen 161, 162
King of the Zombies 65
Koestler, Arnold: *The Ghost in the Machine* 179, 180
Kominski, Peter 109, 112
Kristeva, Julia 89–90
Krueger, Diane, Marianne Fisher 105
Kruuk, Hans 133
Kubrick, Stanley 17–26, 74, 161

LaHaye, Tim 39
Lake Placid and sequels 149
The Land Beyond the Forrest 77
Lang, Fritz: *Metropolis* 176
The Last Exorcism 41
The Last Man on Earth 68
Last Year at Marienbad 15
Lea, Suzanne Goodney 65
LeFanu, Sheridan 77, 78
Left Behind and sequels 39
The Legend of Hell House 160, 162
Legend of the Seven Golden Vampires 85
LeGuin, Ursula 41
Lennon, John 61
Let Me In 78
Lewis, C.S. 154
Lewton, Val 65, 140
Lipton, Judith Eve 110, 123
Locke, John 11
Lorenz, Konrad 9

Lost in Space 178
Lost Souls 40
Lyons, Arthur 29

MacKennon John 13
Maggie 72
Maharishi Mahesh Yogi 24
Maid in Manhattan 105
Malleus Maleficarum, 169
Malthus, Thomas 188
Marlowe, Christopher 41
Maroon 5 146
Matheson, Richard 15, 66, 67, 69
Maturin, Charles: *The Albigenses* 135
Melton, Gordon 76
Melville, Herman 30, 144, 166
Métraux, Alfred 194n15
Miller, Geoffrey 104
Milton, John 12, 29–30
Minetka, Susan 148
Mirror 35
Moby Dick 30, 144
Moody, Raymond 154
Morgan, Jack 152
Morris, Desmond 1, 19, 70, 103
Morrison, Reg 126
Le Morte d'Arthur 101, 105
Munch, Edvard 167
Murnau, F.W.: *Nosferatu* 83–84, 99
Murphy, Charlie 174
My Bloody Valentine 167

New York Review of Books 10–11
Newsom, Carol 29
Newsweek 12
Night of the Living Dead 69–70

The Odyssey 13
Ohman, Arne 148
The Omega Code 40
The Omega Man 68
The Omen and sequels 36, 37–38
One Flew Over the Cuckoo's Nest 88
Open Water 146
Ouija 38

Pal, George 47
Paley, William 6
Perrault, Charles 125
Peterson, Dale 11, 27
Pew Research Religion and Public Life 8
Phelan, Jay 5
Phillip, Kendall 31
Picnic 93
Pinker, Steven 151
Plottel, Jeanine 90
Poe, Edgar Allan: "The Fall of the House of Usher" 158, 159, 160, 162
Pogo 53
Polidori, John: *The Vampyre* 89

Poltergeist 33–34
Pope, Alexander 6
Porter, Cole 100
Practical Magic 175, 176
Predator and sequels 126–129
Pretty Woman 105
Pride and Prejudice and Zombies 72, 105
Prince, Stephen 4–5, 163
Prince of Darkness 31–32
Prom Night 167
Psycho 163
The Puppet Masters 61
Pushkin, Alexander 89

Radcliffe, Anne 3, 195–96n11
Reader, Will 159
Rebecca 114–15
Resident Evil 184
Revenge of the Zombies 65
Revolt of the Zombies 65
Reynolds, W.M.: *Wagner the Were-Wolf* 135
Rice, Ann 95
Richardson, Samuel: *Pamela or Virtue Rewarded* 101
Ridley, Matthew 8, 63
The Romance of the Rose 101
Romero, George 15, 69
Rosemary's Baby 37–39
A Rumor of Angels 154
Russell, Jeffrey 29
Rymer, James Malcolm 77

Salem witch trials 168
Satan 29–30
Saussure, Ferdinand de::90
Schwarz, Barry 53, 116
Sconse, Jeffrey 62
Scream 167
Seabrook, W.B.: *The Magic Island* 65
Senf, Carol 87
The Sentinel 31
Shakespeare, William 12, 105, 123, 152, 166
Shark Exorcism 41
Shaun of the Dead 72
The Shining 161–62, 163
Siegel, Joel 140
Silver, Alan 89
Silver Bullet 162
Singer, Robert 41
Sixth Sense 156
Skinner, B.F. 11
Smith, Charlotte 78, 195n11
Smith, John Maynard 9
Snow White and the Seven Dwarfs 101
Son of Dracula 85
The Sorrows of Satan 44
Sorrows of Young Werther 114
Spielberg, Steven 140–42
Spiritualism 34
Star Trek 61

Star Trek: The Next Generation 52, 178
Star Trek II: The Wrath of Khan 30
Stoker, Abraham 15, 75–81, 94
The Strange Case of Dr. Jekyll and Mr. Hyde (novel and film) 134–135
Summers, Montague 76, 134, 135, 136
Suspicion 116–17
Sussman, Robert 126, 147, 148, 149
Swami Prabhupada 24
Swedenborg, Emanuel 153
Swift, Jonathan 188

Telotte, J.P. 177, 178
The Temptations 123–24
Tennyson, Alfred 7, 61
The Terminator and sequels 184
They Live 50
The Thing 56
The Thing from Another World 55
30 Days of Night 87
Tiger, Lionel 132
Time 12
Tooby, John 14, 187
Tremors 150
Twain, Mark: "The Man Who Corrupted Hadleyburg" 165
2401 162
Twichell, James B. 36
Twilight and sequels 15, 112
2001: A Space Odyssey 17–26, 74, 125, 146, 176, 193n8

Underworld and sequels 94–95
The Uninvited 157
University of California, Santa Barbara Center for Evolutionary Psychology website 5
Ursini, James 89

Vampire 86
Varney the Vampire the Feast of Blood 77
Viser, William 30
Vonnegut, Kurt: *Player Piano* 177
voodoo 64

Waldman, Diane 116
Wall-E 178
Walpole, Horace: *The Castle of Otranto* 78
The War of the Worlds films 45–48
Warm Bodies 72
Weinstock, Jeffrey 97
Welles, Orson 47
Wells, H.G. 45
The Werewolf of London 135
Westworld 180
Wetmore, Kevin 194n6
What Dreams May Come 156
Whedon, Joss 32
White Noise 154
White Zombie 62

"Who Goes There?" 51, 54
Wicca (Neo Paganism) 168, 173–175
Wilbur, Christopher 104
Williams, Tony 71
Wilson, David Sloan 5
Wilson, Edward O. 2, 8, 12–13, 27, 44, 50–51, 53, 69, 74, 148, 187
The Witch 172–173
Witch Board 35
Witch Hammer 169–70
The Witches 171
The Witches of Eastwick 175–76
The Wizard of Oz 168
The Wolf Man and sequels 1, 136–137
Wolfen 139

Wollstonecraft, Mary: *Maria, or the Wrongs of Women* 119
Wood, Robin 38, 164
Workman, Lance 159
World War Z 71
Wrangdon, Richard 11, 27
"The Wurdulak" 97–98
Wuthering Heights 109–11

York, Michael 193n10

Zombie Shark 72
Zombie Strippers 72
Zombieland 72

www.ingramcontent.com/pod-product-compliance
Lightning Source LLC
Chambersburg PA
CBHW032056300426
44116CB00007B/769